*Dreams, Visions &
Prophecies of
Don Bosco*

Dreams, Visions & Prophecies of Don Bosco

Edited by Rev. Eugene M. Brown
Foreword by Morton T. Kelsey
Introductory Essay by Arthur J. Lenti, SDB

Don Bosco Publications
New Rochelle, New York

*Copyright 1986 The Salesian Society, Inc.
All rights reserved.*

Library of Congress Cataloging-in-Publication Data
Dreams, Visions, and Prophecies of Don Bosco.

Includes excerpts from *The Biographical Memoirs of Saint John Bosco* by G.B. Lemoyne.
Includes index.
1. Bosco, Giovanni, Saint, 1815-1888.
2. Dreams—History—19th century.
3. Prophecies—History—19th century.
I. Bosco, Giovanni, Saint, 1815-1888.
II. Brown, Eugene M., 1934 -
III. Lemoyne, Giovanni Battista, 1939-1916. *Memorie biografiche di don Giov. Bosco.* English. Selections. 1986.
BX4700.B75D74   1986   271'.79   86-13533
ISBN 0-89944-085-1   (lib. bdg.)
ISBN 0-89944-086-X   (pbk.)

The Scripture texts used in this book are taken from the *New American Bible*, copyright 1970 by the Confraternity of Christian Doctrine, Washington, D.C., and are used by license of said copyright owner. No part of the *New American Bible* may be reproduced in any form without permission in writing. All rights reserved.

Printed in the United States of America.

January 29th, 1986

There is a wonder world of dreams. Favored people in the history of salvation, such as Joseph of the Old Testament and Joseph of the New, were visited from on high through the medium of dreams.

St. John Bosco is very much of that context and his dream visitations are an integral part of his life and sanctity. It is a joy to know that Don Bosco Publications has assembled a collection of these. All of us will be enriched by reflecting on them.

Timothy Cardinal Manning
Former Archbishop of Los Angeles

Contents

Foreword ix
Introductory Essay xli
Editor's Preface liii

Chapter 1:   The Significance of Dreams in the Life of Don Bosco   1

Chapter 2:   The Mission of Don Bosco and the Future of the Order   7

    THE FIRST DREAM   7
    THE TAILOR'S SHOP   9
    THIS IS MY MOTHER   10
    THE SHEPHERDESS   11
    THE RIBBON OF OBEDIENCE   12
    THIS IS MY HOUSE   16
    ROSES AND THORNS   18
    THE FORTUNE WHEEL   21
    THE WHEEL OF ETERNITY   22
    THE MOUNTAIN   44
    TEN HILLS   45
    THE FIRST SALESIAN MISSION FIELD   50
    THE PEARS ARE FOR YOU   52
    A RAGING BULL   53
    ALL THESE BOYS ARE YOURS   61
    SAINT FRANCIS DE SALES   65
    A SCHOOL FOR BECCHI   68
    HELP US ALSO   69
    FIVE HUNDRED AND FOUR   70
    JOURNEY THROUGH SOUTH AMERICA   72
    LABOR AND REWARDS   84
    THE FAR EAST   91
    NICHE IN SAINT PETER'S   95

Chapter 3: Predictions of Future Events 97

    THE LATIN TEST 97
    A SPIRIT OF PROPHECY 98
    POLICE SEARCH 99
    STATE FUNERALS 100
    THE TWO PINES 103
    THE TWO COLUMNS 105
    THE RED HORSE 108
    THREE PROPHECIES 110
    THE DEATH OF POPE PIUS IX 121

Chapter 4: Dreams About the Boys of the Oratory 125

    GIFTS FOR MARY 125
    FOUR KINDS OF BREAD 129
    THE HANDKERCHIEF OF PURITY 130
    TABLETS, COOKIES AND BISCUITS 132
    A MYSTERIOUS VINE 137
    AN ENORMOUS ELEPHANT 148
    THE SNAKE AND THE ROSARY 156
    FAITH, OUR SHIELD
        AND OUR VICTORY 159
    THE GLOBE 166
    RAGING TORRENT 170
    A LIFE-SAVING RAFT 173
    THERE ARE TEN OF US 182
    FIRST DEATH AT THE ORATORY 184
    DEATH'S MESSENGER 188
    TWO-THIRTY 195
    HE WILL CRY OUT FOR DON BOSCO 196
    THE EAGLE 199
    REQUIEM AETERNAM 201
    THERE IS NO DEAD BOY HERE 205
    THE BOY WITH BLACK SPOTS 206
    A SHORT PATH 208

Chapter 5: **Dreams About Heaven and Hell   211**
TO HELL AND BACK!   211
THE LAND OF TRIAL   228
A PLACE OF SALVATION   233
HIKING TO HEAVEN   239
MAMMA MARGARET   253
DOMINIC SAVIO   255
FATHER PROVERA   267
LUIS COLLE   269
SAINTS PETER AND PAUL   276

Index   279

FOREWORD
The Dream as Religious Experience

by Morton T. Kelsey

In Western Christian society today there is practically no encouragement for a person to attempt to understand dreams as a source of religious insight into life. Most twentieth century Christians simply assume that the idea of finding religious meaning or reality in dreams is a fallacy.

This attitude is strange for several reasons. In the first place, the early Christian Church viewed the dream as one of the most significant and most important ways in which God revealed the divine Presence and will to human beings. Dreams were understood to give people access to a reality that was difficult to contact in other ways.

Not only do we find this view in the Old Testament, in the New Testament, and in the Church Fathers up to the time of Aquinas, but it is the attitude of nearly every other major religion of the world. Some of the most astute observations about dreams were made by the early Christian thinkers, and this evidence has only been systematically presented to the Christian public within the last two decades.

The importance of the dream struck me at a time in which I had come religiously into a dead-end street. As I learned to listen to my dreams and to interpret them I was given a way out of my spiritual stagnation. Indeed I found the prevenient grace of God operating in my life, God became real, and physical and spiritual healing took place within me. I also found myself in a strange position, a priest who believed that God spoke through dreams in a religious environment that had no place for such an idea.

This uncomfortable situation prompted a ten-year study of the religious and *Christian* history of dreams that resulted in a book now published as *God, Dreams and Revelation*.[1] During my research I came across references to the importance of dreams in the life of Saint John Bosco. They were scattered through the twenty volumes of the Italian work *Memorie Biografiche del Beato Giovanni Bosco* and many of these volumes had not been translated into English. Pope Pius IX had instructed Don Bosco to make a record of the way his life had been inspired and directed by God through dreams. Those interested in the religious dream will be very grateful to the editors of this volume for gathering together in the following pages the dreams of this great apostle to the poor and neglected youth of his time. Don Bosco was also the founder of the Salesian Order that still carries out the work that he began.

The dreams that follow are the most impressive and extensive collection of religious dreams within the Christian tradition. The editors have wisely arranged these dreams according to their type: those dealing with the mission of Don Bosco and the order he founded, precognitive dreams, dreams about the various boys in the Oratory and dreams about last things. The only comparable record of the importance of dreams as a direction from God is that of Saint Gregory Nazianzen, the greatest doctor of the early Church, who left us a similar, but shorter record of God's use of dreams in directing his life in his theological poems. In the second book of his poems he wrote:

> And God summoned me from boyhood
> in my nocturnal dreams, and I arrived
> at the very goal of wisdom

Don Bosco could have written these very lines.

In order to do justice to the religious value of the dreams of Don Bosco we shall first look at the present attitude toward dreams and then at the meaning of the dream and vision in physiology and psychology. We shall then suggest a world view in which the dream and vision make sense. Finally, we will give a brief history of the Christian interpretation of dreams and look at the various levels of meaning in dreams. We hope, in light of this, to see how remarkable these dreams of Don Bosco are. We shall conclude with some suggestions for modern people who wish to take seriously this potential method of contact with God and so follow in Don Bosco's footsteps.

Ambivalent Attitudes Toward the Dream

In most academic and popular "intellectual" Western culture the dream is viewed as an essentially meaningless experience, thrown up mechanically, without any kind of order, before the sleeping consciousness. It is the feedback that occurs as consciousness rewinds itself for another day's activity.

Vivid dreams, according to this point of view, result from some immediate stimulus, like dining late on too much chutney or overdoing the mince pie; or they can be caused by something that happens during sleep, like the siren of a passing fire truck, the creaking of a door, or by letting in too much night air. To be concerned about dreams then is silly; it simply indicates a superstitious mind.

This attitude was very nearly universal among the intelligentsia of the eighteenth and nineteenth centuries, and it is still held among those influenced by the positivistic science of this period—in other words, by most of us. It was first suggested 2200 years ago by Aristotle in three little papers on dreaming and was supported by Cicero a few centuries later.

After centuries of unpopularity, this view was revived to become the accepted point of view—without ever being subjected to scientific inquiry. It was considered so obvious and certain that there has been no need to spend time and effort verifying it, or even to spell it out very clearly. In fact, it is hard to find this view fully expressed in written form, although it is assumed in much of the writing in every field of our society. Yet there is nothing in the present careful research on dreaming that particularly supports this point of view. Instead, the actual studies frequently seem to give both analytical and empirical support to the opposite point of view.

On the other hand there is an undercurrent of fascination about dreams. Ever since there were words to talk about them, these strange happenings in the night have been the subject of wonder and discussion wherever people gathered to talk about their hopes and fears. Literature is full of dreams.

Even in this day of sophisticated rejection, after a few cocktails people begin to talk about the funny dream they had the night before. Whenever I lecture and mention my interest in the serious study of dreams, the questions about them begin to come out, and people invariably show their hunger to talk and to hear more about the meaning of their dreams.

I once visited the pastor of a large, smoothly organized urban parish, a man who admitted that he had probably not been bothered by an illogical thought since the first grade. When I mentioned that I was doing some writing on dreams, he could not wait to tell me of the dream that had awakened him a few nights before with the picture of an accident so real that it terrified him.

The next day he had learned to his horror of just such an accident that had claimed the life of a close friend that night. He was still shaken by the experience when I talked with him, and he expressed the hope that someone would write of dreams in religious tradition, for he could find no material relevant to his experience in modern religious writing.

Yet it is easy to forget how many people are still concerned with dreams. The average person in the street is concerned enough to keep a big business going in dream books, which can be found in the paperback racks of almost any newsstand or corner drugstore. There are dozens of these books in print, and they are turned to by millions of people even though the basic ideas in them are highly questionable.

Most popular dream books try to separate out specific dream images and assign meanings to them in order to foretell the future or to explain certain life situations. All this is quite contrary to the legitimate study of dreams. These books, however, are interesting because they do show how great is the popular interest in the subject, and how persistent and pervasive the "commonsense" attitude toward dreams continues to be.

Modern Science Examines the Dream

In the last hundred years the dream has been given serious attention by psychiatry and clinical psychology. Within these fields the dream has been seen as revealing the autonomous depth of human beings called the unconscious. They see the dream as a practical means of understanding and treating various kinds of psychological illness.

Some medical persons also view the dream as revealing the collective unconscious, a vast realm of experience beyond the individual's ken, touching realties of a religious and spiritual nature. The work of Dr. C.G. Jung and his followers in particular has revealed the religious implications of the dream.

This quite different point of view, which finds dreams highly significant and meaningful, has been held in practically all other cultures. Indeed, wherever peoples have not been touched and influenced by our Western world-view with its belief that we are limited to sense experience and reason, the dream has been viewed as the chief medium through which non-physical (or spiritual) powers and realities spoke to people.

Although some dreams were seen as meaningless or unintelligible, it was important for people to consider their dreams, for through them they might obtain intimations of things to come or guidance and confrontation from greater than human powers. All of the major religions of humankind have held this view, and as we have shown, it has never been entirely displaced by the skeptical view of the scientific community.

Instead, the modern support for this view has come from a strange source. Beginning in 1900, with the publication of Freud's carefully documented *Interpretation of Dreams*, the subject has come in for serious consideration by the medical profession. Their research makes it rather hard to avoid the significance of dreams.

Freud first saw dreams as the royal road to understanding our submerged personality, that hidden nine-tenths of the human being which we now know as the unconscious. Jung, if his record can be believed, followed then by witnessing dreams that gave hints of the future and offered suggestions to people superior to their conscious knowledge and attitudes. Recently, the studies of Dement and others carrying on similar research have demonstrated that dreams are so important to mental health that simply being deprived of them may lead to mental breakdown and even psychosis.

In addition, current research on sleep and dreaming has shown that dream experience is universal, and that it occurs in a regular pattern night after night in spite of most people's total amnesia the next morning. The person who is convinced he or she never dreams is simply not aware of what is going on below the level of consciousness. The dreams have been forgotten.

Studies have demonstrated conclusively that something is going on practically all the time we sleep, and about every ninety minutes a vivid dream occurs, completely absorbing almost every reaction of the dreamer. This research suggests how limited most Christians have been in their attitude toward dreams and dreaming.

These findings, particularly those of Jung, certainly suggest that the dream—which has been valued and interpreted by all religious groups, Christianity included—is worthy of serious religious consideration and may be one very important access to knowledge. It is true that in the past this understanding has sometimes led to an uncritical and superstitious concern with dreams. Still, Christian dream-interpretation is an ancient, long-held, and carefully considered religious practice. It deserves to be reviewed and evaluated.

When we are perfectly honest we find the two opposing attitudes toward dreams struggling with each other within us. Much of the time we are dominated by the attitude of the Enlightenment, which devalued dreams as meaningless, and we ignore them.

Then there are times when we awake from a vivid dream strangely moved and troubled, hardly able to shake off its influence throughout the day. Or we read of Lincoln's premonitory dream of his assassination and wonder what it means that dreams sometimes have reality and significance like that. What meaning do dreams actually have? And what is a dream?

Physiology and Dreaming

It may seem hardly necessary to define anything so familiar as a dream, but in defining the familiar we discover how little we know. Most commonly the dream is understood to be a succession of images present in the mind during sleep. And here, as Nathaniel Kleitman has shown in his *Sleep and Wakefulness*, we are getting into one of the least-understood of human activities. We cannot even say precisely what is meant by sleep except in terms of a certain kind of consciousness.

According to Kleitman, sleep is best described as that period in which there is a temporary cessation of the waking state. From time to time in this period anything from a single picture or figure to an elaborate story may be vividly perceived, which is in no sense a direct perception of the outer physical world. Normally this happens four or five times every night, and it can also be "watched" or predicted by keeping track of the sleeper's brain waves, eye movements, and certain other reactions. Indeed, vivid dreams seem to come spontaneously and to be almost as free from our ego control as our perception of the outside physical world.

This process is not the only one that happens in sleep, however. There is a second process closely related to dreaming which can be recalled best between the periods of vivid dreaming. This conceptual activity, simply "thinking," is apparently continuous in the parts of the brain which do not go to sleep. Apparently most of the brain goes right on working whether we are awake or asleep.

Whether we are conscious of it or not, vivid dreaming takes over alternately with conceptual activity, which is constantly at work changing perceptions into thoughts and ideas. The psychologists call these processes "primary-process activity" and "secondary-process mentation," and together they produce the underlying psychic life that seems to be basic to conscious thinking and activity.

It is from this level of psychic life that the sharp and discrete religious intuition probably comes. These intuitions, which are so valued and prized by religious people for direction and guidance, are in most cases the end product of this kind of secondary-process mentation turned upon religious contents. The religious intuition is therefore of the same nature as the dream (and also the vision), and shares in the same reality.

A third form of dream activity is the spontaneous image or vision that appears to a person in the borderland of wakefulness when one is not sure whether one is awake or asleep. These dreams and visions—they are termed hypnagogic or hypnopompic, depending on whether the dreamer is falling asleep or waking up—are usually flash pictures focused on a single impression, but in some cases whole scenes, even fairly long stories may appear.

At times these images coming on the edge of sleep can seem so tangible that the dreamer really does not know whether he is awake or asleep, whether the images belong to the outside world or the figures of the dream. These images are often very significant. And this leads us to the last and closely related form of dreaming.

This final form is the waking dream or vision, in which the dream images break into the waking consciousness. The images themselves are apparently no different from those which can be experienced during sleep, except that they reach the field of consciousness during periods of wakefulness. They rise as spontaneously and with as little ego control as the dream, and genuine visions are involuntary. These are much more common than most people realize.

However, there are persons who are able to cultivate the ability to look inward and observe this spontaneous rise of dream images because they wish to experience them. This experience, which we shall simply call fantasy, seems to be very similar to dreaming; in it the same kind of images and stories arise within one as in dreams. In other cultures and other times the experience of visions has been far more valued than it is among most people today. In fact, as we shall show, the people of other cultures have not distinguished as clearly between the dream and the vision as we do today. Effective meditation can bring us to this level of experience and transformation.

It is quite clear that Don Bosco was a genius in opening himself to this dimension of reality. This ability was probably given to him by inheritance and God's special grace. The important matter is that he developed this ability, used it for God and recorded his experience.

There is an activity, however, which is common in our culture today that is not always so carefully distinguished. This is the daydream, which is different from fantasy. In daydreams the flow of images is not spontaneous, but is directed by the conscious center of personality, the ego. The daydream can be created and also changed at will; fantasy, like the true dream or vision, cannot—it must be met with and observed. At times the line between fantasy and daydreams may be a fine one, but unless it is maintained, fantasy loses the spontaneous quality that is characteristic of both dreams and visions.

Dreams and Visions

One other distinction must be kept quite clear because of the popular modern attitude toward visions. Most people are quite suspicious of visions. They probably would not go so far as to find the dream dangerous or pathological. But the dream is so closely related to the vision that at times the two cannot be distinguished; visions are feared as a sign of mental distintegration.

Many of us automatically assume that any person who experiences a vision must be mentally ill, that any vision must be an hallucination. On the contrary, the real visionary experience is quite different from the hallucination in mental illness.

The true visionary experience is seldom mistaken for giving immediate knowledge of the physical world, but only of the "dream" world, or quite indirectly of the physical one. The vision is superimposed on the physical world, or the two may in some way be synchronized, but they can be distinguished just as easily as the dream is usually distinguished from the experience of waking. However, purely mechanical and materialistic psychology has no place for the vision and tends to link it with hallucination.

Hallucination in mental illness, on the other hand, is a definite sign of pathology. Here the same kind of content one finds in a dream arises spontaneously and is attributed directly to the world outside where it does not belong; the "dream" world is mistaken for the physical world of sense experience.

Persons subject to this kind of hallucination have lost the ability to distinguish between these two kinds of experience and so project their inner images directly upon the outer world. Because they cannot distinguish between the two they are not able to deal adequately with either the outer world or the inner one. Their actions become inappropriate and they are seen as sick. Such hallucination is a common occurrence in several kinds of mental illness where the ego under stress cannot distinguish between experiences that come to consciousness from psychic reality and those that come from the outer world.

It is not possible to discuss dreams without considering the thought process that goes on in sleep, the true vision, and fantasy as well. The four experiences are basically the same in nature. They are intrusions into consciousness of activities over which we have little if any conscious control.

In the past these spontaneous images and thoughts, distinct from outer physical reality, have been valued as a sign of contact with religious reality. Whether the image was presented in sleep or in wakefulness, whether breaking in unexpectedly or sought and cultivated, it was understood to come from a different realm, and nearly all religious groups everywhere have considered that the ability to observe and interpret these images was a religious gift.

This was essentially the common Christian tradition from Biblical times, through the Church Fathers, and up into the seventeenth century; in isolated instances it has continued to the present time. In this tradition dreams were significant because they revealed something beyond humankind which gave purpose and meaning, warning where spiritual disaster impended. In Jung's terminology dreams can express the reality of the collective unconscious, the objective psyche. In religious terms, they kept the people in touch with the purpose and direction of spiritual reality.

Dreams and the Church

At the beginning of the twentieth century there was almost no educated person in our culture who seriously considered this way of looking at human experience. After Freud had broken the ice with *The Interpretation of Dreams*, the reaction to his work showed how deeply people were concerned about this area of their lives. But even when the thaw set in, and people of all kinds began to show an interest in the study of dreams, there was still one major group in our society with almost nothing to say about the subject.

The Christian clergy, particularly the theologians, are largely still silent, and this is surprising in itself in a group not noted for silence. It is more surprising when we realize how much there is about dreams in the Christian tradition from the Old Testament on. It is also surprising when we consider the attention given to other aspects of the inner life.

There are groups of Christians interested in spiritual healing, in speaking in tongues, or preparing for the imminent end of the world, and even in the ritual handling of snakes. But there are few theologians that suggest that Christians should listen to their own dreams or make any particular study of the many dreams in the Bible and in subsequent Church history. However, some recent writers are now pointing to the religious value of dreams.

In fact, I cannot help recalling the consternation I caused in speaking to one group devoted to glossolalia when I spoke about dreams. It seemed to them that the idea of taking dreams seriously was much farther out than the practice of tongue-speaking. What does this mean? Is it just dreams that we have neglected, or is it something more?

The trouble is that the dream comes to us neither from the acceptable material world nor from our well-ordered and controllable reason. To value the spontaneously given content of the dream one must postulate the reality of something in addition to the material world and reason. Depth psychology calls this reality the unconscious; the early Christian community called it the spiritual world; and these two different terms may well refer to the same reality, as the Catholic theologian Victor White has suggested in *God and the Unconscious*. Unless we believe that there is such a realm of reality which can be experienced, we will probably not look very hard for meaning beyond the material world.

Indeed, if there is no meaning beyond the physical world, then what place is there for dreams to come from except the meaningless tag ends of yesterday's sensation? Dreams are then simply the commonest example of the human mind or psyche out of commission. They show how irrational its action can be when logical thinking is switched off.

Of course, sense experience is also nonrational in the sense that it is not guided or directed by reason; it is just given. But since it is believed that there is a real physical world that is revealed in sense experience, this essential irrationality hardly bothers anyone except a few philosophers.

The irrationality of dreams is something else again. So long as we "know" that there is no other world for them to reveal, no world beyond the material one, there is nothing else for dreams to show us but irrationality—our minds at their most irrational, illogical, in fact.

There is no controversy on dreams as there is with glossolalia; the subject simply does not come up for consideration except very rarely. It is very difficult for modern persons to imagine meaningful psychic reality beyond the grasp of his or her reason or his or her physical senses.

Indeed, the greatest thrust of mid-twentieth-century theology is to maintain unequivocally that human beings have no direct or immediate contact with any nonphysical or "supernatural" realm, and so there is no natural religion. This brand of theology also denies the value of depth psychology in human transformation, for once it is admitted that lives are changed in the psychologist's office, then the Church is faced with a realm of reality that is neither physical nor rational, and which is sometimes revealed in dreams.

Once the dream is taken seriously and regarded as having religious significance, then it is inevitable that there is some direct and "natural" contact with reality other than material or rational. Then the door is open and anything can happen, even transformation. Dreams may well be a doorway to religious significance and a new theology, as well as to the unconscious.

Our Western world is so enslaved to this materialistic view of the universe that it is difficult for us even to imagine another dimension of reality. As I show in many places, but particularly in my book *Christianity as Psychology*, the best of modern subatomic physics is not sure about the ultimate nature of this seeming solid physical world in which we live. Some physicists even take over to the Eastern view of reality that says that the material world is truly only illusion. When we do not know what matter is we can no longer seriously maintain that the spiritual world does not exist as long as we are thinking clearly and not just from materialistic *prejudice*.

In order to provide a framework in which dreams and particularly those of Don Bosco have meaning, we suggest a new world view, the view of Jesus of Nazareth, of the early Church, of Plato and also of C.G. Jung and some modern physicists. We are in touch with a real physical world and a real spiritual world. Dreams, visions, and prayer can bring us into touch with this spiritual world. In the following diagram *both* the physical space-time-energy-mass box and the spiritual dimension are real. As we shall see a little later, the dream can refer to many different aspects of this diagram. We have described this world view in several books.[2]

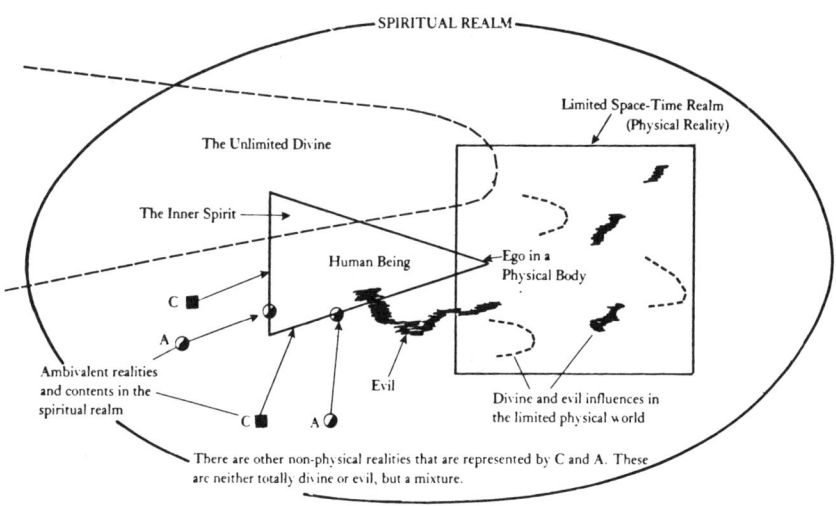

The Christian Interpretation of Dreams

What we do not deem important we do not observe. The Bible is full of dreams, visions, religious intuitions. From Genesis to Revelation we find these intrusions from another dimension. In this brief space available we can only hint at the riches to be found in the Bible. Hebrew has several different words for dreams and visions. The dream is seen almost as the nature of the experience and the vision as its content. We have the dreams of Abraham, Jacob, Joseph, the incredible visionary experiences of Moses. We find the prophets concerned about how to distinguish the true visions and dreams from the false ones. In the book of Job we find Job complaining of God's visitations during his sleep. There are also some critical statements about dreams as they were used in pagan sanctuaries and going there was considered heretical. The general tenor of the Old Testament is that God often speaks through dreams. We find the same attitude in the New Testament and the apocrypha.

In the New Testament there are twelve different words for experiences of the nonphysical dimension of reality; five of them relate to dreams and visions. The very word *apocalpyse* means an uncovering of another aspect of reality. There are dreams surrounding the birth of Jesus and his crucifixion. The resurrection appearances had *both* a physical and a visionary quality about them just as modern physicists view light both as a particle and as energy. In the book of Acts every major development of the nascent Church is marked by a dream, a vision or religious intuition.

Some early Christian writings have come down to us that were not included in the New Testament. These writers who probably knew the apostles carried on the same tradition as we find in the New Testament.

One of the most noteworthy of these early works was the *Shepherd of Hermas*, based on the author's dream-vision. A portion of the book is very similar in subject matter to *Pilgrim's Progress*. The power of this piece and the fact that it was widely read for three centuries shows how deeply symbolic truth was at work in this inspirational book.

Another significant example of the role of the dream or vision in the lives of the early Church Fathers is described in the *Martyrdom of Polycarp*, which shows Polycarp seeing a vision forewarning his capture and death.

These writers also wrote apocryphal gospels and acts of the apostles. These are often fanciful and were not included in the New Testament Canon. The apocryphal writings display the same sort of emphasis on dreams seen in the New Testament. For example, the *Acts of the Holy Apostle Thomas* record that

God gave Thomas missionary instructions through a dream, while *The Testament of Abraham* relates Isaac's dream of Abraham's coming death. *The Clementine Homilies*, written in the second century, show Peter and Simon discussing dreams.

The Post Apostolic Age

Although some people might complain that the writers of the New Testament were not sophisticated thinkers and had been taken in by the illusions of their time, this cannot be said of the Church Fathers. These men faced a hostile empire and using the best thinking of their time they tried to show the reasonableness of their beliefs. They were well trained in philosophy and some of them were the best minds of the Roman Empire. These early Christian theologians based their thinking on philosophy of Plato, the Biblical tradition and their experience of Christ. Many of them witnessed to their belief with their lives. They believed that God spoke directly to human beings through prayer, dreams and visions. How far modern theologians have strayed from these thinkers who laid out the foundations of Christian thought.

Justin Martyr, the first Christian to write down an interpretation of Christianity for the Roman world, was martyred in A.D. 165. He believed dreams allowed human beings to experience spiritual reality and that they were sent by both good and evil spirits.

Irenaeus, bishop of Lyons in the second century, who wrote *Against Heresies*, emphasized the importance of dreams in such New Testament accounts as the Acts 10 story of Peter's dream and the Matthew report of Joseph's dreams.

Two of the most intellectual Church Fathers, Clement and Origen of Alexandria, emphasized the important role of dreams in Christian life. Clement stated that sleep provided human beings a special contact with spiritual reality and was a means for human beings to receive revelations about their destiny.

In his *Against Celsus*, Clement's pupil Origen wrote that the dream was a means of relating to the divine and to future events. It was also Origen who believed the dream spoke symbolically and revealed the nature of spiritual reality. He further maintained that God used the dream as a means of conversion.

Tertullian

Originally from North Africa, Tertullian was a prolific writer whose theory of dreams is expressed in his most important work, *On The Soul*. Tertullian believed that all human beings dream and that in sleep we are overwhelmed by a form of reality different from what we experience in our waking hours as sense experience. Tertullian cited a phenomenal number of references to support his beliefs about dreams—among them Homer, Herodotus, Cicero and others now lost to us.

Tertullian believed that dreams may come directly from God, from demons, or as a result of the natural workings of the depth of the soul. Tertullian emphasized that it was not he alone who believed in dreams, but Christians in general who experienced God in their lives in this way.

Saint Perpetua, only one of many saints who received visions and dreams from God which sustained them in the face of persecution and martyrdom, saw a golden ladder reaching toward heaven, forewarning her own death and that of friends.

Emphasis on the importance of dreams did not stop with the apologists or Tertullian. Such leaders as Cyprian of North Africa and Hippolytus in Rome believed that wisdom was directly imparted through dreams and visions. Cyprian, bishop of Carthage, believed that God guided the Church through visions and he was even prepared for his own martyrdom by a vision.

Two disciples of Origen, Gregory Thaumaturgus and Dionysius, found great comfort and sanctioning of their faith through dreams, and Julius Africanus, also of Alexandria and reputedly bishop of Emmaus, wrote that the king of Persia had foreseen the birth of Christ in a dream.

In Rome, Hippolytus wrote many works dealing with the importance of dreams. In addition to showing that the Biblical prophets had been given instructions through visions and dreams, Hippolytus also analyzed at length the dreams of the prophet Daniel.

Arnobius in the Latin Church was said to have been converted to Christianity by means of a dream, while Lactantius, his disciple, maintained that knowledge of the future came through dreams.

Dreams of the Victorious Christian Church

The issuance of the Edict of Milan in 313 as a result of the victory of Constantine brought a virtual end to the persecution of Christians. The monumental Church leaders who emerged in this period of new freedom believed that God reveals himself to humankind through dreams and visions.

In fact, it was apparently as a result of a dream-vision that Constantine became emperor of Rome. The writer Lactantius tells in his account concerning the battle between Constantine and Maxentius that prior to the engagement, Christ appeared to Constantine in his sleep with the sign of a cross of light, commanding him to use this sign as a safeguard.

Generally speaking, the Church historians of this period were little concerned with dreams. However, one writer, Socrates, did refer to the story of the empress Sominica who received warnings through a dream about the forthcoming death of her child. Another writer, Theodoret, made mention of the fact that the Emperor Theodosius dreamed of receiving the imperial crown. Still another historian, Sozomen, recounted Constantine's directions from God via a dream to give up rebuilding Troy and was then led to erect the marvelous city of Byzantium. Sozomen also detailed his friend Aquilinus's healing one night as a result of a divine vision.

As the Church ceased to be persecuted from outside, problems arose within its own gates—especially problems of heresy. One of the giants in Church history of this period, Athanasius, bishop of Alexandria, believed the dream to be of paramount importance as a means of revelation from God. It was this great churchman who wrote the marvelous *Life of Saint Anthony*, and the effect of the saint's life and extrasensory spiritual gifts upon the author cannot be overstated.

Greek Orthodox Leaders

Three of the most important theologians in the history of Christianity—Basil the Great, Gregory of Nazianzen and Gregory of Nyssa—all believed that God communicated with human beings by means of dreams and visions. In his *On the Making of Man*, Gregory of Nyssa maintained that while we sleep, our reason and sensory functions lie dormant. Then our nonrational side may emerge, and it is through this nonrational side that God speaks to us.

Basil the Great maintained that dreams like the Bible were intended to be obscure so that we would spend more time with God and his truth. In several of his works he discusses God's direct contact via dreams with the Old Testament patriarchs.

It was as a result of the appearance in a dream of two maidens—Temperance and Virginity—that Gregory of Nazianzen decided to lead an ascetic life. He also wrote a book of theological poems telling how God had lead him through his dream life. Another great figure in the Greek church, Saint John Chrysostom, believed that dreams not only reveal spiritual reality to us, but also show us the state of our souls and can affect our actions. He further stressed that we are not held accountable for the subject matter of our dreams. Chrysostom also wrote detailed commentaries on the importance of dreams and visions in the Bible.

Early in the fifth century Synesius of Cyrene, who became bishop of Ptolemais, wrote a sophisticated book on the subject of dreams which made a great impact upon the Eastern world. A complex work which synthesized most of the important Christian thought on the subject, Synesius's study maintained that the meaning of the universe was given its best expression in the dream and that through the dream human beings may know the future, correct bodily malfunctions, gain hope for the future, and come to love the divine. Synesius also suggested that one ought to keep a record of dreams and that there is a vital connection between dreams and mythology. His work was read and commented upon from the fifth century to the fall of Byzantium in 1451.

Doctors in the West

In the Western Church, four influential men emerged who believed in God's revelation through dreams and visions—Ambrose, Augustine, Jerome and Gregory the Great. Ambrose refused to celebrate the eucharist before the Emperor Theodosius because of a dream, and he also discovered the bodies of two martyred saints as a result of directions from a dream. Ambrose's works stated that the Holy Spirit speaks through dreams and that in the Old Testament the great wisdom of Solomon, Joseph and Daniel was seen in their ability to interpret dreams. He also wrote of the continued help that his deceased brother gave him in his dreams.

The man who was to lay the foundation for Western Christian theology for a thousand years, Augustine, believed that there were two basic realities—the material and the spiritual. He maintained that through dreams we may gain entrance to the nonphysical world where spontaneous contents await us. Augustine recounted a dream his mother, Monica, had of the conversion of her son which gave her fortitude to keep praying for him during all his wayward years. In both *The Confessions* and *The City of God* are stories of fascinating, unusual parapsychological dreams.

Jerome of Aquileia on the Adriatic is noted for translating the Bible into the Latin Vulgate. Converted to Christianity by a dramatic dream in which he saw himself surrounded by a bright light before the judgment seat, Jerome became the head of a monastic community in Bethlehem. Jerome believed that dreams must not be sought for their own sake but for the revelations that God is sending through them.

Another later scholar of the Western world, Macrobius, author of *Commentary on the Dream of Scipio*, had a great influence on medieval thought. He spent a portion of his work explaining his classification of dreams into five types—the enigmatic dream, the dream foretelling the future, the oracular dream, the nightmare, and the apparition. It was from the works of Macrobius that the Middle Ages learned what it knew of Platonism, for this author attempted to summarize the wisdom of Greece and Rome and pass it on in a rather oversimplified form.

Another important personage of the fourth century, Saint Martin of Tours, a missionary to Gaul, was the subject of a biography by Sulpicius Severus which detailed Martin's beautiful vision of Christ clothed in the half-cloak he had given to a naked beggar. Saint Martin at the time of his death appeared in glorified form to Severus in a dream.

The next major figure to write about dreams, Gregory the Great, is more closely connected to the Middle Ages than to the classical period, for between his lifetime and that of Augustine and Jerome the Western Empire had fallen, plunging Europe into the Dark Ages. Although his *Morals and Dialogues* discussed the sources of dreams and supported their importance as revelations of the divine, Gregory did not have the critical acumen of his predecessors and his treatment of dreams bears the mark of superstition.

The superstitious and uncritical view of dreams and visions continued through the Dark and Middle Ages. In addition Saint Thomas Aquinas followed Aristotle's view of dreams as unimportant and insignificant. This laid the groundwork for the rejection of the dream by scholasticism; this rejection affected both the Catholic and Protestant Churches. During the same period, however, the dream was still highly valued in the Eastern Church and has continued to be so valued right up to the present time.

Two remarkable studies of the dream, however, do come out of Western Christianity at the time of the Renaissance. Neither of these had been translated from medieval Latin and medieval French in which they were written. Jung's reference to these books led me to them. The first is the remarkable book of the Jesuit Benedict Pererius published in 1598 and entitled: *De Magia: Concerning the Investigation of Dreams and Concerning Astrological Divination. Three Books. Against the False and Superstitious Arts.* I have read few wiser studies of the meaning of the dream. Gaspar Peucer wrote from a Calvinistic and humanistic point of view. His book *Les Devins, ou commentaire des principles sortes de divination* covers much the same ground as Pererius. Both men followed a generally accepted and well-known body of sophisticated opinions about dreams available at that time.

Some Modern Dreams

With the rise of scholastic thought on the one side and the development of the materialism of the Enlightenment on the other, the dream soon fell into eclipse as a study for the "Enlightened." Nevertheless, God continued to touch human beings through the dream. We mention three important modern religious figures touched by the dream and then a young man with no background in the historical importance of the dream. However, the most significant modern or ancient Christian witness to the importance of the dream is still Don Bosco.

The first dream, that of a Baptist minister named A.J. Gordon, occurred at the end of the nineteenth century. In the dream, Gordon was standing before his congregation about to begin preaching when a stranger of compelling presence entered the church and sat down. Although Gordon wished to greet the man at the end of the service, Gordon could not get to him before he left. When Gordon asked one of his parishioners who the man was, the parishioner replied, "Did you not recognize him? It was Jesus."

The impact of this dream—with the sorrowful expression on the stranger's face—radically changed Gordon's life and ministry. He later wrote, "It was a vision of the deepest reality. Apparently we are most awake to God when we are asleep to the world."

The second dream, that of Anglican minister John Newton, author of "Amazing Grace," was by his own testimony the most important event of his life and the inspiration for that hymn. Captain of a slave-trading ship at the time of the dream, Newton saw himself on a sailboat in Venice. Suddenly a strange man presented him with a ring, telling him that happiness was his as long as he possessed the ring.

Later in the dream, accosted by a man who ridiculed the worth of the ring, Newton dropped it into the sea. Just then he looked up, observing a huge fire in the Alps. Fearfully he stood gazing at the raging fire and reflecting on his stupidity for parting with the ring. Suddenly the stranger appeared who rescued the ring from the water and promised to hold it in trust for Newton so that he could always feel its power. Newton left his abominable profession of slave trading, went back to England, took orders in the Church and became one of the greatest hymn writers of all times.

The third dream, that of Saint Therese of Lisieux, who died in 1897 at the age of twenty-four, took place during the course of a long illness and subsequent depression. In the dream, three deceased Carmelite nuns and the mother superior of the convent appeared to her. She asked to remove the veil from the face of one of them. Granted permission, she recognized the nun as Mother Ana of Jesus, a saint who had introduced the reform orders into France. As an incredible light shone from the nun's face, Therese felt a great love and warmth surround her. As a result of this experience, Therese was able to write, ". . . I knew beyond doubt that heaven was a reality. . . . My heart melted in her love and I became inflamed in love, joy, and thankfulness, not only to her but to the whole of heaven."

Just as dreams have been sources of guidance and revelation to the early Church Fathers, to ministers and saints, so too they can provide encouragement and direction for men and women today.

The following series of dreams was experienced by a young man reared in the Catholic Faith who had rejected his religious heritage. Alienated from his family, he had left home and was living in a commune in Indiana. His life was practically devoid of meaning and he felt directionless.

The first dream of the series showed the young man returning home, encountering his weeping father. His brothers and sisters, by contrast, were joyful at his arrival.

This dream was pointing out the young man's basic problem—his confrontation with his father, the outer symbol of the youth's inner father, or the old traditional way of doing things. Because the young man realized he needed to separate himself from his distorted father image, he turned to his inner child, who responded.

The insights from this dream enabled the young man, who was attending college out of a sense of duty, to drop out of school and deal with his personal life.

The second dream pictured the youth in the desert, encountering a wise old Indian chief. The desert in this dream portrayed the young man's directionless state, but the Indian chief was a hopeful symbol—an important figure representing an alive spiritual reality. Subsequent dreams showed the young man that he must give up the reality he knew and explore his identity and life pathway more thoroughly.

Shortly after these dreams the young man left Indiana and hitchhiked across the country, a trip which brought him insights and altered his personality.

While staying at a monastery in New Mexico, the youth had a dream that he was dying of a heart attack, but that after the "death" experience his spent heart was replaced by a larger, stronger one. This dream is symbolic of the death of the old ego adaptation, making way for a new life.

The next dream found the youth in the mountains contemplating some nearby cliffs. Even the Indians who had inhabited these mountains showed fear in their legends when they spoke of these cliffs. But the young man decided to climb the cliff alone. Proud that he had conquered the heights alone, he eventually looked down on the people below and began sneering at them for never daring the climb. A few minutes later, however, the cliff gave way beneath him, and he fell into an abyss.

Paradoxically, if the young man had not had the courage to climb the mountain, he never would have fallen nor experienced the transformation which it brought about. It almost seems that the sin of pride brings about redemption here. The experience is reminiscent of Paul's question in Romans 6: "Should we sin that grace should abound?" Paul was almost grateful for his own failures for they permitted grace to work in his life.

As the dream continued, the cliff cracked and the young man changed into a weed, symbolic of the valueless, the unusable. The young man was incapable of recognizing his own limits and mortality. In order to come to a new view of himself, he had first to try to achieve so much that he fell into an abyss as a weed. Then the youth saw the weed burn up and the ashes spread over the bottom of the abyss. This image is reminiscent of the Phoenix, which rises from its ashes and is often used in Christian symbolism. And now, from the depth of the dream, a great but gentle voice came forth pleading, "Jesus, Jesus," and with the sound of this voice the young man was resurrected.

The next dream showed the father figure again, but under

a new guise—that of a strong, tall, black-clad cleric. This image was representative of the traditional, severe, religious attitude in which the young man had grown up. This black-clad figure came toward him, poked a finger at him, and derided the resurrection experience of the previous dream.

The young man, deciding to confront this negative figure, turned to him and said, "No, you are wrong." As a result of facing his own inner doubt in this manner, the youth's life started to change. He was able to actualize the potential pointed out to him through his unconscious by God.

The young man returned to Indiana and began to take his Church life seriously in spite of its negative side. He returned to the university to finish his education and began a genuine Christian journey. The full text of these dreams is found in my book *The Other Side of Silence* and is also discussed at length in John Sanford's *Healing and Wholeness*.

The dream continues to speak to human beings just as it did to the members of the early Church, making us conscious of the workings of the Spirit within us and helping us attain God's potential for our lives.

Different Kinds of Dreams

Often when I am lecturing on dreams I am asked if all dreams are important and significant. My answer is that they all reveal something from the depth of us. However, some dreams reveal far more than others. If we analyze ordinary garden dirt far enough we can discover much about the nature of matter, but uranium and radium reveal the volatile and energetic nature of physical reality much more dramatically. And some dreams are radium dreams revealing the depth and wonder of the spiritual dimension of reality. Other dreams need to be worked on and analyzed if they are to be understood.

Dreams refer to many different aspects of our total experience. In attempting to understand dreams it is helpful to see what the dream is pointing to most significantly. In the following diagram we have enlarged a part of the diagram presented before and show the part that deals with the human psyche and its potential for experiencing. In this diagram the right side represents the physical world and our ordinary conscious perception of it. The left side represents the nonphysical world and the depth of the human psyche.

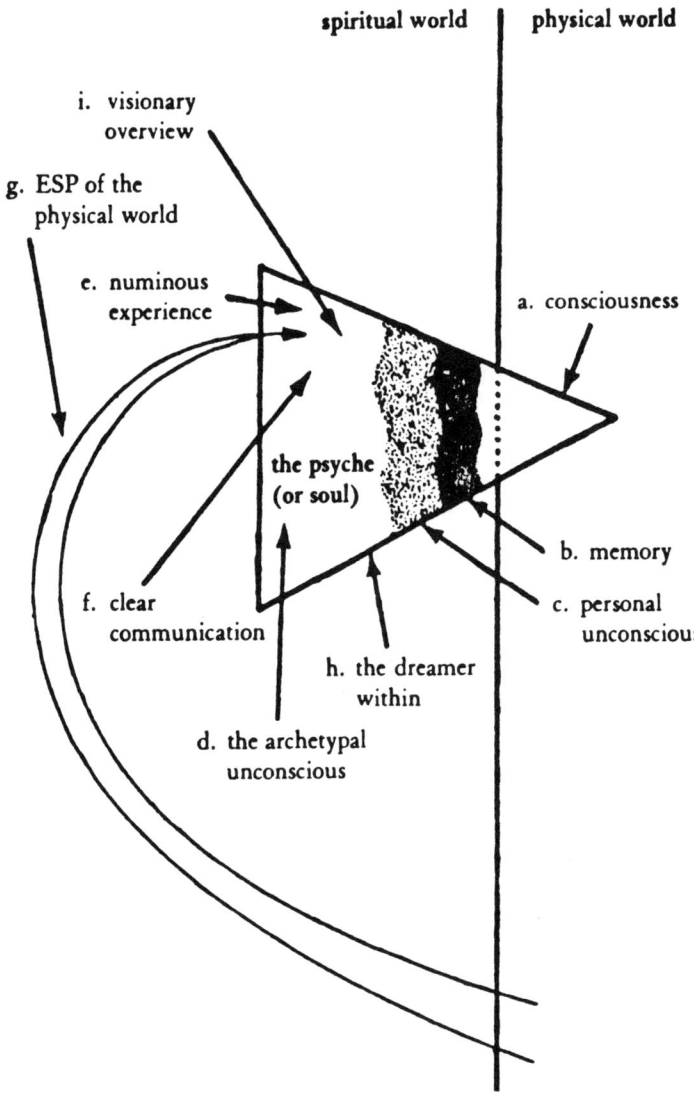

It is valuable to discern which part of the psyche and the spiritual world is being expressed in a dream. What part of me is speaking most clearly? All nine levels may be present in a dream, but one needs to decide which one is presenting the dominant message. Most people find these nine levels within them from time to time, although some are far more rare than others.

a. Sometimes a dream refers mainly to yesterday's events and their significance, but seldom without some alteration in the scene. One can always ask one's self why this particular event from a former day has been seized upon and highlighted by the dreamer within. In thirty-five years of listening to my own dreams and thirty of listening to others' dreams, I have found that dreams which merely repeat yesterday's events are really quite rare, in spite of the old wives' tale to the contrary.

b. A dream can reproduce anything from memory, even a scene quite inaccessible to conscious recall, for instance a scene from second grade in school, in full color with names and faces. Nothing in one's life seems to be lost beyond remembrance to the dreamer within. But why does this content of the past arise now?

c. Sometimes a dream brings forth actions and thoughts of the past which we have repressed and forgotten because they cause us pain. The personal unconscious is not locked to the dreamer within. This kind of dream can bring up important material and help us become whole.

d. One of the great discoveries of both Freud and Jung was that there are universal symbols which bubble up out of the soul and tell us of its very nature and structure. This area of the soul has been named the "collective unconscious" by Jung. Understanding this level requires much study and application.

e. Some dreams are charged with numinous or awe-inspiring power. When something beyond our soul touches us and is known, there is usually a sense of awe and holy fear. This can bring terror if it is some evil or demonic reality, amazement if it is some deceased person or an angelic or neutral spiritual reality, or ecstasy if God is the one who touches our soul. We call such visions of the night "numinous dreams."

f. Sometimes the message of a dream comes through clearly in a direct and understandable sentence or two. I have argued with God that he should speak like this more often. The answer which has come to me is that God is more interested in relationship with me than in giving me information. When I puzzle over a dream I spend more time with God as Saint Basil suggested.

g. Dreams are the natural altered state of consciousness, and *very occasionally* we are given knowledge in dreams of the physical world which we do not get through ordinary sensory channels. This information can cross space and time, and even tell of the future. *One of the most dangerous uses of dreams is to expect that they are always or usually speaking of the future.* Only one or two percent of dreams have this meaning, and no one can tell which ones foretell the future until after an event has occurred. Most superstitious and silly uses of dreams involve using them for fortune telling. But occasionally they do give this kind of information. One of the most interesting confirmations of this ESP quality of dreams is found in an article in the *Journal of Chemical Education* by R. A. Brown and R. G. Luckock entitled "Dreams, Daydreams and Discovery." (Volume 55, Number 11, Nov. 1978) This well documented study shows that many important scientific discoveries have been directed by dreams.

h. From some deep center of reality a dreamer within speaks to us. This reality knows everything about us, has a wisdom greater than ours, and provides these nightly dramas for our transformation. These dramas tell us who we are, where we have been, where we have strayed from the path, how we can get back on the path and where our destiny would lead us. I believe this dreamer within is no other than the Holy Spirit which God gives us as our inner guide, friend and comforter. Sometime this Spirit presents us in our dreams with the dazzling light of God's presence or with the risen Christ or with the Virgin Mary or one of the saints to guide us on our journey.

i. Once or twice in a life, often near the end of it, we human beings are given a glimpse of life beyond us, a visionary overview of reality, of the divine center of love at the core of existence. These, of course, are the great revelatory experiences for which we all hope. They seldom come or are appreciated, however, unless we have been working on and listening to our dreams. Seldom do we experience the more significant and important kinds of dreams unless we have valued them, seen them as invaluable friends, recorded them and thought about them.

The Dreams of Don Bosco

Undoubtedly Don Bosco had many dreams described in these first four categories of dreams. These require considerable work to understand. They need to be interpreted and Don Bosco had a natural understanding of the meaning of symbols. However, what makes the dreams of this saint so significant is the great number belonging to the last five classifications that we have delineated. His openness to this spiritual realm, his closeness to it, enabled God to flood him with this kind of experience.

Often when someone begins analysis the first dream will spell out the course of analysis and of that person's life. Bosco's first dream set the course of his entire life and occurred when he was just nine years of age. It told in symbolic form what was to be his life's mission. Even though he did not understand it, he couldn't forget it. When he was asked by Pope Pius IX to speak of the supernatural influences in his life, it was this dream that impressed the Pope so much that he ordered Don Bosco to write down his dreams for the encouragement of his Congregation and the rest of us.

Often in these dreams we find that the figures within them give interpretations of the symbols that are present. In addition to this, Don Bosco was comfortable with symbols and pictures and instinctively knew their meaning. As you read through these dreams you will perceive his uncanny ability to understand what the dreams were saying to him. You will see that they present him with the whole range of the spiritual world, the forces of evil, the deceased and the angelic powers as well as experiences of Christ and God.

The pages that follow are filled with numinous encounters. Don Bosco's dreams were really part of his prayer life, his spiritual encounters. I known of no other record of dreams that contains more dreams of this kind.

I have seldom seen more examples of the clear dream than we find in the record of dreams that Don Bosco has left us.

Sometimes the directions seem ridiculous and yet time bore out the correctness of following these instructions that were given him. Many of us long to get such clear and direct answers to our questions and to receive directions on our paths as we find in the following pages. Don Bosco was a particularly gifted human being and few of us have experiences like this.

Few dreams are more fascinating than dreams that give us extrasensory information, ESP dreams. These dreams can be telepathic and tell us of what is going on in another's mind. How often Don Bosco knew what was in the hearts and minds of the students of his Oratory. In his dreams he was given insights that he did not have in his conscious, waking life. In addition, he often had clairvoyant dreams; he saw what was happening at a great distance from him. Most impressive of all is the precognitive dream where the dreamer gets a glimpse of the future. Here again Don Bosco was given a vision of many things that were hidden by time, but the most amazing vision of the future related to the development and expansion of his order that seemed impossible from a human point of view. When such information received through dreams can be verified it makes us realize that truth can be presented through them and gives us more confidence in the spiritual contents of dreams that cannot be verified.

Not only did his dreams direct Don Bosco, lead him and direct him, they also gave him wisdom and guidance by which he was able to help and guide others upon their ways. He seemed to be in close touch with the Holy Spirit which presented him dreams that showed him where he came from, where he had failed, how he could rectify any mistakes he made, how he could make the greatest use of his potential. His dreams also gave him this information about others and from the record the data given him was almost unerringly correct.

What most people get from dreams only a few times in their lives as they listen to their dreams, Don Bosco received again and again. His visions of heaven were magnificent and he had them frequently. His dreams of hell, however, present a God slightly different from the loving one that he so well exemplified. I wonder if the use of fear so often present in education at his time may not have influenced the pictures that these dreams present. I know the reality of evil and its awfulness and it is just this power that these dreams present with frightening reality. Seldom, however, are people brought to Christ through fear of hell. Christ came to save us from the powers of evil and death by his defeat of them in his crucifixion and resurrection, ascension and in the giving of the Holy Spirit. In interpreting dreams, particularly when they seem to present horror and fear, it is important for us to be sure that our fears and doubts have not added a personal element. But the readers must assess the material for themselves.

There is no other such record of Christian dreams with which I am acquainted. They are also verified by the work that he did among the poor and dispossessed youth in Italy of his time, a work that went out all over the world. The order that he founded has continued this work into our time. In Don Bosco's dreams spirituality and social concern are blended together and are of one piece. Here is genuine Christianity.

Our Response to Don Bosco's Dreams and Visions

If we wish to emulate Don Bosco in his concern for the dream and follow him, what do we do? Several obvious suggestions immediately come to mind. First of all, we need to have a view of the world that sees the spiritual world interpenetrating the physical and influencing it—the view of the world common to what Jesus had and most of the saints of the Church including Don Bosco. Without this view our concern with dreams can become simply a toying with the mysterious. And then we need to believe that God can speak through the dream and present us with all the dimensions of the physical and spiritual worlds. And third, we need to begin to keep a *written record* of our dreams. Our written record is evidence of our belief that dreams are important and that God can touch us in this way. What we do is a better indication of what we truly believe than merely what we say. And then we need to have a spiritual guide or friend with whom we can talk over these strange and wonderful visitations of the night as well as our occasional visions. And then we can pray to God for help in understanding our dreams. In my book *Dreams, A Way to Listen to God,* I tell the story of a woman who found the meaning of a life-changing dream praying before the reserved Sacrament. God still touches us in this way. Those who have found real meaning and answers in prayer will often find meaning in their dreams by bringing them before God with a prayerful attitude. When Joseph was asked in Egypt who there was who could interpret dreams, he replied, "Surely, interpretations come from God." (Gn 40:8)

Often we do not understand the symbols of dreams. We have forgotten the language of myths and symbols and need to learn a whole new language. One can look at individual dream symbols or patterns of them and ask, Do the symbols have any particular or significant meaning? There are volumes written on some dream symbols. Sometimes it helps to look up the meaning of symbols which leave one completely in the dark. J. E. Cirlot has provided us with *A Dictionary of Symbols* (Philosophical Library, 1972). It can be helpful if one uses the suggestions *only* as suggestions. In the indices of the *Collected Works* (Princeton) and of *The Visions Seminars* (Spring Publications, 1976) of C. G. Jung one can find many helpful explanations of the meaning of many symbols. *It is of great importance to remember that one's personal associations with dreams take precedence over the meanings provided by another person or found in any book.* We need to remember that only when the meaning of a symbol or dream "clicks" with the individual who dreamed it is it correct.

It is also wise to remember that usually when we dream of others we are dreaming of an aspect of ourselves that the other person represents rather than of that person. Few people have the incredible telepathic dreams of others that came so frequently to Don Bosco. We always need to deal with ourselves before we deal with others' lives and we should deal with others only when they have asked us to do so or when God has put them in our care.

Many books have been written about understanding and interpreting our dreams. These suggestions are about as adequate as any twenty or thirty pages would be on the subject of prayer and meditation. They are beginnings and if the readers wish to go further they can follow up on the suggestions we have offered. After reading through the dreams of Don Bosco, they can start reading some of the books we have suggested and taking the above suggestions seriously. The important matter is that

God still speaks and that he often speaks through the dream. We may be missing something of great value if we do not listen to them. What the world would have missed if Saint Paul had not listened to his vision of the night at Troas and began his work in Europe, or if Saint John Bosco had ignored his dreams and been a sheepherder or a tailor.

NOTES

1. This book was originally published in 1968 as *Dreams: The Dark Speech of the Spirit.* The original has an extensive appendix with translations of many relevant passages from the Church Fathers and a comprehensive index. In 1978 I published a short guide to the Christian interpretation of dreams entitled *Dreams: A Way to Listen to God.* A summary of both of these books is found in chapters 5, 6 and 7 in *Transcend: A Guide to the Spiritual Quest,* published in 1981. In *Adventure Inward* I give seventeen suggestions in a chapter on dream interpretations. I draw on all these sources. The books of John Sanford, *Dreams, God's Forgotten Language, The Kingdom Within* and *Healing and Wholeness,* are very helpful in understanding the religious function of the dream.

2. Much of this material has been drawn from chapter 5 of my book *Transcend.* The diagram is take from page 57 of my book *Resurrection.*

Introductory Essay

by Arthur J. Lenti, S.D.B.

We wish to thank Rev. Eugene Brown and Don Bosco Publications for this new, handy collection of Don Bosco's dreams in English apart from the *Biographical Memoirs*,[1] one which will make them available to a wider readership.

The *Biographical Memoirs* themselves record some one hundred and fifty dreams of Don Bosco, and the Salesian tradition as a whole has handed down an even larger number. No doubt many dreams were never told or recorded. For over sixty years, from childhood to his death at the age of seventy-two, dreams were a constant occurrence for Don Bosco, and he related them to his followers and to his youngsters for the purpose of edification, instruction and admonishment. Obviously, only significant dreams are recorded here. His normal dreaming activity must have been as intense as anyone else's. Don Bosco was indeed a dreamer, in fact a visionary. His own attitude toward these dreams was at first a doubting one, but he soon developed a healthy respect for them. (See Chapter 1 of this collection, page 3.) He further states that some dreams were a factor in important personal decisions and in setting the direction of his apostolate.[2]

Importance of Don Bosco's Dreams for a Study of the Saint's Life and Work

Great importance is given to dreams, and much use is made of them, in modern psychology and, recently, in spiritual direction. Therefore, such a large body of material, mostly pertaining to the Saint's inner life and apostolate, should not be neglected. A careful study of the dreams should yield valuable insights into Don Bosco's spiritual life, his educational and apostolic experiences and concerns, his fears and hopes for Church and society, and generally his thought and convictions. Don Bosco's writings, including his autobiographical memoirs, do not yield much in this respect. He was fairly reticent about himself, and he kept no personal journal. His dreams, read in continuity and in conjunction with his writings and recorded words of the same period, constitute a valuable source for a study and an understanding of his life and work.

Critical Questions

At this point certain critical questions are raised. Do these narratives represent actual dream experiences? If they do, to what extent, that is with what fidelity, do they record Don Bosco's original dreams? Finally, what precisely was the nature of these experiences? A brief comment on each of these questions is in order.

First, do these narratives represent actual dream experiences? In view of the didactic and educational thrust of many of these narratives, especially such as are exclusively concerned with the spiritual condition and welfare of the youngsters, one is tempted to ask whether these so-called dreams might not be mere didactic parables created by Don Bosco out of his ever-present preoccupation with his children's spiritual welfare. A reputable biographer of the Saint writes:

> Dreams were a recurring experience throughout sixty of the seventy-three years of Don Bosco's life. Of these dreams a good number may be regarded simply as edifying and didactic parables. They are an attempt to express symbolically ideas, tendencies, hopes that were part of Don Bosco's spiritual and educational world. When, however, the future of his work is revealed in a dream with uncanny accuracy and a long time in advance of totally unforeseeable developments, then we are dealing with a different phenomenon.[3]

The *Dream of the Two Columns* of 1862 is narrated by Don Bosco as an "apologue or parable," according to the earliest witness and according to Lemoyne in *Monumenti* (who depends on them),[4] although in the *Biographical Memoirs* Lemoyne has Don Bosco calling it a dream, we know not on what authority.

Obviously, any judgment in this matter can only be tentative. It may be assumed that in most cases we are confronted with true, if not with extraordinary, dream experiences.

Secondly, if these narratives report true dreams, to what extent and with what fidelity do they represent Don Bosco's original experiences? What happens when a considerable lapse of time has intervened between the experience and the telling of the dream? Vivid dreams might persist in the memory in most of their details, but usually images are blurred and details quite soon forgotten. Certain stresses and slants might be introduced into the narrative, by way of interpretation, as a result of subsequent events. Moreover, even when the narration takes place immediately, it might be affected by certain purposes and concerns (didactic, educational) extraneous to the original dream. Finally, one should take into account the limitations inherent in all reporting. The *Lanzo Dream* of 1876 (pp. 255-266 of this collection) is an interesting example in that it is one of the few dreams for which there is extant in the Central Salesian Archives a manuscript draft in Don Bosco's own hand, presumably prepared in view of the telling. This autograph did not become available to Lemoyne (nor to his successors), who relied on notes taken by himself and by others at the time of Don Bosco's narration for the text edited in the *Documenti*. This is also the text of the *Biographical Memoirs* (by Ceria). These reports are likewise preserved in the Central Salesian Archives. On the one hand, Don Bosco's autograph differs significantly, though not substantially, from both the manuscript reprots and the edited text in point of sequence and in a number of details. On the other hand, we witness an editorial development by conflation and rewriting from the first reports to the final text.[5] The case of the already mentioned *Dream of the Two Columns* of 1862 is also revealing. Of it there are extant in the Central Salesian Archives three reports, which were available to Lemoyne and on which he bases the text edited in *Documenti*. But the text edited by him in the *Biographical Memoirs* gives a scenario which goes considerably beyond both the reports and the *Documenti* text—on what authority, again, he does not tell us.[8] To the extent that it is possible to check the biographer's method in this matter, it appears that the final texts are rewritten composites of known reports, in some cases with further changes and additions. Speaking of this method and with reference to the *Lanzo Dream* of 1876, Stella remarks:

> ... The Lemoyne texts carry us considerably beyond the Don Bosco autograph. Some elements included in the text of the *Biographical Memoirs* are much later than Don Bosco's death and can hardly be regarded as part of the tradition stemming from the oral exposition of December 22, 1876. It seems that at times the prevailing concern was to produce a text suitable for public reading rather than one that adhered faithfully to the oral exposition. It should be borne in mind that Fr. Lemoyne, better than anyone else, would know what liberties he could take in the compilation. For he had on occasion been asked by Don Bosco to write up a dream on the basis of the latter's oral exposition made to him. His usual method seems to be that described with respect to a dream of 1868. Fr. Lemoyne says: 'We have faithfully recorded what we ourselves heard at length from Don Bosco or what was testified to us orally or in writing by various priests after coordinating it into one single narrative. It was a difficult task because we wished to record most accurately every word, every link between scenes, and the sequence of incidents, warnings, reproaches, and whatever else he said but did not explain and was perhaps misunderstood.'[7]

Thirdly, what was the nature of these experiences? Ceria speaks of three types:

> This common designation lumps together experiences of a very different order—dreams that were not really dreams; dreams that were nothing but dreams; and dreams of a

revelatory character. Certain dreams were true visions, because they took place in a waking state. Such were, for instance, Don Bosco's prophetic vision at young Cagliero's sick bed and the vision of 1870 on the future of Italy, France, Rome and Paris . . . At other times Don Bosco related, in the family, his common dreams . . . But by far the largest and most characteristic group is that made up of dreams that contain revelatory elements—elements that lay beyond the interpretive power of Don Bosco's own mind . . . The question as to the origin of such dreams is legitimate . . . [8]

While maintaining that "true divine revelations in dream form are relatively infrequent . . . and of difficult interpretation . . .", he goes on to argue for the divine origin of these dreams—from the fact that they show a logical and purposeful plan and development (which is not the case in common dreams); from the fact that the predictions contained in them were later fulfilled; from the fact of knowledge transcending human insight; and from the fact that Don Bosco himself attached great importance to these dreams, was guided by them, and did not object when the word "vision" was used to describe them.[9]

Without passing judgment on the validity of these and similar criteria, I will only remark that in practice, in the case of a particular dream, the criteria of knowledge transcending human insight and of truth-fulfillment are difficult to verify, while the criteria of complexity-continuity and of Don Bosco's personal conviction do not appear determining. Methodologically, therefore, it seems best not to approach the narrative with a preconceived notion about the nature of the experience, but rather to accept it as it stands, seeking to illuminate it with all the critical tools at one's disposal. If, after a thorough study of the dream narrative, it seems appropriate or useful to pass judgment on the nature of the experience, one might then prudently do so.

Typology of Don Bosco's Dreams

Establishing some kind of typology for Don Bosco's dreams, that is to order them according to kind, is a good preliminary measure before a study, or a serious reading, of the dream is undertaken. This may be done on the basis of various criteria.

For example, Don Bosco's dreams may be ordered on the basis of content and function. With this criterion we may distinguish the following groups:

(1) Vocation Dreams—The dream of 1824-1825 and that of 1844, (pp. 7-9 and 11-12 of this collection) are among the most important in this category.

(2) Educational Dreams—These are set in the educational environment in which Don Bosco was personally involved, beginning in the mid-1850's. They deal mostly with problems arising in the educational setting—discipline, morality, Christian life and virtues. In these dreams, predictions of deaths among the youngsters are frequent.

(3) Prophetic Warnings—These related to persons, as well as to Church, State and society, in the time of the liberal revolutions.

(4) Dreams About the Salesian Society—These pertain to the present state and the future of the Salesian Society and its work.

Some dreams are of a composite type, and some do not qualify for these categories, but most do fall under one or more of these four. It may be further noted that one type may be more characteristic of one period in the Saint's life than of another because of the concerns that preoccupied him in that period.

More important for a study of the dreams in establishing a typology on the basis of the tradition and authority of the text itself. Some aspects of this problem have already been covered in our discussion of the critical questions. With this criterion we may identify the following types:

(1) Dream narratives that carry Don Bosco's authentication in the sense that there is extant in the Central Salesian Archives either an autograph manuscript by the Saint, or an allograph manuscript corrected by him. In this category belong

the dreams narrated or mentioned by Don Bosco in his autobiographical memoirs,[10] and ten dream narratives critically edited recently from archival manuscripts.[11]

(2) Dream narratives for which there is extant no autograph manuscript or annotations by Don Bosco, but only reports by persons who heard the Saint's narration. It is a fact that from a certain time on early Salesians around Don Bosco began to write down everything about the Saint that seemed in any way extraordinary. Thus dreams narrated by the Saint in "good nights" or in other situations were written down, usually by several persons, and the reports preserved.[12] From these two types of tradition were derived at one time transcriptions, adaptations, summaries, etc., chiefly for use within the Salesian family. But in the main this activity ceased with the publication of the all-encompassing work of the *Biographical Memoirs*.

(3) A third type would consist of a number of dreams for which there is extant no early report.

Some Conclusions

From what has been discussed thus far, some methodological conclusions for the study, or simply for the reading, of Don Bosco's dreams may be drawn. The critical scholar will actually use such methodology in his or her study of particular dreams. The ordinary reader will bear in mind such points and take them as a guide in evaluating the dream in question.

As a starting point, it seems preferable to assume that the experience lies within the category of dreams in general and is, at least partially, explainable in these terms. In doing so, one does not preclude the possibility that the dream could be a mere apologue or parable (at one end of the scale) or a divine communication (at the other). We are only saying that any determination in this respect, when possible or necessary, is to be made at the end, not at the beginning, of the process.

Secondly, from all available evidence a critical text of the dream narrative must be researched and established. The text of the *Biographical Memoirs* should be evaluated in the light of archival manuscripts, as has already been pointed out.

Thirdly, the dream must be examined and compared with the context in which the dreamer lived. Images, scenes, plot, persons, statements, ideas, language, etc. should be elucidated through comparison with the dreamer's cultural context—in our case, with Don Bosco's social, philosophical and theological ideas: the books he read and wrote; his educational, catechetical and pastoral endeavors at the time; events involving the Salesian Congregation, the Church and society at large, and much more. In other words, one should seek to identify both the materials out of which the dream is fashioned and the stimuli (the internal, if not the external ones) that set the dream in motion. This kind of investigation will enable us not only to clarify the elements of the dream by uncovering the precise references, but also to form at least a preliminary judgment as to the nature of the experience itself.

Fourthly, when dealing with predictions and visions of the future, the student should try to establish the exact parameters of the statements and then investigate how such predictions and forecasts have been fulfilled. It should be noted that the language of these prophecies is often stereotyped, indefinite and highly symbolic. Sometimes this language is patterned on that of the almanacs and prophetic books in circulation.[13] Then again, prophecy often has a conditional character, even when this is not specified. All this makes verification of fulfillment difficult. For instance, the "dawn of glory" predicted for the Congregation in the *Lanzo Dream* of 1876 cannot be identified with certainty. Don Bosco's autograph manuscript reads (with no time specification):

> A glorious day will dawn for the Salesian Congregation from the four corners of the earth. Battle and triumph. Its soldiers will grow in numbers, if its leaders will not allow the chariot in which rides the Lord to stray off the road.[14]

The text of the *Biographical Memoirs* reads:

> The Lord is preparing great things for you. In the coming year your Congregation will see a dawn of glory so resplendent that it will light up the four corners of the earth.

A great splendor lies in the offing. But see to it that the Lord's chariot is not led by your Salesians off its course, out of its set path.[15]

On the basis of the latter text, the worldwide "dawn of glory" has been identified as the launching of the Salesian Cooperators and of the *Salesian Bulletin* in 1876-77. But this must remain problematic.[16] Moreover, it may be asked on the basis of the first text, could Don Bosco merely have forecast the worldwide growth of the Salesian Society in the indeterminate future?

Supernatural Revelations

Don Bosco was a totally committed person. He was consumed with zeal for God, for the Church, for souls, for society. These concerns so completely absorbed his waking hours and the little sleep he allowed himself that dreaming about matters that constituted the sole reason of his existence was for him an activity no different from his habitual expression of these concerns in speech and action. One might say that much in Don Bosco's dreams is explainable in terms of the context in which he lived and worked. Moreover, he was in the highest degree insightful and sensitive. He was a psychic, endowed with powers that pertain to the field of extrasensory perception, such as clairvoyance and precognition. But when all is said and done in the way of critical appraisal, there are numerous aspects that seem to defy natural, scientific explanations.

In particular, the contents of Don Bosco's dreams leave us wondering. Time and again his dreams deal with social and political events, or with situations within his experience, in a fashion both elaborate and logically calculated. It has been observed that people usually do not dream in that way.

> Hall investigated dream content on the basis of more than 10,000 dreams by hundreds of subjects. He found that people tend not to dream about current events of political, social, or economical nature. Nor do they dream about their work, business, and occupations. The content of

dreams is usually very personal and intimate, and has to do with one's attitudes toward oneself and toward important persons in one's environment. The cast of the dream is the subject himself and people who play an important role in his life. The setting is more often recreational, involving activities of a leisurely nature...[17]

It must be admitted that Don Bosco's recorded dreams do not comply with this natural pattern of dreaming. They are not personal and intimate, and do not have to do with Don Bosco's attitudes towards himself. As has been remarked above, some dreams may well be didactic stories created with logic and calculation; some predictions of deaths among the Oratory youngsters in dreams might well be natural acts of precognition. In spite of these possibilities, a great number of Don Bosco's recorded dreams defy such explanations. Therefore, one is left to wonder: Is the finger of God at work here?

NOTES

1. G.B. Lemoyne, A. Amadei and E. Ceria, *The Biographical Memoirs of Saint John Bosco*. D. Borgatello, ed., New Rochelle, NY: Salesian Publishers, 1965-1985 (14 volumes). This is the English translation of the first 14 volumes of the 19-volume (Italian) *Memorie Biografiche di San Giovanni Bosco. The Biographical Memoirs* (hereafter *BM*) are the monumental work of Fr. G.B. Lemoyne and his successor, Frs. A. Amadei and E. Ceria. Fr. G.B. Lemoyne joined Don Bosco at the Oratory as a priest in 1864. After serving in various important posts, he was appointed secretary to the General Council of the Society in 1883 and remained at Don Bosco's side until the Saint's death in 1888. Through all those years, with the collaboration of many helpers, he amassed a huge fund of historical material on Don Bosco and the Salesian Society in view of a projected comprehensive history of the Founder and his work. Later, as official historian of the Society he edited this material in the privately printed Documenti (45 volumes). From these and additional materials he published 8 volumes of the *Biographical Memoirs* between 1898 and 1912, volume 9 appearing one year after his death in 1916. Volume 10 and volumes 11-19 were published by Frs. A. Amadei and E. Ceria respec-

tively between 1930 and 1939, on the basis of both Lemoyne's work and their own further research.

2. Don Bosco's autobiographical memoirs: *San Giovanni Bosco, Memorie dell'Oratorio di San Francesco di Sales dal 1815 al 1855.* E. Ceria, ed. Torino: SEI, 1946, p. 136, (hereafter *MO*). These memoirs were composed by Don Bosco, upon injunction from Pius IX, between 1873 and 1876. In them are described, "in retrospect," Don Bosco's early years, schooling and vocation, the founding and early history of the Oratory up to 1855. Of the *MO* there are extant in the Central Salesian Archives an autographed rough draft by Don Bosco and a good copy by Fr. Berto, his secretary, and corrected by Don Bosco.

3. A. Caviglia, *Don Bosco.* Torino: L.I.C.E., 1934, pp. 35-36.

4. Cf. P. Stella, *Don Bosco nella storia della religiosità cattolica,* Vol. II. Roma: LAS, 1981, 565ff.

5. Compare the critically edited text of Don Bosco's autograph in C. Romero, *I sogni di Don Bosco.* Leumann (Torino): LDC, 1978, pp. 40-44 with *BM* XII: 432-441; and cf. P. Stella, *op cit.*, pp. 510-517.

6. Compare documents in P. Stella, *op cit.*, pp. 563-569 with *BM* VII: 107-109; and cf. P. Stella, *op cit.*, pp. 547-554.

7. P. Stella, *op cit.*, pp. 516-517. The reference for the Lemoyne quote is *BM* IX: 100.

8. *BM* (Italian) XVII: 7-8. For the vision at Cagliero's bedside cf. *BM* V: 67-68. For the vision of 1870 cf. *BM* 10: 49-55.

9. *BM* (Italian) XVII: 12.

10. *MO* pp. 22, 43-44, 79, 80, 134, 136. These are the vocation dreams referred to above. For a description of the *MO* cf. note 2.

11. C. Romero, *op. cit.* (cf. note 5). The ten critically edited dream texts are: the Prophecy of 1870; the Message to Pius IX of 1873; the Message to the Emperor of Austria of 1873; the Lanzo (Salesian Garden, or Savio) Dream of 1876; the Message to Leo XIII of 1878; the Dream on Future Salesian Vocations of 1879; the (San Benigno) Dream of the Diamonds of 1881; the Provera Dream of 1883; the Dream on the South American Missions of 1883; and the Dream of the Handmaid of the Lord, in two parts, of 1887. The messages are not properly presented as dreams, but as divine communications.

12. A number of chronicles and other reports by such early Salesians as Berberis, Berto, Bonetti, Ruffino, etc. are preserved in the Central Salesian Archives. For the formation and activity of "historical committee" of 1861 cf. *BM* VI: 505-507.

13. Cf. P. Stella, *op. cit.*, pp. 535-539.
14. C. Romero, *op cit.*, p. 43.
15. *BM* XII: 439.
16. Ibid., pp. 441-442. Cf. P. Stella, *op cit.*, pp. 521-522.
17. A.M. Cuk, "Dreams," in *Catholic Encyclopedia* (1966) 4: 1054.

Editor's Preface

All but eleven of the dreams in this book were taken, usually verbatim, from the 14 volumes in English (as of the date of this writing) of *The Biographical Memoirs of Saint John Bosco*, Rev. Diego Borgatello, S.D.B., Editor-in-chief. The introduction and comments of the author of the Memoirs have often been included for reasons of clarity and continuity. The remaining dreams (not necessarily in order) can be found in volumes 15 through 20 of the Italian edition: *Memorie Biografiche del Beato Giovanni Bosco*. I am indebted to Rev. Hugh McGlinchey, S.D.B., for the English translation of the other eleven dreams; they were selected and edited from his unpublished work entitled: *Dreams to Hope By*.

The division of the dreams of this book into categories is my own; even though some dreams do not fit neatly into one classification or another, it is hoped that the reader will find this helpful. In the narration of some of the dreams, passages from Scripture and other quotations were given in both Latin and English. The Latin has been omitted in this edition.

Rev. Eugene M. Brown
Don Bosco Multimedia

CHAPTER 1

The Significance of Dreams in the Life of Don Bosco

Father Giovanni Battista Lemoyne (1839-1916) was the original chronicler of the life of Don Bosco. In the first volume of what was to become a 20 volume set (in Italian) of biographical memoirs, he writes:

An unbroken tradition has made [Don Bosco's dreams] history at the Oratory. When asked about them, Don Bosco never denied them. Furthermore, he told us of many other similar happenings, some really marvelous. A biographer cannot ignore them, because it would be like writing the life of Napoleon without mentioning any of his victories. *Don Bosco* and the word *dream* are correlative. If this biography were to ignore this fact, his former pupils by the thousands would ask: "What about his dreams?"

It is truly astounding how this phenomenon went on in his life for sixty years. After a day marked by many worrisome problems, plans, hard work, he would no sooner rest his weary head on his pillow than he would enter a new world of ideas and visions that would exhaust him until dawn. No other man could have endured this continuous shifting from a natural to a preternatural or supernatural level without serious mental injury. Don Bosco could; he was always calm and deliberate in all his actions.

We are mindful of the words of Sirach: "Empty and false are the hopes of the senseless, and fools are borne aloft by dreams. Like a man who catches at shadows or chases the wind, is the one who believes in dreams." (Sir 34:1-2) ". . . Divinations, omens and dreams all are unreal; what you already expect, the mind depicts. Unless it be a vision specially sent by the Most High, fix not your heart on it: for dreams have led many astray, and those who believed in them have perished. The law is fulfilled without fail, and perfect wisdom is found in the mouth of the faithful man." (Sir 34:5 8)

That is very well and to the point. But it is also true that in both the Old and New Testaments, as well as in the lives of innumerable saints, the Lord in His fatherly love gave comfort, counsel, commands, a spirit of prophecy, threats and messages of hope and reward both to individuals and to entire nations through dreams. Were Don Bosco's dreams like those? We repeat that we shall not venture an opinion. Others will have to pass judgment. We say only that Don Bosco's life was an intricate pattern of wondrous events in which one cannot but perceive direct divine assistance. Hence, we must reject the notion that he was a fool, or that he labored under illusions, or that he was vain and deceitful. Those who lived at his side for thirty and forty years never once detected in him the least sign that would betray a desire to win the esteem of his peers by pretending to be endowed with supernatural gifts. Don Bosco was a humble man, and humility abhors insincerity. His stories were always and solely directed to the glory of God and the salvation of souls, and were marked by a simplicty that won all hearts. We never heard anything that might suggest a disturbed mind or a desire for effect in describing scenes concerning Catholic truths. Discussing his dreams, Don Bosco said to us many times: "Call them dreams, call them parables, call them whatever you wish, I am sure that they will always do some good." (Vol. I, pp. 190-191)

Many of the dreams of Don Bosco could more properly be called visions, for God used this means to reveal His will for Don Bosco and for the boys of the Oratory, as well as the future of the Salesian Congregation. Father Lemoyne continues:

Although Don Bosco attached great significance to these dreams, he always spoke of them with sincere humility. It was obvious that he was not in any way trying to glorify himself. In fact, before narrating one of these dreams, he would always preface his talk with some words designed to banish any semblance of merit or privilege on his part. Often he would even adopt a witty tone and play down the extraordinary elements so as to make them appear quite natural and matter-of-fact to his listeners; however, they knew better. Nevertheless, what he did showed how important he believed them to be. He did not spare himself in preaching, hearing confessions, or listening to the boys who came to him privately, anxious to know what he had learned about their present or future state. Unfailingly, his dreams instilled a healthy horror of sin far more effectively than a spiritual retreat. All the boys would go to confession with genuine sorrow, and many would make a general confession. A greater number than usual would also receive Communion, to their own spiritual benefit. It could not have been otherwise, because the boys realized that the predictions of one who could read their innermost thoughts would unfailingly come true. Nevertheless, Don Bosco once confided to us: "At first I was hesitant about giving these dreams the importance they deserved. I often regarded them as mere flights of fancy. As I was narrating these dreams and predicting deaths and other future events, several times I wondered if I had rightly understood things, and I became fearful that what I said might actually be untrue. Occasionally, after narrating a dream, I could no longer remember what I had said. Therefore, in confessing to Father Cafasso, I sometimes accused myself of having spoken perhaps rashly. The saintly priest would listen to me, think the matter over, and then say: 'Since your predictions come true, you need not worry. You may continue to make them.' " (Vol. V, pp. 242-243)

Canon Hyacinth Ballesio writes of the effects of Don Bosco's dreams on the boys of the Oratory:

Don Bosco lived for us. Even his very scanty sleep was crowded with thoughts of his children as he dreamed of them. Were they dreams or visions? He called them dreams, but we were convinced that they were nothing less than visions. I remember the dream in which he saw his boys, numbering more than four hundred students and artisans, in various poses symbolizing their spiritual condition. He narrated it on successive evenings after night prayers, so vividly and forcefully that it rang forth like a prophecy. In this dream he saw some pupils resplendent with light, others with a heart full of pure gold, and still others with hideous, horrid features or looking like animals with hearts full of clay. He had seen youngsters surrounded, besieged or assailed by wild animals, typifying temptations, dangerous occasions and sins. Don Bosco told us this dream with simplicity, gravity and fatherly affection, giving it maximum importance. Its impression on all of us was unique and most wholesome. One after another we each went to him to learn in what condition he had seen us. To our astonishment, everyone had to admit that what Don Bosco had seen was true.

The effect of this dream on the boys' conduct was so great that the most powerful spiritual retreat scarcely could have equaled it. These extraordinary things which I mention cannot be explained by Don Bosco's natural insight or the knowledge he derived from his confidential talks with the boys or from his co-workers' reports. Don Bosco's words and actions were such that, under the circumstances, we who were no longer children could see no rational or plausible explanation other than to accept the fact that these were heavenly charisms. Considering just this dream or vision, how could he have otherwise seen and remembered so unerringly the spiritual condition of each of his four hundred pupils? Among them were newcomers who had recently arrived at the Oratory and others who had never gone to confession to him; yet, on hearing Don Bosco's vivid, intimate description of their souls, of their inclinations, and of their most secret doings, they had to admit that what he said was true. (Vol. VI, pp. 545-546)

Bishop John Cagliero, who had been a student at the Oratory during its early days, writes:

I was there in 1861 when Don Bosco narrated the dream of "The Wheel of Eternity," in which he had seen the future of the fledgling Salesian Congregation. He told us about these dreams after consulting Father Cafasso, who advised him to keep giving them importance "with a clear conscience," for he judged them to be for God's greater glory and the good of souls. Don Bosco disclosed this to us, his closest co-workers, some years before Father Cafasso's death.

The boys' attention to his words was surprisingly impressive. On his part, Don Bosco unerringly and unhesitatingly would privately tell each one who asked him—and very many of us did—what he was doing in the wheat field and what it meant. It took Don Bosco three consecutive evenings to relate this dream, which we discussed among ourselves and with our beloved father for quite some time, convinced that it had given him a clear knowledge of the Oratory's future and that of the

Salesian Congregation. Privately, in the company of his closest co-workers, he delighted in repeating the description of the golden wheat ripening in that mysterious field and the various poses of the reapers and of those who were handing out the sickles. He also assured us that, contrary to expectations, our Congregation, despite great opposition and persecution, would be approved, survive, prosper, and extraordinarily expand, to the astonishment of many good, prudent people who thought otherwise. All these things I have repeatedly heard from companions and from Don Bosco himself. (Vol. VI, p. 546)

Biographers of Don Bosco have noted the profound influence of Pope Pius IX on his life and mission. Don Bosco had great respect for the office of the papacy and for the person of Pius IX. The pope had taken a keen interest in the progress of the Oratory, and over the course of time encouraged Don Bosco to found a new religious order. Pope Pius IX gave official Church approval to the Constitution of the Society of St. Francis de Sales on April 3, 1874.

At an audience some years before (March 21, 1858), Pope Pius IX had told Don Bosco:

"When you get back to Turin, write down these dreams and everything else you have told me, minutely and in their natural sense. Save all this as a legacy for your Congregation, so that it may serve as an encouragement and norm for your sons." (Vol. V, p. 577)

Nearly nine years later (January 12, 1867), Pope Pius IX asked Don Bosco:

"Well, did you follow my advice? Did you write down those things which had a bearing in inspiring you to found your Society?" "Your Holiness," Don Bosco replied, "I truthfully lacked the time. I was so taken up with . . ." "Well, then, I not only advise you but order you to do it. This task must have priority over everything else. Put aside the rest and take care of this. You cannot now fully grasp how very beneficial certain things will be to your sons when they shall know them." Don Bosco promised to do that, and he kept his word.

(Vol. VIII, p. 256)

Father Angelo Amadei became Father Lemoyne's assistant in the research and compilation of *The Biographical Memoirs*, and continued this work after Father Lemoyne's death in 1916.

Father Amadei states that there were over 140 reported dreams and visions of Don Bosco. We present here a selection of these, under the following categories:

1) The mission of Don Bosco and the future of the Order
2) Predictions of future events
3) Dreams about the boys of the Oratory
4) Dreams about Heaven and Hell

CHAPTER 2

The Mission of Don Bosco and the Future of the Order

From his very first dream at the age of nine, and continuing, apparently, for the remainder of his life, Don Bosco was favored by God with dreams which gave him clear directions for his life and ministry. God revealed to Don Bosco that he would become a priest; that he would work with boys and bring them closer to Jesus and to His mother; that he would establish a religious order which would spread throughout Italy and Europe and would eventually send missionaries to many other countries of the world. These dreams contained many details which proved, years later, to be completely accurate and correct.

THE FIRST DREAM

"When I was about nine years old I had a dream that left a profound impression on me for the rest of my life. I dreamed that I was near my home, in a very large playing field where a crowd of children were having fun. Some were laughing, others were playing and not a few were cursing. I was so shocked at their language that I jumped into their midst, swinging wildly and shouting at them to stop. At that moment a Man appeared, nobly attired, with a manly and imposing bearing. He was clad with a white flowing mantle and his face radiated such light that I could not look directly at him. He called me by my name and told me to place myself as leader over those boys, adding the words:

" 'You will have to win these friends of yours not with blows, but with gentleness and kindness. So begin right now to show them that sin is ugly and virtue beautiful.'

"Confused and afraid, I replied that I was only a boy and

unable to talk to these youngsters about religion. At that moment the fighting, shouting and cursing stopped and the crowd of boys gathered about the Man who was now talking. Almost unconsciously I asked:

" 'But how can you order me to do something that looks so impossible?'

" 'What seems so impossible you must achieve by being obedient and by acquiring knowledge.'

" 'But where, how?'

" 'I will give you a Teacher, under whose guidance you will learn and without whose help all knowledge becomes foolishness.'

" 'But who are you?'

" 'I am the Son of Her whom your mother has taught you to greet three times a day.'

" 'My mother told me not to talk to people I don't know, unless she gives me permission. So, please tell me your name.'

" 'Ask my mother.'

"At that moment I saw beside him a Lady of majestic appearance, wearing a beautiful mantle glowing as if bedecked with stars. She saw my confusion mount; so she beckoned me to her. Taking my hand with great kindness she said:

" 'Look!'

"I did so. All the children had vanished. In their place I saw many animals: goats, dogs, cats, bears and a variety of others.

" 'This is your field, this is where you must work,' the Lady told me. 'Make yourself humble, steadfast and strong. And what you will see happen to these animals you will have to do for my children.'

"I looked again; the wild animals had turned into as many lambs, gently gamboling lambs, bleating a welcome for that Man and Lady.

"At this point of my dream I started to cry and begged the Lady to explain what it all meant because I was so utterly confused. She then placed her hand on my head and said:

" 'In due time everything will be clear to you.'

"After she had spoken these words, some noise awoke me; everything had vanished. I was completely bewildered. Somehow my hands still seemed to ache and my cheeks still stung because of all the fighting. Moreover, my conversation with that Man and Lady so disturbed my mind that I was unable to sleep any longer that night.

"In the morning I could barely wait to tell about my dream. When my brothers heard it, they burst out laughing. I then told my mother and grandmother. Each one who heard it gave it a different interpretation. My brother Joseph said:

" 'You're going to become a shepherd and take care of goats, sheep and livestock.'

"My mother's comment was: 'Who knows? Maybe you will become a priest.'

"Dryly, Anthony muttered: 'You might become the leader of a gang of robbers.'

"But my very religious, illiterate grandmother, had the last word: 'You mustn't pay any attention to dreams.'

"I felt the same way about it, yet I could never get that dream out of my head. What I am about to relate may give some new insight to it. I never brought up the matter and my relatives gave no importance to it. But in 1858, when I went to Rome to confer with the Pope about the Salesian Congregation, Pius IX asked me to tell him everything that might have even only the slightest bearing on the supernatural. Then for the first time I told him the dream that I had when I was nine. The Pope ordered me to write it in detail for the encouragement of the members of the Congregation, for whose sake I had gone to Rome." (Vol. I, pp. 95-96)

THE TAILOR'S SHOP

Don Bosco told this confidentially to a few at the Oratory, among them Father John Turchi and Father Dominic Ruffino.

"Can you imagine," he said, "how I saw myself during my first year of philosophy?"

"Was it in a dream?" someone asked.

"That doesn't matter," Don Bosco replied. "I saw myself as a priest wearing surplice and stole. I was sitting in a tailor's shop, not sewing new clothes, but mending old ones torn and full of patches. Then and there I did not grasp its meaning. I mentioned this to someone or other but never fully disclosed it until I was a priest, even then only to my spiritual director, Father Cafasso."

This dream or vision remained indelibly engraved in Don Bosco's memory. It meant that he was called not just for a select group of innocent boys in order to shield them from evil and make them advance in virtue, but also that he was to gather around himself wayward boys, already tainted by evil and lead them again to the practice of virtue and make them good citizens. (Vol. I, p. 285)

THIS IS MY MOTHER

Don Bosco saw the valley below the Susambrino estate transformed into a big city. Gangs of boys were running through the streets and squares shouting, playing and cursing. John could not stand that, and quick-tempered as he was by nature, he scolded them and threatened to hit them if they would not stop it. They paid no attention whatever and so he began to strike out. They lost no time in jumping him and pounding him fiercely. John had to take to his heels. But suddenly he met a Man who ordered him to stop and go back to teach those boys how to be good and avoid evil. John complained that they had already beaten him up and would do it again and worse if he went back. Then this Man introduced him to a Lady of very noble aspect who was coming forward. He told John: "This is my Mother. Listen to Her."

The Lady looked at John intently and lovingly and then said. "If you wish to win over these boys, do not hit them: be kind and appeal to their better selves."

Then, as in his first dream, he saw the boys transformed into wild animals and then again into sheep and lambs, and he himself their shepherd by the Lady's order. The Prophet Isaiah had envisioned something similar: "Wild beasts honor me, jackals and ostriches, for I put water in the desert and rivers in the wasteland for my chosen people to drink, the people whom I formed for myself that they might announce my praise." (Is 43:20-21)

Perhaps this was the time when he envisioned the Oratory with all its buildings ready for him and his boys. One of his fellow seminarians, a Father Bosio of Castagnole, who later became pastor at Levone Canavese, paid his first visit to the Oratory in 1890. The Superior Chapter accompanied him on a tour of the House. Passing through the courtyard, the priest looked around at the many buildings enclosing it and then exclaimed: "What I see is not new to me. In the seminary Don Bosco described it all to me, as if he had seen with his own eyes what he was telling me. It is just as he described it." And the good priest was greatly moved while reminiscing about his schoolmate and friend. (Vol. I, p. 316)

THE SHEPHERDESS

A wonderful thing happened during those days to comfort Don Bosco, by disclosing future events to him. Let us narrate it in his own words from the pages of his memoirs:

On the second Sunday of that year (1844) I was to tell my boys that the oratory was being transferred to the Valdocco area. I was, however, truly worried because I was uncertain about the exact location, the means and the people [to help me]. On Saturday night, I went to bed feeling uneasy, but that night I had a new dream which seemed to be a sequel to the one I had had at Becchi when about nine years old. I think it best to put it down literally.

I dreamed that I was in the midst of a multitude of wolves, goats, kids, lambs, sheep, rams, dogs and birds. The whole menagerie raised an uproar, a bedlam, or, better, a racket that would have frightened even the bravest man. I wanted to run away, when a Lady, dressed as a shepherdess, beckoned me to follow Her and accompany the strange flock She was leading. We wandered aimlessly, making three stops along the way, at each of which many of those animals changed into lambs, so that the number of lambs continually increased. After a long trek, I found I was in a meadow, where those animals were grazing and frolicking, making no attempt to bite each other.

I was exhausted and wanted to sit by the roadside, but the Shepherdess invited me to keep walking. A short distance away, I came upon a large playground surrounded by porticoes, with a church at one end. Here I noticed that four fifths of those animals had become lambs. Their number was now very large. At that moment many young shepherds came to watch over them, but they remained only a short time and walked off. Then a marvelous thing happened: many lambs turned into shepherds, and they, in increasing numbers, took care of the flock. When the shepherds became too many, they parted and went elsewhere to herd other strange animals into pens.

I wanted to leave, because I thought it was time for me to say Mass, but the Shepherdess asked me to look to the south. On doing so, I saw a field in which maize, potatoes, cabbage, beets, lettuce and many other vegetables had been planted. "Look again" She said. I did so, and beheld a monumental church. In the choirloft I saw choristers and musicians who seemed to be inviting me to sing Mass. On a white streamer inside the church there was emblazoned in large letters HERE IS MY HOUSE AND HENCE MY GLORY WILL COME FORTH. Still dreaming, I asked the Shepherdess where I was, and the meaning of all this walking, the stops, that house, the church and then another church. "You will understand everything," She answered, "when with your bodily eyes you will behold all that you now see in your mind." I thought I was awake, and so I said, "I see clearly, and with my bodily eyes; I know where I am going and what I am doing." Just then the bell of Saint Francis of Assisi Church rang the *Ave Maria* and I awoke.

The dream lasted nearly the whole night and there were many other details. At the time I understood little of it because, distrusting myself, I put little faith in it. As things gradually began to take shape, I began to understand. In fact, later on, this dream, together with another, formed the basis of my planning while at the *Rifugio*. (Vol. II, pp. 190-191)

THE RIBBON OF OBEDIENCE

Strange dreams, lasting through the night, came to comfort Don Bosco ... In these mysterious visions a series of interlaced scenes kept recurring along with various new ones. But the previous scenes never wholly faded from view. They blended with the marvels of new dreams, all seeming to converge on one point only: the future of the oratory.

I seemed to be in a vast meadow with a huge crowd of boys who were fighting, swearing, stealing, and doing other blameable things. The air was thick with flying stones, hurled by youngsters who were fighting. They were all abandoned boys, devoid of moral principles. I was about to turn away when I saw a Lady beside me. "Go among those boys," She said, "and work."

I approached them, but what could I do? I had no place to gather them, but I wanted to help them. I kept turning to some people who were watching from a distance, and who could have come to my aid, but no one paid attention or gave me any assistance. I then turned to the Lady. "Here is a place," She said, and pointed to a meadow.

"That's only a meadow," I said.

She replied: "My Son and His Apostles did not even have a place to lay their head." (cf. Mt 8:20) I began to work in that meadow, counseling, preaching, hearing confessions, but I saw that almost all my efforts were in vain. I had to have some building where I could gather and house those abandoned by their parents and those despised and rejected by society. Then the Lady led me a little further to the north and said: "Look!"

I did so and saw a small church with a low roof, a small courtyard, and a great number of boys. I resumed my work, but since the church was becoming too small, I again appealed to the Lady and She pointed out another church, much larger, and a house adjacent to it. Then She took me closer, to a field that was tilled and that lay almost opposite the facade of this new church. "In this place," She added, "where the glorious martyrs of Turin, Adventor and Octavius, suffered martyrdom, on those clods soaked and sanctified by their blood, I wish that God be honored in a very special manner." So saying, She put out Her foot and pointed to the exact spot where the martyrs had fallen. I wanted to leave a marker there so as to find the place again when I returned, but I could not see a single stick or stone. Nevertheless, I kept the place clearly in mind. It coincides exactly with the inner corner of the chapel of the Holy Martyrs, previously known as St. Anne's Chapel; it is the front left corner as one faces the main altar of the church of Mary Help of Christians.

In the meantime, I found myself being surrounded by a very vast and ever increasing number of boys, but, as I kept looking to the Lady, the premises and the means were also growing accordingly. I saw then a very grand church on the very spot She had pointed out as the place where the soldiers of the Theban legion had been martyred. There were a great many buildings all around, and in the center stood a beautiful monument.

While these things were taking place and I was still dreaming, I saw that priests and clerics were helping me, but after a while, they left. I tried everything to get others to stay, but after a while they too left me alone. Then I turned once more to the Lady for help. "Do you want to know what to do to keep them?" She asked. "Take this ribbon and bind their foreheads with it." Reverently I took the white ribbon from Her hand and noticed the word *Obedience* written on it. I immediately gave it a try and began to bind the foreheads of these volunteers. The ribbon worked wonders, as I went ahead with the mission entrusted to me. All my helpers gave up the idea of leaving me, and stayed on. Thus was our Congregation born.

I saw a great many other things, but there is no need to relate them now. (Maybe he was referring to important future events.) Suffice it to say that ever since, I have walked on sure ground as regards the Oratories, the Congregation, and the manner of dealing with outsiders, irrespective of their position. I have already foreseen all the difficulties that will arise and I know how to overcome them. I can see perfectly, bit by bit, what is to take place, and I go forward without hesitation. It was only after I had seen churches, schools, playgrounds, boys, clerics and priests helping me, and I had learned how to advance the entire apostolate, that I began to mention it to others and speak of it as a reality. That is why so many people thought that I was talking foolishly and believed I was insane.

Here then was the source of that unshakeable faith in the ultimate success of his mission, of that sureness that seemed temerity, in tackling all sorts of obstacles, that taking on of colossal undertakings which were more than any man could handle and bring to completion.

As for the spot pointed out by the Blessed Virgin to Don Bosco as the place of the martyrdom of Saints Adventor and Octavius, from which Saint Solutor fled, wounded by a lance, to die at Ivrea as he vowed allegiance to Jesus Christ, we can give a lengthier explanation.

Don Bosco was determined never to tell anybody of this dream, and even less inclined to manifest what he knew about the precise spot of that glorious event. Therefore, in 1865, he suggested to Canon Lawrence Gastaldi that he write the lives of these three Theban martyrs, after doing some research; and that, with the help of history, tradition and topography, he point out the probable spot where they were martyred. The learned canon agreed, and published an historical study on these three martyrs. After a lengthy examination of the evidence, he concluded that it was not possible to designate exactly where they were martyred, that it was certain they had sought safety outside the city gates near the Dora River, but had been discovered and martyred near their hiding place. He also stated that the vast stretch of land extending from the city gates to the Dora River, west of the borough of that name, was in ancient times known by the name of *vallis or vallum occisorum*, the valley of the slain, and is now popularly known by the first three syllables, *Vald'occo*, possibly with reference to the three martyrs who were killed there. It was also undeniable that this area had obviously been blessed by God, since wonderful works of charity and devotion had risen there, another clue that the spot had been bathed by the blood of those brave Christians. The author added that, after carefully studying the ancient topography of the city, he was of the opinion that the Oratory of Saint Francis de Sales was built near that hallowed spot, or perhaps enclosed it within its walls.

Don Bosco was delighted with this information which, in a way, confirmed what he had learned in his dream. Even from the very beginning of the Oratory, he showed a particular devotion to these holy martyrs. Every year on the feast day of Saint Maurice, the commander of the Theban legion, he linked his name to that of his glorious legion and to his three soldiers, and saw to it that their feast was celebrated with many Communions in the morning and with solemn vespers in the evening, with a homily in their honor, and Benediction of the Blessed Sacrament. (Vol. II, pp. 232-235)

THIS IS MY HOUSE

Don Bosco seemed to be at the northern edge of the *Rondò* or Valdocco Circle. Looking toward the Dora River, along the tall trees which at that time lined the boulevard now known as *Corso Regina Margherita*, he happened to see, about 200 feet away, near the present *Via Cottolengo*, three handsome youths, resplendent with brilliance. They were standing in a field then planted with potatoes, maize, beans and cabbage, and they stood precisely on the spot which in a previous dream had been pointed out to him as the place where the three soldiers of the Theban legion had gloriously suffered martyrdom. They gestured to him to come and join them. Don Bosco hurried over and, with great kindness, they took him to the farther end of that field, where the majestic church of Mary Help of Christians now stands.

During that brief walk Don Bosco saw wonder upon wonder, and finally he stood before a Lady remarkably beautiful and majestic, splendidly clothed, around whom stood venerable men who resembled a senate of princes. Hundreds of people in glittering array formed Her retinue as though She were a queen, and other similar throngs were visible as far as the eye could see. The Lady, who stood where the main altar is now located, beckoned to Don Bosco to draw nearer. When he was close to Her, She told him that the three young men who had accompanied him were the martyrs Solutor, Adventor and Octavius, and he interpreted this to mean that they would be the patron saints of that place.

Then, with an enchanting smile and affectionate words, She encouraged him never to abandon his boys, but to carry on the great work he had begun with even more determination. She informed him that he would encounter many serious obstacles, but that they would all be overcome and swept aside by his firm faith in the Mother of God and Her Divine Son.

Finally She pointed out to him a house which really did exist and which he later found out belonged to a man named

Pinardi. She also showed him a small church on the same spot where the church of Saint Francis de Sales and its adjacent building now stand. She then raised Her right hand and in an infinitely melodious voice said: *This is my house: hence my glory will come forth.* On hearing these words Don Bosco was so moved that he woke up. The Blessed Virgin, for truly that was She, and the entire vision faded slowly from view as the mist at dawn. (Vol. II, p. 268)

Difficulties never deterred Don Bosco from his resolve: this was a lifetime trait of his. Once he had reached a decision, after long reflection and consultation with his superiors and other prudent people, he never withdrew until he had completed his task. But he started nothing from purely human motives. While asleep he was favored with visions that offered enlightenment. These he narrated to Father [Michael] Rua and others in the first years of his work.

Sometimes he would find himself gazing upon some buildings and a church, the whole complex identical to the present Oratory of St. Francis de Sales. On the facade of the church there was the legend: *This is my house: hence my glory will come forth.* Boys, seminarians, and priests were coming and going through its portals. This vision sometimes gave way to another: in the same place there would appear the little Pinardi house, and around it porticoes adjoining a church, and a large number of boys, clerics and priests. "But this can't be," Don Bosco told himself; "that is too good to be true. Is this a diabolical illusion?" Then he distinctly heard a voice saying to him, "Do you not know that the Lord can enrich His people with the spoils of the Egyptians?"

At other times he seemed to be in *Via Cottolengo.* On his right, there stood the Pinardi house in the midst of a vegetable garden, surrounded by fields; on his left, almost opposite the Pinardi house, was the Moretta house with the adjacent playgrounds and fields, where the Daughters of Mary Help of Christians were later to establish themselves. Two pillars rose at the main gate of the future Oratory of Saint Francis de Sales, and over them Don Bosco could read the following inscription: *"From here and from there my glory will come forth."* This was evidently the first intimation of a sister congregation which was to flourish beside the Salesians. If he saw the latter, is it not likely that he also saw the Sisters? Be that as it may, he was sparing with words in these matters, so he said nothing at that time.

Meanwhile, the first dream he had had at the *Convitto* was about to be verified. Don Bosco was to make three stops before finding a permanent residence. The first had been at the *Rifugio* and the second at the *Molini Dora.* The Moretta house with its meadow was to be the third. May God be blessed!

(Vol. II, p. 318)

ROSES AND THORNS

Don Bosco first related this dream in 1864 when one night, after prayers, as was his custom at times, he gathered the members of his infant Congregation in his anteroom for a conference... After speaking of detachment from the world and from one's own family to follow Our Lord's example, he continued:

I have already told you of several things I saw as in a dream. From them we can infer how much Our Lady loves and helps us. But now that we are all together alone, I am going to tell you not just another dream, but something that Our Lady Herself graciously showed me. I am doing this that each of us may be convinced that it is Our Lady Herself who wants our Congregation. This should spur us to work even harder for God's greater glory. She wants us to place all our trust in Her. I am taking you into my confidence. Please do not mention what I tell you to anyone else in this house or to outsiders, lest you give evil tongues occasion to wag.

One day in 1847, after I had spent much time reflecting on how I might help others, especially the young, the Queen of Heaven appeared to me. She led me into a beautiful garden. There stood there a rustic but wide and charming portico built as a vestibule. Its pillars were dressed with climbing vines whose tendrils, thick with leaves and flowers, stretched upward together and knitted a graceful awning. The portico opened on a lovely walk that soon became, as far as the eye could see, a breathtakingly beautiful pergola, whose sides were lined with enchanting roses in full bloom. The ground too was covered with roses. The Blessed Virgin said to me: "Take off your shoes!" When I had done so, She added: "Walk under that rose pergola, for this is the path you must take." I gladly removed my shoes because it would have been a pity to step on such gorgeous roses. I took but a few steps and immediately felt very sharp thorns piercing my feet and making them bleed. I had to stop and turn back.

"I had better wear my shoes," I told my guide.

"Yes, indeed," She replied, "Sturdy ones." So I put my shoes on again and returned to the rose pergola, followed by a number of helpers who had just showed up and asked to go along with me. They followed me under the indescribably beautiful pergola, but as I went along I noted that it was becoming narrow and low. Many of its branches were draped like festoons; others instead just dropped straight down. Some branches, here and there, jutted sideways from the rose stalks, while others formed a thicket which partly blocked the path; still others crept along the ground. All the branches, however, were thick with roses. There were roses about me, roses above me, and roses under my feet.

As my feet made me wince with pain, I could not help brushing against the roses at my sides, and even sharper thorns pricked me. But I kept walking. My lacerated legs, though, kept getting entangled in the lower branches. Whenever I pushed aside a bough barring my way, or skirted the sides of the pergola to avoid it, the thorns dug into me and made me bleed all over. The roses overhead also were thick with thorns which pricked my head. Notwithstanding, I went forward, encouraged by the Blessed Virgin. Now and then, however, some sharper thorns pierced me more than others and caused greater pain.

Meanwhile those who were watching me walk under that bower—and they were a crowd—passed comments, such as, "How lucky Don Bosco is! His path is forever strewn with roses! He hasn't a worry in the world. No troubles at all!" But they couldn't see the thorns that were piercing my poor legs. I called on many priests, clerics, and laymen to follow me, and they did so joyfully, enthralled by the beauty of the flowers.

When, however, they discovered that they had to walk over sharp thorns and that there was no way to avoid them, they loudly began complaining, "We have been fooled!"

I answered: "If you are out for a nice time, you had better go back. If not, follow me."

Many turned back. After going on for a while, I turned to look at my followers. You cannot imagine how I felt when I saw that some had disappeared and others had already turned back and were walking away. I went after them and called them back, but it was useless; they would not even listen to me. Then I broke into tears and wept unrestrainedly as I asked myself: "Must I walk this painful path all alone?"

But I was soon comforted. I saw a group of priests, clerics and laymen coming toward me. "Here we are," they said. "We are all yours and ready to follow you." So I led them forward. Only a few lost heart and quit; most of them followed me through.

After walking the whole length of the pergola I found myself in another enchanting garden, and my few followers gathered around me. They were exhausted, ragged and bleeding, but a cool breeze healed them all. Another gust of wind came and, like magic, I found myself surrounded by a vast crowd of boys, young clerics, coadjutor brothers and even priests, who began helping me care for all those boys. Many of these helpers I knew, but many more were strangers.

Meanwhile I had come to a higher spot in the garden, where a very imposing, majestic building stood. I entered and found myself in a spacious hall so grandiose that I doubt one could find its like in any royal palace. Fresh thornless roses, set all through the hall, filled it with a most delicate fragrance. The Blessed Virgin, who had been my guide all along, now asked me: "Do you grasp the meaning of what you now see and of what you saw before?"

"No," I said. "Please explain it to me."

She replied: "The path strewn with roses and thorns is an image of your mission among boys. You must wear shoes, a symbol of mortification. The thorns on the ground stand for sensible affections, human likes and dislikes which distract the educator from his true goal, weaken and halt him in his mission, and hinder his progress and heavenly harvest. The roses symbolize the burning charity which must be your distinguishing trait and that of your fellow workers. The other thorns stand for the obstacles, sufferings and disappointments you will experience. But you must not lose heart. Charity and mortification will enable you to overcome all difficulties and lead you to roses without thorns."

As soon as the Mother of God finished speaking, I awoke and found myself in my room.

Don Bosco understood the purport of the dream and concluded by saying that from then on he knew exactly the path he had to follow. Already known to him were the obstacles and snares with which his adversaries would attempt to block his progress. Many would be the thorns on his path, but he was sure, absolutely sure, of God's will in the matter and of the ultimate success of his great undertaking. (Vol. III, pp. 25-27)

THE FORTUNE WHEEL

Don Bosco had the gift of prophecy to a remarkable degree. His predictions—fully realized—were so varied and numerous as to lead us to believe that this charism was habitual in him. He often told us of his dreams concerning the Oratory and the Salesian Society. Among others, I recall this in particular, around the year 1856. Don Bosco said:

"I dreamed that I was in a square where I saw a fortune wheel of some kind symbolizing the Oratory. A man was holding its handle. He called me over and said: 'Watch!' He then gave the wheel a turn and I heard a slight click, hardly audible beyond where I stood. The man asked me: 'Did you see what I did? Did you hear anything?'

'Yes, I saw you spin the wheel and I heard a click.'

'Do you know what a turn of the wheel means?'

'No.'

'It means a decade of your Oratory.'

"Four more times he spinned the wheel and asked the same questions, but every time the click was louder. I thought that at the second spinning it could be heard all over Piedmont;

at the third, all over Italy; at the fourth, all over Europe; at the fifth, all over the world. The man then said: 'You have seen the future of your Oratory.' "

Now, as I consider the growth of Don Bosco's work—Father Rua continued—I see it limited in the first decade to the city of Turin; in the second, it spreads throughout Piedmont; in the third, its fame and influence grow throughout Italy; in the fourth, throughout Europe; in the fifth, finally, Don Bosco's work is known and sought in all parts of the world.

(Vol. V, p 297)

THE WHEEL OF ETERNITY

"The wise man's heart," we read in Holy Scripture, "knows times and judgments; for there is a time and a judgment for everything. Yet it is a great affliction for man that he is ignorant of what is to come; for who will make known to him how it will be?" (Eccl 8: 5-7)

That Don Bosco knew when to toil and when to pause and explain, that he was not ignorant of things past and future concerning his mission, is further proven by the unswerving dedication inspiring the chronicles of Father Ruffino and Father Bonetti and the memoirs of Bishop John Cagliero, Father Chiala, and others who were privileged to hear Don Bosco's words.

With remarkable accord, they report another dream in which Don Bosco saw the Oratory and its beneficial results, the spiritual condition of his pupils, their vocation—as Salesian priests or brothers or as laymen in the world—and, lastly, the future of his budding Congregation.

Don Bosco's dream occurred during the night of May 1, 1861 and lasted about six hours. At dawn on May 2, he arose and jotted down the dream's highlights and the names of some of the various people he had seen in it. He narrated it after night prayers on three successive nights from the little rostrum in the porticoes. The first night, May 2, he spoke for nearly forty-five minutes. The introduction, as usual, seemed somewhat obscure and strange....After announcing his topic, he continued:

This dream concerns the students only. Very much of what I saw simply defies description. I seemed to have just started out of my house at Becchi on a path leading to Capriglio, a village near Castelnuovo. I wanted to see a field belonging to my family in a little dale behind a farmstead called "Valcappone." As a boy I had often worked there. The field was very sandy and its yield barely equaled the taxes on it. As I was nearing it, I met a man in his forties, of average height, suntanned, and with a long, well-trimmed beard. He wore a tunic reaching to his knees and fastened around his waist, and a white beret. He seemed to be waiting for somebody. He greeted me cordially, like an old acquaintance, and then asked, "Where are you going?"

"To a nearby field of mine," I answered, "And what brings you around here?"

"Don't be so curious," he replied. "You don't have to know that."

"Very well. Will you at least tell me your name? You seem to know me, but you are a stranger to me."

"You don't have to know that, either. Just come along with me."

I followed him and after a few steps saw a large fig orchard. "Look at those figs!" the man exclaimed. "Aren't they luscious? Go ahead, help yourself!"

Taken aback by the sight, I replied, "That's funny! There never were figs here before!"

"There are now!" he replied.

"But this isn't the season for figs! They can't be ripe."

"But some are! If you want to pick them, hurry because it's getting late." I did not stir and so my friend insisted: "Hurry, don't waste time because it will soon be dark."

"Why do you rush me? Besides, I don't want any. I like to look at them and give them away, but I personally don't care very much for them."

"In that case, let's go on. But remember what St. Matthew's Gospel says about great events menacing Jerusalem: 'From the fig tree learn a parable: When its branch is now tender and leaves break forth, you know that summer is near.' (Mt 24:32) It's all the nearer now that the figs are already beginning to ripen."

23

We resumed our walk and came to a vineyard. "Perhaps you care for grapes," the man said. "Take some!"

"Not now! In due time I'll pick them from my own vineyard."

"But you have grapes right here!"

"Not now!"

"Can't you see how ripe they are?"

"I can hardly believe it. This isn't the season for grapes!"

"Hurry because it's getting dark. You can't afford to lose time."

"What's the hurry? It will be soon enough if I get home before dark."

"Hurry, I say, because night is coming."

"So what? Morning will follow!"

"You are wrong. There will be no morning!"

"What do you mean?"

"I mean that night is coming."

"What kind of night? Are you trying to say that I have to pack up for eternity?"

"I repeat: Night is coming! You haven't much time left."

"Tell me, at least, if it will be very soon."

"Don't be so curious. Don't try to know more than is good for you."

"That's what my mother used to say about nosy people," I thought. Then I said aloud: "All right, but I still don't want any grapes!"

So we continued along the road and soon came to my field. My brother Joseph was there loading a wagon. He greeted us both, but, seeing that the stranger ignored him, asked me if he was a schoolmate of mine.

"No," I answered. "I never saw him before."

My brother then turned to him. "Would you please tell me your name?" There was no response. In amazement my brother again asked me, "Who is he?"

"I don't know. He won't tell!"

We both again pleaded with the stranger to identify himself but he kept repeating, "Don't try to know more than is good for you."

My brother gave up and left us alone. The stranger then

turned to me and said, "Would you like to see something unusual?"

"Certainly!" I replied.

"Would you like to see your boys as they are now and as they will be in the future? Would you want to count them?"

"Very much so!"

"Come here then."

From I don't know where he pulled out a strange contraption housing a large wheel and set it on the ground.

"What's this wheel?" I asked.

"The wheel of eternity," he replied, and, seizing the handle, he gave it a spin.

"Now, you try it," he said.

I did so.

"Look inside."

I looked and saw a large lens encased in the wheel. The lens was about five feet in diameter, and its edge bore the inscription: "This is the eye that sees the lowly things in heaven and on earth."

I immediately looked through the lens. What a sight! All the Oratory boys stood there before my eyes. "How can this be?" I said to myself. "I have never before seen anyone around here and now the place is full of boys. Aren't they in Turin?" I carefully examined the whole contraption; only through the lens could I see anybody. I looked at the stranger in amazement. After a few moments, he ordered me to turn the handle once more. Something startling happened: the boys were separated into two groups: the good and the bad; the former beaming with joy, the latter—not many, thank God—a sorry sight. I recognized them all. How different they were from what their companions believed them to be! Some had tongues pierced through with holes, others had pitifully squinting eyes, and still others had ugly sores covering their heads or worms gnawing at their hearts. The longer I looked, the more I grieved for them. "Can these possibly be my boys?" I asked. "What can these strange ailments mean?"

"I will tell you," the stranger replied. "Pierced tongues symbolize foul talk; squinting eyes indicate a lack of appreciation of God's graces by setting earthly things above the heavenly. Sores on the head show that they neglect your advice and cater to their own whims; worms symbolize evil passions gnawing at their hearts. There are boys, too, who do not want to hear your words lest they have to put them into practice."

At a nod from him, I spun the wheel again and pressed my eyes to the lens. Four boys bound with heavy chains came into view. I looked at them carefully and recognized them. I asked the stranger what that meant. "That shouldn't be hard to figure out," he replied. "These are the boys who pay no attention to your advice. If they do not mend their ways, they run the risk of ending up in jail and rotting there for their crimes."

"Let me jot their names down lest I forget," I said, but the stranger objected, "You don't have to! Their names are in this book."

I noticed then that he carried a notebook. At his word I gave the wheel another turn and looked. This time I saw seven other boys, defiant and distrustful, their lips padlocked. Three were also clamping their ears shut with their hands. Again I wanted to write their names down, but again the stranger firmly forbade it.

Painfully amazed to see those boys in their predicament, I asked why their lips were padlocked.

"Can't you see it for yourself?" the stranger replied. "These are the boys who refuse to tell."

"Tell what?"

"They won't tell, that's all!"

I understood then that he meant confession. These are boys who, even when questioned by their confessor, will not answer or will answer evasively or contrary to the truth. They say "no" when the answer should be "yes." My friend then went on: "Do you see those three clamping their hands over their ears? Aren't they a sorry sight? Well, they are boys who not only do not tell their sins, but even refuse to listen to their confessor's advice, warnings, and orders. They hear your words, but pay no heed to them. They could unplug their ears, but won't. The other four boys, instead, listened to your exhortations and warnings but did not put them into practice."

"How can they get rid of that padlock?" I inquired.

Let pride be cast out of their hearts, he replied.

"I will speak to these boys," I went on, "but there is little hope for those who willfully shut their ears." That stranger then advised that whenever I say a few words by way of sermon, half those words should be on making a good confession.

I promised that I would. I don't mean to say that I will carry out that injunction to the letter because I would make myself tiresome, but I will do my best to impress the importance and need of good confessions upon all and as often as possible. In fact, more people are eternally lost through bad confessions than in any other way because even the worst people occasionally do go to confession. There are very many, however, who make bad confessions.

When, at the stranger's command, I gave the wheel another turn, I was horrified to see three boys gripped from behind by three husky monkeys armed with horns. Each beast gripped its victim's throat by its forepaws so tightly that the boy's face became flushed and his blood-shot eyes almost popped out of their sockets. Moreover, the beast's hind legs and long tail bound the boy's thighs and legs so as to almost completely immobilize him. These were boys who go through a spiritual retreat and still remain in mortal sin, guilty especially of impurity, of a serious offense against the Sixth Commandment. The devil chokes them to keep them from speaking when they should; he makes them blush to the point of losing their heads so that they no longer realize what they are doing. A false shame then overwhelms them and leads them to perdition. The devil has them by their throats so tightly that their eyes seem to pop from their sockets, and they can no longer see their miserable condition and the way to get out of their horrible mess. A senseless fear and repugnance keep them from the sacraments. The devil grips their thighs and legs to make it impossible for them to take a step in the right direction. So strong are their bad habits that these boys become convinced they can no longer help themselves.

I assure you, my dear boys, that I wept at that sight. I wanted to rescue those unfortunate lads, but as soon as I drew away from the lens I could see them no more. I also wanted to take down their names, but my friend would have none of it. "It's unnecessary," he kept saying, "because they are all written down in this notebook."

Grieved by this sight beyond words, I tearfully turned to

my companion, sobbing, "How is this possible? How can these boys be in such miserable shape after I lavished so much care on them in confession and out of confession?"

"*Labor, Sudor, Fervor,*" was his scrambled, mumbled reply.

"I didn't get it," I said. "Please speak more clearly."

Again he muttered, "*Labor, Sudor, Fervor.*"

"It's no use," I said. "As long as you keep mumbling, I can't make out what you are saying."

"Are you making fun of me?" he asked.

"Not at all! I just can't understand you."

"Listen, you know your grammar. Just pay attention: *Labor—comma; Sudor—comma; Fevor—period.* Do you get it now?"

"I get the words," I replied, "but what's the message?"

"All right, I'll make it clearer: *Constant hard work; Incessant, painstaking mortification; Fervent and persevering prayer.* For these boys, however, your sacrifices, no matter how great, will be of no avail. You will not win them over, because they do not want to shake off Satan's yoke of slavery."

Meanwhile I kept staring through the lens, fretting and thinking, "How is this possible? Are those boys really doomed, even after a spiritual retreat? Were all my sacrifices, efforts, sermons, suggestions, and warnings to no avail? Were all their promises a sham? What a letdown!"

These thoughts utterly disheartened me. My friend noticed it. "How proud and conceited you are!" he chided me. "Do you expect your boys to be converted just because you work for them, to respond to your cares just because you love them? Do you perhaps think that you love, work, and suffer more than Our Blessed Savior? Do you expect your words to be more effective than His? Do you preach better than He did? Do you believe you have been more loving and anxious for your boys than Our Lord was for His Apostles? Aren't you aware that they lived constantly with Him, endlessly benefited from all kinds of graces and favors, heard His admonitions and precepts, and witnessed His divine example? Shouldn't all this have effectively spurred them to saintly lives? Didn't He do all He could for Judas? And yet Judas betrayed Him and died impenitent. Are you better than the Apostles? Didn't they carefully choose seven deacons? They chose but seven and one of them went astray. Are you surprised and upset if among five hundred boys a few will not respond to your care? Are you so conceited as to expect that none of your boys will turn out badly and be lost? How proud can you be?"

These words silenced me, but for all that I still felt very much disheartened.

"Cheer up!" my friend went on. "Turn the wheel again and see how generous God is! See how many souls He wants to give you! Look at all those boys."

I peered again into the lens and saw a very large number of boys totally unknown to me.

"I see them," I remarked, "but I don't know any of them."

"Well," he replied, "the Lord will give you all these boys to make up for the fourteen who do not cooperate with you. For each one of them He will give you a hundred!"

"Poor me!" I exclaimed. "The Oratory is full already. Where shall I put them?"

"Don't worry. Right now that's no problem. Later, He who sends them will make room for them."

"I'm not too worried about that," I said. "My greatest worry is feeding them!"

"Don't worry about that either! The Lord will provide."

"In that case, I am quite happy!" I replied in deep relief.

Delightedly I kept looking at those boys, studying the features of very many so as to be able to recognize them if I ever met them.

Thus ended Don Bosco's talk on the night of May 2, 1861.

Don Bosco resumed his story on the following night, concisely and vividly. Through the lens he had also seen the vocation of each of his boys. However, he did not disclose any names and postponed to a later account the questions he had put to his guide and the latter's answers concerning symbols and allegories of the dream.

The cleric Dominic Ruffino was nevertheless able to gather a few names confidentially from the boys themselves to whom Don Bosco had more privately manifested what he had seen about them. Ruffino recorded the names in 1861 and gave us the list. To make our narration clearer and avoid repetitions, we shall insert names and explanations, mostly in non-dialogue form, while still reporting the chronicle word by word. Don Bosco resumed his narration on May 3, as follows:

I was rejoicing to see so many new boys when the stranger, still standing by his apparatus, asked me: "Would you like to see something even more delightful?"

"Certainly!" I replied.

"Then give the wheel another turn."

I did and peered through the lens. I saw the boys separated into two groups, some distance apart, in a broad area. At my left I could see a vast field, in which all sorts of vegetables were growing, and a meadow lined at its edge with a few rows of wild vines. The first group of boys was working this field with spades, hoes, picks, shovels, and rakes. They were broken up into squads, each with a foreman. The whole group took orders from Chevalier Oreglia who was busy handing out tools and prodding sluggish workers. Farther away, near the edge of the field, I saw other boys sowing seed. A second group was working on my right in a vast field covered with golden wheat. A long trench separated this field from other fields which stretched out as far as the eye could see. All the boys were busy harvesting—bundling into sheaves, piling them, gleaning, carting, threshing, sharpening sickles, and handing them out. Some boys were also playing guitars. I assure you, it was quite a scene. Nearby, in the shade of ancient trees, were tables laden with food; a little farther off, one could see a gorgeous garden with all kinds of flowers in full bloom. The two groups of boys symbolized different vocations: the lay state and the priesthood. I did not know this at the time, and so I asked, "What's the meaning of all this?"

"Can't you see it yet?" he replied. "Boys tilling the soil are those who work for themselves alone. They are not called to be priests."

I understood then that this applied to the artisans. In their state of life they only think of saving their own souls and feel no special obligation to work at saving the souls of others.

"And the second group?" I asked. But then it dawned on me that these boys were called to be priests. Now I knew who were called to the priesthood and who were not.

As I watched very interestedly, I noticed that Provera was handing out sickles. I took this to mean that he might become the rector of a seminary, a religious community, or a house of studies; perhaps he might become something even more important. I observed that not all the reapers received their sickles from him. The boys who did are those who are destined to join the [Salesian] Congregation. The others, instead, are to become diocesan priests. The sickle symbolized the Word of God. Another detail: Provera did not readily give a sickle to all who asked. Some he just ordered to take either one or two morsels of food. The first morsel signified piety, the second knowledge. James Rossi was sent to take one. The boys had to report to the cleric [Celestine] Durando who was in the little grove setting tables and serving the reapers- the task of those who are particularly destined to promote devotion to the Most Blessed Sacrament. Matthew Galliano was busy serving beverages. Costamagna, too, asked for a sickle, but was first sent to Provera to pick two flowers from the garden. The same happened to Quattroccolo. Rebuffo was promised a sickle on condition that he first pick three flowers. Olivero also was there.

Meanwhile, all the other boys were scattered here and there in the wheatfield, some working abreast with larger or narrower rows to cultivate. Father Ciattino, the pastor of Maretto, was using a sickle he had received from Provera. Francesia and Vibert were cutting wheat. So too were Hyacinth Perucatti, Merlone, Momo, Garino, and Jarach—an indication that they would save souls by their preaching if they persevered in their vocation. Some reaped more than others. Bondioni was cutting wheat like mad, but how long could he last? Others hacked at the wheat with all their strength but cut nothing. Vaschetti took hold of a sickle, began to cut, and went at it zestfully until he found himself working in another field. He wasn't the only one, either. Some sickles were dull or blunted or in such poor condition that they actually did more harm than good.

Dominic Ruffino had a long row to take care of. His sickle was very sharp, but blunted at the point, signifying lack of humility and an ambition to outdo his companions. He went to Francis Cerruti to have his sickle fixed. The latter had been given the task, a symbol that one day he would become a teacher and instill knowledge and piety into students. Hammering, in fact, is the task of those charged with forming priestly candidates. Provera handed the blunted sickles to Cerruti and the dull ones to Rocchietti and others—an indication that they would one day form priestly vocations to piety. Viale came up for a sickle and picked out a dull one, but Provera made him take one he had just sharpened. I also saw Rinaudo servicing farm tools.

While all this was going on, Fusero was tying sheaves. This meant that his task would be to keep souls in God's grace, particularly the souls of those called to the priesthood. In other words, he would one day form young clerics.

Others were helping him; among them I saw Turchi and Ghivarello. This meant that they would work especially in setting consciences right, as, for example, in hearing confessions, particularly of priests or priestly candidates.

Others were loading sheaves on a wagon symbolizing God's grace. Converted sinners must climb upon this wagon in order to make a start on their way to heaven. When the wagon was fully loaded, oxen—a symbol of strength and perseverance—started pulling it. Some boys led them, following Rua. This means that Rua's task will be to lead souls to heaven. [Angelo] Savio trailed behind, gleaning ears of wheat or sheaves which fell from the wagon.

Scattered about the field were John Bonetti, Joseph Bongiovanni, and others, busily gleaning. Their task will be to rescue obstinate sinners. Bonetti, especially, is called by God to seek such unfortunate people.

Fusero and Anfossi were preparing sheaves for threshing. Perhaps this suggested a teaching career. Others, like Father Alasonatti, stacked them; they are those who administer finances, watch over the observance of rules, and teach prayers and hymns—in short, those who materially and morally contribute in directing souls to heaven.

One strip of land had been cleared and smoothed out for threshing. John Cagliero, who had just gone to the garden for flowers and had handed them out to his companions, betook himself to the threshing area, still holding a little bouquet of flowers. Threshing grain symbolizes God's call to instruct the common people.

Far off, black columns of smoke were rising to the sky. Some boys had gathered cockle and were burning it outside the field. This symbolized those who would remove the bad from the good as directors of our future houses. Among them I saw Francis Cerruti, John Baptist Tamietti, Dominic Belmonte, Paul Albera, and others, who are now studying in the lower Latin grades.

All the above scenes kept unfolding simultaneously. I saw some boys in that crowd hold lighted lanterns, though it was broad daylight. Evidently they were destined to be beacons, giving good example to other workers in the Lord's vineyard. Among them was Paul Albera, who, besides carrying a lamp, also played the guitar. This means that not only will he guide priests, but he will also encourage them to persevere. It suggested, too, some high post in the Church.

Amid so much hustle and bustle, however, not all the boys were busy. One fellow was holding a pistol, an indication that he was inclined to a military career, though he was as yet uncertain. Others just stood about idly, watching the reapers, with no intention of joining them. Some looked undecided; being too lazy for action, they couldn't make up their minds. Others instead ran for a sickle, but a few of these did nothing on reaching the field. There were also some who swung the sickle wrongly. Molino was one of them. These are boys who always do the opposite of what they should. Quite a few others kept roaming about or picking wild grapes, denoting those who waste their time in tasks not pertaining to them.

The boys tilling the soil in the field at the left were also an odd sight. While most of those sturdy lads worked very diligently, a few were using their hoes the wrong way or only pretending to work. Some knocked the blade off the handle at every blow. The handle symbolized the right intention.

I also observed artisans reaping wheat and students hoeing. I again tried to jot down some notes, but my guide would immediately show me his notebook and stop me. I could also see that very many boys stood idly about because they couldn't make up their minds. Instead, the two Dalmazzo brothers, Primo Gariglio, Monasterolo, and many others seemed determined to make a decision one way or the other. I saw some quit hoeing to go and do some reaping. One boy was in such a hurry that he forgot to get a sickle. Shamefacedly, he went back for one, but the person in charge refused to give it to him despite his insistence. "It's not time yet!" he told him.

"Yes, it is!" the lad insisted. "I want it now!"

"Not now!" was the reply. "First go to the garden and pick two flowers."

"All right," he exclaimed, shrugging his shoulders. "I'll pick all the flowers you want."

"Two will do!"

He ran to the garden but, on getting there, realized he had not asked which two flowers he should pick. He rushed back to ask.

"Pick the flower of charity and that of humility," he was told.

"I've got them already."

"You only *think* you have them!"

The boy fumed, clenched his fists, and raged.

"This is no time for a tantrum," the one in charge told him, and he absolutely refused to hand him a scythe. The lad bit his fists in rage.

After this I stopped looking through the lens, which had enabled me to learn so much. I felt stirred, too, by the moral applications my friend had suggested. I again asked for a few more explanations. The stranger repeated: "The wheat field is the Church; the harvest is the fruit reaped; the sickle is the tool—the Word of God especially—to harvest the fruit. The dull blade means lack of piety; the blunted point signifies lack of humility. Leaving the field while reaping means leaving the Oratory and the Salesian Society."

The following night, May 4, 1861, Don Bosco concluded his narrative. The first part had shown him the Oratory pupils, especially the students; the second indicated those who were called to the priesthood. The third part was a succession of visions: the Salesian Society in 1861, its prodigious growth, and the gradual disappearance of the first Salesians and their replacement by others. Don Bosco spoke thus:

After I had leisurely taken in the richly varied harvest scene, the obliging stranger said, "Now give the wheel ten turns and look."

I obeyed. Marvelously, those very lads whom I had patted as children a few days before were now virile, bearded men, some with greying hair.

"How could this happen?" I inquired. "That man was a mere youngster the other day!"

My friend answered, "Don't be surprised! How many turns did you give the wheel?"

"Ten."

"Then they are all ten years older. We have gone from 1861 to 1871."

"Oh!" Through that mysterious lens I saw new places, new houses of ours, and many pupils in the care of my dear Oratory boys, now priests, teachers, and directors.

"Give the wheel ten more turns, and we shall reach 1881," the stranger told me. I complied and peered into the lens. Now I saw only about half the boys I had seen before. Nearly all were grey-haired, a few stooping.

"Where are the others?" I asked.

"Gone into eternity," he replied.

This striking loss grieved me considerably, but I was consoled by the sight of an immense tableau of new and unknown regions and a multitude of boys led by teachers unknown to me but pupils of my first boys, some already mature in years.

I gave the wheel ten more turns and then saw only one-fourth of the boys I had seen but a few moments before. They were much older and white-haired.

"Where are the others?" I asked.

"Gone into eternity. This is now 1891."

I then beheld a very touching sight. My toil-worn priests were surrounded by boys I had never seen; many were of a different race and color.

I turned the wheel ten more times. I could only see a few of my first boys, tottering and bent with age, gaunt and thin. Among others I remember seeing Father Rua, so old and haggard as to be hardly recognizable.

"What about all the others?" I asked.

"Gone into eternity! We are now in the year 1901."

I saw many houses of ours, but none of my old Salesians.

The directors and teachers were all unknown to me. The multitude of boys kept growing, as was the number of houses and personnel.

"Now," the stranger said, "turn the wheel ten more times, and you will see things that will both cheer and sadden you." I complied.

"Nineteen hundred and eleven!" my friend exclaimed.

My dear boys, I saw new houses, new boys, new directors, and teachers dressed differently from us. And what about my first Oratory boys? I searched and searched through the great multitude and could find only one of you, white-haired, bent with age. Surrounded by boys, he was telling them about the Oratory's beginnings and repeating things he had learned from Don Bosco, while pointing out to them his picture hanging on the parlor wall. And what about the first pupils and superiors that I had just seen as old men? . . .

At a nod from the stranger, I again gave the wheel several turns. All I could see was a vast solitude, with nobody in sight. "Oh!" I gasped. "There is nobody here! Where are all the cheerful, lively, strong boys that are at the Oratory with me right now?"

"Gone into eternity! Remember that a decade goes by with every ten turns of the wheel."

I figured that I had given the wheel fifty turns and that around 1911 the boys that are now at the Oratory would all be gone into eternity.

"Now," the stranger said, "would you like to see something really startling?"

"Yes," I replied.

"Watch! Give the wheel as many turns counterclockwise as you did clockwise."

I did so.

"Now look!" the stranger cried.

I saw an immense crowd of boys of countless nations, features, and tongues. So vast was the throng that I could single out only a small fraction with their superiors.

"I don't know any of them," I said to the stranger.

"Still," he replied, "they are all your sons. Listen. They are talking about you and your first boys, their superiors, now long dead, and the teaching you and your first sons handed down to them."

Again I looked intently, but on removing my gaze from the lens, I saw the wheel begin to spin by itself so fast and so noisily that I awoke and found myself in bed, exhausted.

Now that I have told you all these things, you may think that Don Bosco is an extraordinary man, a great man, a saint, no doubt! My dear lads, before you entertain such foolish notions about me, feel absolutely free to believe or not believe these things and to make whatever you want of them. I only ask that you do not make fun of them, whether among yourselves or with outsiders. Bear in mind, though, that Our Lord can manifest His will in many ways. Sometimes He makes use of the most unsuitable, unworthy instruments, as when He made Balaam's donkey speak and even used Balaam himself—a false prophet—to foretell many things concerning the Messiah. Such may be the case with me. I warn you, then, not to follow my example blindly. What you must do is to pay close attention to all I say because that at least, I hope, will always be in accordance with God's will and helpful to your souls.

As for what I do, never say, "Don Bosco did it and so it has to be good." Examine it first. If you see it is good, do likewise, but if it were, perchance, bad, beware of imitating it. Don't! Good night!"

In regard to the three pupils who had monkey-like creatures on their shoulders, Father Francis Dalmazzo testified under oath:

I remember well that, in speaking of these boys, Don Bosco said that if they wished to know more, they were to ask him. More than fifty pupils, disturbed by their conscience, did so, but Don Bosco told each one, "It's not you." Later, in meeting those three boys in the playground at different times, he warned them of their miserable condition. One was a classmate of mine, and he confidentially told me of his astonishment at Don Bosco's knowledge. On the other hand, I have had personal proofs of Don Bosco's discernment of hearts, because time and again he revealed my own interior state to me without me saying a word. I also had similar proofs from my companions who candidly admitted that, despite their silence on serious sins in confession, Don Bosco had unerringly pointed them out to them.

Concerning the four boys whom Don Bosco had seen in chains, we came to know about one of them through Father [John] Borel.

In 1866, while ministering in the city jails, he came across a convict, an army deserter named B ... who asked him to get him a copy of *The Companion of Youth* from Don Bosco and to give him this message: "Do you remember telling me that in the dream of 'The Wheel' you saw me in chains? Well, I was one of those four boys. Fortunately, I have committed no crime. I just couldn't stand army life and took off." Don Bosco visited him and brought him the prayer book. Aside from the dream, he had predicted other matters to this lad when, on finishing secondary school at the Oratory, he had come to say good-bye to Don Bosco and had told him that he intended to enter religious life.

"Stay with us," was the advice of Don Bosco, who had previously tried to persuade him to remain. "Here you will find all you desire." However, the youth was determined to go.

"All right," Don Bosco concluded, "you may go. You will join the Jesuits and will be dismissed. Then you will try the Capuchins, but you will not succeed. Eventually, after a lot of trouble, you will be hungry and come back here."

This made no sense at the time, for the youth's family was wealthy and prominent. Yet Don Bosco's prediction was literally fulfilled. The boy first joined the Jesuits and then the Capuchins, but he could not adapt himself to their rules and after a while had to leave. Many years later, after squandering his patrimony, he showed up at the Oratory in a miserable condition. He stayed there for a time but then, driven by wanderlust, left. All these details he told us himself. He was still living in 1901.

Meanwhile, since May 4 clerics and pupils had continued to crowd around Don Bosco to find out whether he had seen them among the tillers or the reapers and to learn what they were actually doing, and he obliged. We have already reported many of his replies as we narrated the dream. Several had all the earmarks of genuine predictions.

Don Bosco had seen the cleric John Molino, sickle in hand, idly watching those who were reaping; he then had walked to the ditch surrounding the field, leaped across it, and throwing his hat away, run off. Molino asked Don Bosco for an explanation. "You will study not five but six years of theology," Don Bosco replied. "Then you will give up your clerical habit." The cleric was shocked by this seemingly strange and unlikely reply, but future events proved the truth of Don Bosco's words. This cleric actually did study theology for six years—four at the Oratory and two at the Asti seminary. Then, after the spiritual retreat preparatory to his ordination, he went to San Damiano d'Asti, his native town, for one day ostensibly to settle some business; once there, he lay aside his cassock and never returned.

The cleric Vaschetti was considered one of the main pillars of the Giaveno junior seminary, and indeed he was. When Don Bosco revealed that he had seen him leap over the ditch and quit, he replied somewhat peevishly, "You *must* have been dreaming!" Actually, at that time it had never entered his mind to leave Don Bosco. Later, however, he did withdraw, for he was free to do so. As a priest, he one day called on Don Bosco, and the latter reminded him of his prompt but filial outburst.

"I remember," Vaschetti answered. "You were right!"

Then Don Bosco added, "God wanted you here. Anyway, I hope He will help you with His grace. However, you will have your problems." God did assist Vaschetti, who did much good as a pastor.

The cleric Joseph Fagnano originally had no intention of asking Don Bosco what part he had played in the dream. Having recently come to the Oratory from the Asti seminary and being wary by temperament, he was somewhat skeptical about the whole thing. However, having been urged by his companions, he too asked Don Bosco what he had seen of him through that lens. Don Bosco replied, "I saw you in the field, but you were so far away that I could hardly recognize you. You were working among naked men."

Fagnano did not attribute much significance to these words, but they flashed back to his mind years later as, on the feast of Mary Help of Christians, he was stranded on the shores of the Strait of Magellan, surviving on mollusks for two days, because stormy seas prevented the ship that he was to board from entering the harbor. Later he found himself working among naked Indians in Tierra del Fuego, his mission field.

To Angelo Savio, Don Bosco said that he had seen him too, in far distant regions. To Dominic Belmonte he said, "You will give God glory with music." Then he added a word which instantly made a deep impression upon him. However, no sooner had he stepped away from Don Bosco than he immediately forgot it, and no amount of effort could bring him to recall it. Don Bosco had also seen him leading a wagon drawn by five mules. He worked most successfully, first as a teacher and general assistant at Mirabello, then as a teacher at Alassio, as prefect and, later, as director at Borgo San Martino, and as director and pastor at Sampierdarena. In all these places he also taught music and added splendor to the liturgy. Finally [in 1886] he became Prefect General of the Salesian Society and director of the Oratory of St. Francis de Sales. Always and everywhere he enjoyed the love and full confidence of both confreres and pupils. We read in the chronicle:

Don Bosco also told Avanzino about his part in the dream, adding, "This is what God wants you to do." Avanzino did not disclose the work for which he seemed destined because it was not to his liking, but later he told his friends, "Don Bosco bared things to me which I had never revealed to any living person."

To G . . . too Don Bosco said, "You should be a priest, but you lack three virtues: humility, charity, and chastity." He added, though, that he had not been called to get his sickle from Provera. Ferrari, a boy who kept saying that he wanted to be a priest, never went to ask what part he had played in the dream, though many were pressing him to do so. He ridiculed the whole thing, but eventually he found himself cornered. Don Bosco told him that he had seen him in the wheat field and that, despite repeated exhortations to pick more flowers, he had started harvesting wheat very briskly; when he was through, and had turned back to look at his work, he found nothing.

"What does that mean?" the lad asked.

"It means that if you don't mend your ways and if you

continue to follow your whims instead of letting yourself be guided, you will end up as an unfrocked priest or religious."

The Oratory boys, however, were not satisfied merely with personal communications. They wanted more detailed, public explanations of the dream and a clarification of certain points which they had not fully understood. Their curiosity kept them in suspense and had to be relieved. These boys were unconstrained, bright, and studious, and their questions could have posed a difficult problem for anyone unsure of the truth of what he was saying. But Don Bosco had no fear of being caught in contradictions. The chronicle continues:

> On the evening of May 4, Don Bosco allowed everyone to ask questions, as he too wished to explain whatever part of the dream was still unclear to them. There were a good number of questions at the "Good Night" on May 5.
> "What does 'night' mean?" they inquired.
> "That death is drawing near. 'The night comes on when no one can work,' said Our Lord. (Jn 9:4) The boys took this as a hint he was giving them that perhaps his end was near. After a brief, painful silence they asked whether there was any way by which they could prolong his life. "Yes," he replied. "First, I should stop having these dreams because they sap my strength; secondly, people who stubbornly persist in evil should stop forcing Our Lord, in a manner of speaking, to have to use such drastic measures to make them give up sin."
> "How about the figs and grapes?"
> "The figs and grapes, partly ripe, partly unripe, show that certain events preceding the 'night' have already come to pass and others are still due. Those which have already taken place I will tell you in due time. The figs especially symbolize great events which will soon take place at the Oratory. I could tell you much on this score too, but I had better not just now. I'll tell you later. I will add that the ripe figs, taken as a symbol for boys, can signify that they are ripe either for God's service or for eternity."

We shall here assert our belief that some figs must have been bitter and that for this reason Don Bosco did not pick them, though he justified his refusal with a pretext. The prophet Jeremiah described a vision of his in these words: "The Lord showed me two baskets of figs placed before the temple of the Lord . . . One basket contained excellent figs, the early-ripening kind. But the other basket contained very bad figs, so bad that they could not be eaten." (Jer 24:1-2) The first basket symbolized those who had repented of their transgressions and had earned God's mercy; the second represented those who would be exterminated by God because of their impenitence. "I will make them like rotten figs, too bad to be eaten," says the Lord. (Jer 29:17)

As reported in Ruffino's chronicle the questioning went on:

"What did those monkey-like creatures on the boys' shoulders symbolize?"

"The demon of impurity," Don Bosco replied. "When this demon wants to enslave someone, he does so behind his back to hide the ugliness of this sin and make it appear to be a mere nothing. These demons throttle their victims when they attempt to confess their sins. The significance of eyes bursting from their sockets is that anyone possessed by the demon of impurity no longer sees the things of heaven. My dear boys, remember those three words: *Labor* (Hard work), *Sudor* (Constant mortification), and *Fervor* (Fervent prayer), and you will be able to overcome this demon."

"And how can the padlock be removed from the mouth?"

Don Bosco repeated what the stranger had said: "Let pride be cast out of their hearts."

Questions were asked about the work each boy was doing in the field and its meaning.

"What else could you tell us about the wheat field?" one boy asked.

"Those who were working there have a priestly vocation. Now I know which of you should study for the priesthood and which should not. Do not think, though, that all those tilling the soil were totally excluded from harvesting, or vice versa. Among the harvesters there were some artisans. I recognized them and shall assign them to study. I also saw one of you asking for a sickle, but the one in charge refused to give it to him because he still lacked some virtues. If he will acquire them, it will be a clear sign that the Lord is calling him. It will be up to him not to make himself unworthy of that call. But both tillers and harvesters were doing God's will and were on the path of salvation."

"What did the food and the flowers represent?"

"There were some who wanted to harvest, but Provera would not give them a sickle because they weren't as yet good enough for that. He would tell them: 'You still lack a flower' or 'You need two flowers. You must eat more food . . .' These flowers symbolize charity, humility, or purity, while food stands for study or piety. After these boys picked flowers or ate their food, they went back to Provera and got their sickles."

Don Bosco was also asked about what he saw at every tenth turn of the wheel, especially in regard to the growth of the Salesian Society. "There was," he answered, "a long interval at every tenth turn of the wheel to give me time to examine thoroughly every detail of those scenes. From the very first few turns I saw the [Salesian] Congregation already formed and well established, along with a great number of confreres and pupils in different houses. New scenes appeared at every turn of the wheel. Many boys I had seen before were no longer present; others had aged; still others were new to me. The boys' number kept growing rapidly and enormously."

Some boys were struck by the fact that the mysterious stranger had said: "You will see things that will gladden you and others that will sadden you." They asked him whether at every tenth turn—that is, every tenth year—he had seen them doing the same kind of work, holding the same office, or conducting themselves in the same way. Were they better or worse than in the previous decade? Don Bosco did not want to answer this question. Nevertheless, he sighed, "It is sad and discouraging to see what one goes through in a lifetime. If, as a boy, I had foreseen what I have gone through these last few years, I would have been disheartened."

The boys also expressed their astonishment at the number of houses and hospices which Don Bosco claimed he would have one day. At this time the Oratory was his only house. "You will see, you will see!" he replied.

Thus Don Bosco spoke familiarly to the whole community.

Certain things, however, he disclosed only to his young clerics. For example, he told them that two of those he had seen in the wheat field would become bishops. This news spread through the Oratory like wildfire and stirred up a great deal of talk. Since Don Bosco refused to say more, the boys tried guessing and evaluated all their clerical companions. Eventually they settled on John Cagliero as probably one bishop and Paul Albera as the other. These rumors flew about the house for a long time.

Thus reads the witness of Ruffino's chronicle. We can add that nobody then thought of James Costamagna, and he himself was very far from suspecting that God had a mitre in store for him. (Vol. VI, pp. 530-553)

THE MOUNTAIN

A frequent utterance of Don Bosco was that "the Lord would do everything through boys who have been brought up at the Oratory." Meanwhile he kept up his conferences to the Salesians. Father Paul Albera recalls one of this period which deeply impressed the members:

In a dream Don Bosco saw himself surrounded by boys and priests, and he suggested that they all set out to climb a nearby mountain. All agreed. At its summit, tables were set for a delicious repast, amid music and entertainment. Here and there along the way, various obstacles made the climb so difficult and frustrating that at one point Don Bosco and the tired climbers sat down. After a rest, he encouraged them to go on and resumed the climb at a hurried pace. At a certain point he looked back and discovered that all his followers had abandoned him. He quickly retraced his steps to look for them. He found them and led them again up the rocky slopes, but once more they all deserted him.

"Then," Don Bosco continued, "I thought to myself: *I must get to the top of the mountain, but with many followers. This is my goal, my mission. How am I to accomplish it? I know! My first followers were picked at random. They were virtuous and willing, but untested, and not imbued with my spirit. They were not used to hard going and were not bound to each other or to me by special ties. That is why they left me. I will remedy this. My disappointment is too bitter to be forgotten. I know now what I must do. I can rely only on those whom I have trained myself. Therefore I shall now go down to the foot of the mountain. I will gather many boys, win their affection, and train them to face hardships and sacrifices bravely. They will gladly obey me; together we shall climb the Lord's mountain."*

Then, looking at those about him, he told them that he had put his hopes in them. Speaking at length and with emotion, he exhorted them to be faithful to their vocation in view of Our Lady's countless graces, and of the unfailing reward prepared for them by the Lord. (Vol. VII, pp. 198-199)

TEN HILLS

We read in the Book of Daniel that four noble youths, brought as slaves from Jerusalem to Babylon by Nabuchadnezzar, remained faithful to God's laws, and for this reason "To these young men God gave knowledge and proficiency in all literature and science, and to Daniel the understanding of all visions and dreams." (Dn 1:17) By God's grace, Daniel could tell whether dreams were supernatural or not and what message they carried from God. To a great extent at least, for the same reason, the Lord granted this grace also to Don Bosco in the dreams which we have already narrated and obviously—in our opinion—also in the dream we are about to relate. It came to him the night of October 21, and he narrated it the following night. [Surprisingly] C.B. ... a boy from Casale Monferrato, had the same dream, during which he seemed to be with Don Bosco, talking to him. In the morning the boy was so deeply impressed that he went to tell it all to his teacher, who urged him to report to Don Bosco. The youngster met Don Bosco as he was coming down the stairs to look for the boy and tell him the very same dream. Here is the dream:

Don Bosco seemed to be in a vast valley swarming with thousands and thousands of boys—so many, in fact, that their number surpassed belief. Among them he could see all past and present pupils; the rest, perhaps, were yet to come. Scattered among them were priests and clerics then at the Oratory.

A lofty bank blocked one end of the valley. As Don Bosco wondered what to do with all those boys, a voice said to him: "Do you see that bank? Well, both you and the boys must reach its summit."

At Don Bosco's word, all those youngsters dashed toward the bank. The priests too ran up the slope, pushing boys ahead, lifting up those who fell, and hoisting on their shoulders those who were too tired to climb further. Father Rua, his sleeves rolled up, kept working hardest of all, gripping two boys at a time and literally hurling them up to the top of the bank where they landed on their feet and merrily scampered about. Meanwhile Father Cagliero and Father Francesia ran back and forth encouraging the youngsters to climb.

It didn't take long for all of them to make it to the top. "Now what shall we do?" Don Bosco asked.

"You must all climb each of the ten hills before you," the voice replied.

"Impossible! So many young, frail boys will never make it!"

"Those who can't will be carried," the voice countered.

At this very moment, at the far end of the bank, appeared a gorgeous, triangular-shaped wagon, too beautiful for words. Its three wheels swiveled in all directions. Three shafts rose from its corners and joined to support a richly embroidered banner, carrying in large letters the inscription *Innocence*. A wide band of rich material was draped about the wagon, bearing the legend: *With the help of the Most High, Father, Son and Holy Spirit.*

Glittering with gold and gems, the wagon came to a stop in the boys' midst. At a given order, five hundred of the smaller ones climbed into it. Among the untold thousands, only these few hundred were still innocent.

As Don Bosco kept wondering which way to go, a wide, level road strewn with thorns opened before him. Suddenly there also appeared six white-clad former pupils who had died at the Oratory. Holding aloft another splendid banner with the inscription *Penance*, they placed themselves at the head of the multitude which was to walk the whole way. As the signal to move was given, many priests seized the wagon's prow and led the way, followed by the six white-clad boys and the rest of the multitude. The lads in the wagon began singing *"Praise the name of the LORD; Praise, you servants of the LORD,"* (Ps 135:1), with indescribable sweetness.

Don Bosco kept going forward, enthralled by their heavenly melody, but, on an impulse, he turned to find out if the boys were following. To his deep regret he noticed that many had stayed behind in the valley, while many others had turned back. Heartbroken, he wanted to retrace his steps to persuade those boys to follow him and to help them along, but he was absolutely forbidden to do so. "Those poor boys will be lost!" he protested.

"So much the worse for them," he was told. "They too received the call but refused to follow you. They saw the road they had to travel. They had their chance."

Don Bosco insisted, pleaded, and begged, but in vain.

"You too must obey," he was told. He had to walk on.

He was still smarting with this pain when he became aware of another sad fact: a large number of those riding in the wagon had gradually fallen off, so that a mere hundred and fifty still stood under the banner of innocence. His heart was aching with unbearable grief. He hoped that it was only a dream and made every effort to awake, but unfortunately it was all too real. He clapped his hands and heard their sound; he groaned and heard his sighs resound through the room; he wanted to banish this horrible vision and could not.

"My dear boys," he exclaimed at this point of his narration, "I recognized those of you who stayed behind in the valley and those who turned back or fell from the wagon. I saw you all. You can be sure that I will do my utmost to save you. Many of you whom I urged to go to confession did not accept my invitation. For heaven's sake, save your souls."

Many of those who had fallen off the wagon joined those who were walking. Meanwhile the singing in the wagon continued, and it was so sweet that it gradually abated Don Bosco's sorrow. Seven hills had already been climbed. As the boys reached the eighth, they found themselves in a wonderful village where they stopped for a brief rest. The houses were indescribably beautiful and luxurious.

In telling the boys of this village, Don Bosco remarked, "I could repeat what St. Teresa said about heavenly things—to speak of them is to belittle them. They are just too beautiful for words. I shall only say that the doorposts of these houses seemed to be made of gold, crystal, and diamonds all at once. They were a most wonderful, satisfying, pleasing sight. The fields were dotted with trees laden simultaneously with blossoms, buds, and fruit. It was out of this world!" The boys scattered all over, eager to see everything and to taste the fruit.

(It was in this village that the boy from Casale met Don Bosco and talked at length with him. Both of them remembered quite vividly the details of their conversation. The two dreams had been a singular coincidence.)

Here another surprise awaited Don Bosco. His boys suddenly looked like old men: toothless, wrinkled, white-haired, bent over, lame, leaning on canes. He was stunned, but the voice said, "Don't be surprised. It's been years and years since you left that valley. The music made your trip seem so short. If you want proof, look at yourself in the mirror and you will see that I am telling the truth." Don Bosco was handed a mirror. He himself had grown old, with his face deeply lined and his few remaining teeth decayed.

The march resumed. Now and then the boys asked to be allowed to stop and look at the novelties around them, but he kept urging them on. "We are neither hungry nor thirsty," he said. "We have no need to stop. Let's keep going!"

Far away, on the tenth hill, arose a light which grew increasingly larger and brighter, as though pouring from a gigantic doorway. Singing resumed, so enchanting that its like may possibly be heard and enjoyed only in paradise. It is simply indescribable because it did not come from instruments or human throats. Don Bosco was so overjoyed that he awoke, only to find himself in bed.

He then explained his dream thus: "The valley is this world; the bank symbolizes the obstacles we have to surmount in detaching ourselves from it; the wagon is self-evident. The youngsters on foot were those who lost their innocence but repented of their sins." He also added that the ten hills symbolized the Ten Commandments whose observance leads to eternal life. He concluded by saying that he was ready to tell some boys confidentially what they had been doing in the dream: whether they had remained in the valley or fallen off the wagon.

When he came down from the stand, a pupil, Anthony Ferraris, approached him and told him within our hearing that, the night before, he had dreamed that he was with his mother and that when the latter had asked him whether he would be coming home next Easter, he had replied that by then he would be in paradise. He then whispered something else in Don Bosco's ear. Anthony Ferraris died on March 16, 1865.

We jotted down Don Bosco's dream that very evening, October 22, 1864, and added this note: "We are sure that in explaining the dream Don Bosco tried to cover up what is most mystifying, at least in some instances. The explanation that the ten hills symbolized the Ten Commandments does not convince us. We rather believe that the eighth hill on which Don Bosco called a halt and saw himself as an old man symbolizes the end of his life in the seventies. The future will tell."

The future is now past; facts have borne out our belief. The dream revealed Don Bosco's life-span. For comparative purposes, let us match this dream with that of *The Wheel of Eternity*, which we came to learn only years later. In that dream each turn of the wheel symbolized a decade, and this also seems to be the case in the trek from hill to hill. Each hill stands for a decade, and the ten hills represent a century, man's maximum life-span. In his life's first decade, Don Bosco, as a young boy, begins his mission among his companions at Becchi and starts on his journey; he climbs seven hills—seven decades—and reaches the age of seventy; he climbs the eighth hill and goes no farther. He sees beautiful buildings and meadows, symbols of the Salesian Society which, through God's infinite goodness, has grown and borne fruit. He has still a long way to go on the eighth hill and therefore sets out again, but he does not reach the ninth because he wakes up. Thus he did not live out his eighth decade; he died at the age of seventy-two years and five months.

What do our readers think of this interpretation? On the following evening, Don Bosco asked us our opinion of the dream. We replied that it did not concern only the boys, but showed also the worldwide spread of the Salesian Society.

"What do you mean?" a confrere countered. "We already have schools at Mirabello and Lanzo, and we'll have a few more in Piedmont. What else do you want?"

"No," we insisted. "This dream portends far greater things." Don Bosco smiled and nodded approval.

(Vol. VII, pp. 467-471)

THE FIRST SALESIAN MISSION FIELD

The following dream made Don Bosco decide on his missionary apostolate in Patagonia. He first narrated it in March 1876 to Pius IX. Later he told it privately to a few Salesians. The first to be so honored was Father Francis Bodrato on July 30 of that year. That very evening, Father Bodrato repeated it to Father Julius Barberis at Lanzo, where the latter had gone to spend a few days of vacation with a group of clerical novices.

Three days later, Father Barberis was back in Turin at the Oratory. While conversing with Don Bosco in the library, the latter told him the dream as they paced back and forth. Father Barberis did not disclose that he had already heard it, not only because he was delighted to hear it again from Don Bosco's own lips, but also because, in retelling his dreams, Don Bosco would add new and interesting details.

Father Lemoyne, too, heard it from Don Bosco himself, and he and Father Barberis wrote it down. Father Lemoyne stated that Don Bosco confided to them that they were the very first ones to whom he had narrated this kind of vision *in detail*. We report it almost to the letter:

I seemed to be in a wild region I had never before seen, an immense untilled plain, unbroken by hills or mountains, except at the farthest end, where I could see the outline of jagged mountains. Throngs of naked, dark-skinned, fierce-looking, long-haired men of exceptional height and build swarmed all over this plain. Their only garments were hides strung across their shoulders. Their weapons were long spears and slings.

These throngs, scattered about, presented varied sights to the spectator: some men were hunting, others were carrying bloodied chunks of meat at spear point, still others were fighting among themselves or with European soldiers. I shuddered at the sight of corpses lying all over the ground. Just then many people came into sight at the far edge of the plain. Their clothing and demeanor told me they were missionaries of various orders who had come to preach the Christian faith to these barbarians. I stared intently at them but could recognize no one. They strode directly to those savages, but the latter immediately overwhelmed them with fiendish fury and hatred, killing them, ripping them apart, hacking them into pieces, and brandishing chunks of their flesh on the barbs of their long spears. Now and then, fighting broke out again among the savages or against neighboring tribes.

After witnessing this horrible bloodshed, I said to myself: *How can one convert so brutal a people?* Then I saw a small band of other missionaries, led by a number of young boys, advance cheerfully toward those savages.

I feared for them, thinking, *They are walking to their death.* I went to meet them; they were clerics and priests. When I looked closely at them, I recognized them as our own Salesians. I personally knew only those in front, but I could see that the others too were Salesians.

How can this be? I exclaimed. I did not want them to advance any farther because I feared that soon their fate would be that of the former missionaries. I was about to force them back when I saw that the barbarians seemed pleased by their arrival. Lowering their spears, they warmly welcomed them. In utter amazement I said to myself: *Let's see how things will turn out!* I saw that our missionaries mingled with them and taught them, and they docilely listened and learned quickly. They readily accepted the missionaries' admonitions and put them into practice.

As I stood watching, I noticed that the missionaries were reciting the rosary as they advanced, and that the savages, closing in from all sides, made way for them and joined in the prayers.

After a while, our Salesians moved into the center of the

throng and knelt. Encircling them, the barbarians also knelt, laying their weapons at the missionaries' feet. Then a missionary intoned: *Praise Mary, Ye Faithful Tongues,* and, as with one voice, the song swelled in such unison and power that I awoke, partly frightened.

I had this same dream four or five years ago, and it sharply impressed me because I took it as a heavenly sign. Though I did not thoroughly grasp its specific meaning, I understood that it referred to the foreign missions, which even at that time were one of my most fervent aspirations.

Thus the dream dated back to about 1872. At first Don Bosco believed that it referred to the tribes of Ethiopia, later to the regions around Hong Kong, and finally to the aborigines of Australia and of the East Indies. It was only in 1874, when he received most pressing requests to send Salesians to Argentina, that he clearly understood that the natives he had seen in his dream lived in Patagonia, an immense region then almost entirely unknown. (Vol. X, pp. 46-48)

THE PEARS ARE FOR YOU

I seemed to be standing in a garden near a fruit tree with extraordinarily large fruit on it. The tree was heavy with three kinds of fruit: figs, peaches, and pears. Quite suddenly a strong wind arose and it started hailing; the hailstones were mixed with real stones that hit my shoulders. I tried to find shelter, but someone came up and said, "Hurry, pick the fruit!" I looked for a basket, but the one I found was too small. The man scolded me and said, "Get a bigger one."

I changed my basket for another, but no sooner had I picked two or three of the fruit than the basket was full. Again the person chided me saying, "Hurry, or the hailstones will ruin all of them."

I resumed picking the fruit, but to my great astonishment I saw that some of the enormous figs I had picked were rotten on one side. The stranger then shouted, "Hurry, sort them!"

I began to sort out the good fruit, making three separate stacks in my basket, putting the figs on one side, the peaches on the other, and the pears in the middle, but all the fruit—figs, peaches, and pears—were so big (they were bigger than a man's two fists) that I could not stop staring at them—they were not only large but beautiful. The stranger then said, "The figs are for the bishops, the pears are for you, the peaches are for South America." He then clapped his hands and said, "Courage, *bravo, bravo*, well done, *bravo!*" and disappeared.

I woke up; the dream made such a deep impression on me that I cannot get it out of my mind.

It is not known whether Don Bosco immediately tied in this dream with the project that was then so dear to him; but in time the connection became more and more apparent. Careful choice was necessary, especially at the beginning, so that unsuitable candidates would not compromise the whole project. The large basket that could hold so much stood for the size of the school to be set aside for the project; the figs for the bishop symbolized young men for the diocesan seminaries; the peaches for South America, the Salesian missionaries; the pears in the middle, the Salesians for the Headquarters of the Congregation. What about the hailstones that bruised his shoulders? They signified the strong, high-placed opposition that he would encounter... (Vol. XI, pp. 22-23)

A RAGING BULL

It has been said that we are to pay no heed to dreams, and I assure you that most of the time I too agree. Nevertheless, though dreams may not reveal future events to us, they can at times help us to see our way through intricate problems and to act wisely in different matters. Therefore we may accept what they have to offer us that is good.

Just now I want to tell you about a dream that absorbed my mind, you might say, all through the retreat and that especially last night upset me. I will tell it as I saw it, because I think that it has many valuable lessons, but I will condense it here and there so as not to be too lengthy.

Well, then, it seemed we were all together on our way from Lanzo to Turin, aboard some vehicles—either coaches or railway cars, but just which I am not sure. At a certain point on our way, I can't recall where, our vehicles stopped. I got off to see what had happened and faced a man who defies all description. He seemed to me both tall and short at the same time, stout and slim, red and white, walking on the ground and floating in the air. Totally confused and bewildered, I made bold to ask, "Who are you?"

His only answer was, "Come with me!"

I first wanted to know who he was and what he wanted, but I had no time to find out. "Hurry!" he said. "Let's get the vehicles into this field." The astonishing thing was that he spoke loudly and softly at the same time and in different tones, so that my amazement knew no bounds.

The field was very vast and, to all appearances, quite flat, unplowed and as smooth as a threshing floor. Not knowing what to say and seeing his determination, we turned the vehicles around into that vast field, and once there we ordered everyone to get down. They all did so very quickly, and no sooner were all off than the vehicles immediately disappeared, leaving no trace.

Not knowing how to conduct myself with that stranger, I stammered, "Will you now tell us why you made us stop here?"

"To save you from very great danger!" he replied.

"What danger?"

"A raging bull which leaves not a living person in its path: 'A roaring bull seeking whom to devour.' " (cf. 1 Pt 5:8)

"Easy, my friend!" I retorted. "You apply to a bull what St. Peter says of a lion—a roaring lion."

"That does not matter in the least. There it was a roaring *lion,* here it is a roaring *bull.* What matters is that you had better be on guard. Call all your followers about you and immediately and very seriously tell them to be on guard and very alert. As soon as they hear the roar of a bull, an unusual and thundering roar, they are immediately to fling themselves face down upon the ground and stay that way until the bull has passed. God help anyone who will not obey you. Whoever refuses to lie face to the ground as I have ordered will be as good as dead. Holy Scripture tell us that the lowly shall be exalted and the proud will be humbled."

Then he immediately added, "Quickly, quickly! The bull is

on its way! Shout as loud as you can to fall to the ground!"

I did so and he insisted, "Louder! Louder!"

I yelled so loudly that I'm sure I frightened Father Lemoyne who sleeps next door to me. I was shouting at the top of my voice.

In an instant the bellow of a bull was heard, and the man told me, "On guard! On guard! Make them all lie next to one another in two straight rows, with an aisle for the bull to pass between them!" I shouted out his orders. In a flash everyone lay flat on the ground, and we could see the bull far off, thundering forward in a fury. Although just about everyone lay flat on his face, a few remained standing in order to have a good look at the bull.

"Now you will see what happens to them," the man told me. "You will see what they get for refusing to lie low."

I wanted to warn them again, to shout, and to run to them, but he forbade me. I insisted that he let me go to them, but he answered sharply, "Obedience applies to you too! Lie down!"

Before I could get down, I heard a thundering bellow, awesome and frightening. The bull drew closer. Terror seized all, and they kept asking, "Who knows? Who knows?"

"Do not fear!" I shouted. "Stay down!"

And my friend kept yelling: "He who humbles himself shall be exalted and he who exalts himself shall be humbled ... he who humbles himself ... he who humbles himself...." (cf. Lk 14:11)

I found one thing strange and astonishing. Pressed flat to the ground as I was, face to the earth and eyes in the dust, I could still clearly see everything happening about me. The bull had seven horns set almost in a circle, two below the snout, two in the place of eyes, two in a normal position, and one on the crest. Even more amazing was the fact that the horns were very tough but mobile, and the bull kept turning them as he wished, so that to gore and fling his victim to the ground he did not have to turn from side to side. He kept running forward without a turn, knocking down anyone he encountered. The horns below the snout were the longest, and they wrought frightful havoc.

The bull was now upon us. The man shouted, "Now you

will see the power of humility." Instantaneously, to our astonishment, we found ourselves lifted high into the air, so that the bull could not possibly reach us. Those few who had refused to lie flat on the ground were not raised up. The bull rushed them and in a flash tore them to pieces. Not one was spared. Meanwhile, hanging in the air, we were scared stiff at the thought of what our fate would be if we fell to the ground. We could see the angry bull straining toward us and leaping high to sink his horns into us, but he could not do us the least harm. More furious than ever, he rent the air with a frightful roar as if to tell us he was leaving to seek reinforcements. And so "in great wrath" (cf. Rv 12:12) he stormed off.

Then we instantly found ourselves again on the ground. "Face the south!" the man shouted. We did so, and suddenly, to our amazement, everything changed around us. To the south we saw the Blessed Sacrament exposed and many candles burning on either side. The field was gone, and we seemed to be in a very vast church, all beautifully decorated.

While we were all kneeling in adoration before the Blessed Sacrament, a host of most horrid, roaring bulls appeared, their heads bristling with horns. They came close to us, but since we were in adoration before the Blessed Sacrament, reciting the chaplet in honor of the Sacred Heart of Jesus, they could do us no harm. After a while, I don't know how, we turned around and saw that the bulls had left. Looking back to the altar, we saw that the candles had disappeared, the Blessed Sacrament was no longer in sight, and the church itself had vanished from sight, and we found ourselves back in the field where we had been before.

You know well enough that the bull symbolizes the devil, our spiritual enemy, who in rage against us continually tries to harm us. The seven horns are the seven capital sins. We can be rescued from the horns of this bull, that is, from the devil's assaults, and not fall into those sins mainly by humility, the bedrock of virtue. Meanwhile, we kept looking at each other, confused and amazed. No one spoke, for we did not know what to say. Everyone expected me or the dream personage to say something. Drawing me aside, he said, "Come, I will show you the triumph of the Congregation of St. Francis de Sales. Climb that rock and you will see!"

A huge boulder stood in the middle of that boundless field, and I climbed on it. A limitless panorama spread before me. I would never have thought that the field was so immense; it seemed to cover the entire earth. People of every race, color and nation were gathered there. They were such a multitude that I never thought the world could hold so many. I carefully observed the first who came into my view. They were dressed like us. Those in the front ranks I could recognize. I saw many Salesians leading groups of boys and girls; they were followed by other Salesians with more groups, and more came after them and still more whom I did not know, until they became a huge blur. They were numberless. To the south I could see Sicilians, Africans, and an innumerable host of people I did not know. All had Salesians in the lead, but I could recognize only those in the first few ranks.

"Turn around," the man ordered. My gaze met countless masses of other people wearing animal skins and a kind of cloak of velvet sheen, brilliantly dyed in various colors. I was told to face the four points of the compass. Among other things, in the east I saw women whose feet were so tiny they could barely stand or walk. The wonder of it all was that everywhere I saw Salesians leading squads of boys and girls and countless crowds of adults. I always recognized those in the front ranks, but not those who followed, not even the missionaries. At this point I must cut short many things because it would take too long.

Then my guide said to me, "Look and pay close attention, even though you will not understand what I am now telling you. What you have seen is the harvest awaiting the Salesians. Do you see how immense a harvest it is? This vast field you stand on is the Salesians' field of labor. The Salesians whom you see are already at work and you know them, but then the horizon extends as far as you can see, filled with people yet unknown to you. This means that not only in this century but also in the next and in future centuries, Salesians will labor in fields of their own. Do you know under what conditions the achievements you have seen are to be reached? I will tell you. Take heed: you must have these words engraved on your coat-of-arms as your watchword, your badge. Note them well: *Work and temperance will make the Sa-*

lesian Congregation flourish. Have these words explained repeatedly and insistently. Compile and print a handbook that will clearly explain that work and temperance are the legacy you are bequeathing to the Congregation, and will be also its glory."

"I will most willingly do so," I replied. "It is wholly in keeping with our purpose. It is what I keep insisting upon day after day and stress upon every occasion."

"Are you really quite convinced? Have you thoroughly understood me? This is the heritage you will leave them. Tell them clearly that as long as they live by it, they will have followers from the south, the north, the east and the west. Now bring the spiritual retreat to a close and send them on their way. These will set the norm; others will follow."

Then coaches suddenly appeared to take us all to Turin. I kept looking at them. They were quite peculiar, the strangest I have ever seen. Everybody began to step aboard, but since they had neither railings nor sides, I feared that our boys might fall off, and so I didn't want to let them go. But my guide told me, "Let them go. They are quite safe if they faithfully abide by the words: 'Stay sober and alert.' (1 Pt 5:8) If these words are diligently carried out, no one will fall, even though the coach has no handgrips and is in rapid motion." They left and I remained alone with that man. "Come," he said quickly. "I want to show you a very important thing. Oh, you have so much to learn! Do you see that coach out here?"

"Yes."

"Do you know what it is?"

"I can't see it that well."

"Draw closer then. Do you see that placard there? Go closer and look at it carefully. There is an emblem emblazoned on it. It will tell you what the coach is."

I went up to the placard and saw four very thick spikes painted on it. I turned to him and said, "Unless you explain, I cannot understand."

"Don't you see those four nails? Look at them closely. They are the four nails which pierced and so cruelly tormented Our Divine Savior's body."

"And so?"

"They are also the four nails which plague religious Congregations. If you can keep these four nails away, that is, if your Congregation is not plagued by them, if you are wise enough to shunt them off, things will go well and all of you will be safe."

"I am still no wiser than before," I replied. "What do these nails symbolize?"

"If you want to know, go inside this coach. It has four compartments, one for each nail."

"What do the compartments mean?"

"Look at the first." I did so and read the words, "Their god is their belly." (Phil 3:19) "Ah, now I begin to understand," I exclaimed.

My guide remarked, "This is the first nail, which plagues and destroys religious Congregations. If you are not careful, it will create havoc among you also. Fight it relentlessly, and you shall see that things will go well with you.

"Now read the inscription on the nail of the second compartment: 'They are busily seeking their own interests rather than those of Jesus Christ.' (cf. Phil 2:21) This refers to those who seek their own comfort and ease, scheming for their own advantage and perhaps that of their family, rather than for a Congregation which is working for Jesus Christ. Be on guard, drive scourge far from you, and you will see the Congregation prosper."

On the third compartment I saw the third nail's inscription. I read: "Theirs is the tongue of an asp." My guide said: "A fatal nail for any Congregation will be grumblers and complainers, those who, right or wrong, are forever criticizing."

The fourth compartment read: "Chamber of idleness." The guide remarked: "Here idlers abound. When idleness gains a footing in a community, it totally destroys it. On the other hand, as long as your men work hard, you will face no danger. Now take note of another thing which is too often overlooked. I want you to give it special attention. Do you see that little cubicle which belongs to no compartment and yet reaches a little into all?"

"I see it but it's just a heap of leaves and grass, tall and short, all tangled together."

"Good! Take a close look at it!"

"But why?"

"Read carefully the nearly half-hidden inscription."

I peered intently and read: "The snake lurks in the grass."

"What are you driving at?"

"Look, there are some people who lie low. They clam up and never confide in their superiors; they keep their secrets to themselves. Be on guard, for the snake lurks in the grass. They are a real scourge, a plague for any Congregation. Bad as they might be, once discovered, they might be corrected, but, no, they remain hidden and we are unaware of them, and the evil becomes worse and poison builds up in their hearts. By the time they are found out, it is too late to repair the damage they have already done. So, then, learn well what things you must keep far from your Congregation. Keep well in mind what you have heard. Give orders to have these things explained at length again and again. If you do so, you can rest secure that your Congregation will increasingly prosper."

Then, lest I forget anything he told me, I asked him permission to write it all down.

"You can try if you want to," he answered, "but I doubt that you have time. Be alert!"

As he was talking and I was all set to write, I seemed to hear a confused roar, a rumble all about me, and the very ground seemed to quake. I swiftly looked around to see what else was happening and saw that the boys who had departed shortly before were all dashing toward me from every direction in utter fright. Just behind them came a roar and then a bellowing bull in pursuit. His very reappearance struck me with such terror that I awoke.

I have told you this dream on this occasion before we return to our houses because I am well convinced and can say in all truth that we would worthily close this retreat if we were to resolve to live up to our motto, *Work and temperance*, and strive to a man to keep from us the four great nails which plague religious life. They are gluttony, comfort and ease, grumbling and idleness. To this we might add that each one is to be always open, truthful and trusting with his superiors. In this way we shall not only benefit our own souls but also help to save those whom Divine Providence will entrust to our care.

(Vol. XII, pp. 335-341)

ALL THESE BOYS ARE YOURS

I dreamt that I saw an area which did not resemble the open meadowlands outside Turin. A small rustic cottage facing a small threshing yard seemed to beckon me to its shelter. It was a bare cottage, like that of peasants, and the room in which I stood had doors opening into several other rooms both above and below its level. All around I saw racks for farm tools, but no people. I looked through the rooms, but they were all empty. The house was totally deserted. Then, hearing the voice of a small boy singing loud and clear, I stepped outside and saw a lad, ten or twelve years old, sturdily built, dressed like a farmhand. He was standing erect and motionless, staring at me. Beside him stood a peasant woman neatly dressed. The youngster was singing in French:

Ami respectable,	[Respectable friend,
Soyez notre père aimable.	Be our kind father.]

"Come in, come in," I said from the doorway. "Who are you?" Still staring at me, the young lad repeated his song. "What do you wish from me?" I asked. The same song was his answer.

"Please say something," I insisted. "Do you want me to let you in? Do you want to tell me something? Would you like a present, a medal perhaps, or money?"

Ignoring my question, the youngster looked about him and then started to sing another ditty:

Voilà mes compagnons	[Behold my companions
Qui diront ce que nous voulons.	Who will tell you what we want.]

Instantly, a multitude of boys appeared from nowhere, heading toward me through the untilled fields. They sang in unison:

Notre perè de Chemin,	[Father of the Way,
Guidez-nous dans le Chemin;	Guide us along the Way;
Guidez-nous au jardin,	Lead us to the garden,

Non au jardin des fleurs,   Not to a flower garden,
Mais au jardin de bonnes moeurs.   But the garden of good morals.]

"But who are you all?" I asked in astonishment, as I got close to them. The same lad again replied in a ditty:

Notre Patrie   [Our country
C'est le pays de Marie.   Is the land of Mary.]

"I don't understand!" I said. "What are you doing here? What do you want from me?"
    They all chorused:

Nous attendons l'ami   [We are awaiting the friend
Qui nous guide au Paradis.   Who will lead us to Paradise.]

"That's fine!" I exclaimed. "Do you want to come to my schools? You are too many, but we shall manage somehow. If you want to learn your catechism, I will teach you; if you want to come to confession, I am at your disposal. Or would you like me to train you in singing or teach you or give you a sermon?" Gracefully they again chorused:

Notre Patrie   [Our country
C'est le pays de Marie.   Is the land of Mary.]

    While listening, I asked myself: *Where am I? In Turin or in France? Just yesterday I was at the Oratory! How strange this is! I don't understand!* As I was immersed in these thoughts, the good woman took the youngster by the hand and, pointing to a farther, more spacious farmyard, told the crowd, *Venez avec moi* [Come with me], and led the way.
    All the boys who had clustered about me followed her. As I joined them, new groups of boys arrived carrying sickles, hoes and other farm tools and joined the crowd. I gazed at them more astonished than ever. Surely I was neither at the Oratory nor at Sampierdarena. I kept saying to myself: *I can't be dreaming because I am walking.* If occasionally I slowed down,

the throng surrounding me jostled me forward.

Meanwhile, I kept my eyes on the woman who was leading us and who aroused my keenest curiosity. Modestly dressed, she wore a red kerchief around her neck and a white blouse characteristic of young highlanders or shepherdesses, but I sensed an air of mystery about her, although her appearance was quite ordinary. Adjacent to the larger farmyard stood another rustic cottage, and not far from it was a very beautiful home. When all the boys were gathered in the farmyard, the woman turned to me and said, "Look at these fields, this house! Look at these boys!"

I looked. The boys were a multitude—well over a thousand times as many as at first had appeared.

"All these boys are yours!" the woman went on.

"Mine?" I echoed. "By what right can you give them to me? They are neither yours nor mine. They belong to God!"

"By what right?" the woman continued. "They are my children and I entrust them to you."

"But how can I look after so many energetic youngsters? Don't you see how wildly they chase each other through the fields, leap over ditches, and climb trees? Look at those boys fighting. How can I keep order and discipline alone?"

"Shall I tell you?" she exclaimed. "Look!"

Wheeling about, I saw a second huge crowd of boys surging forward. Over them the woman cast a broad veil, covering them entirely. I had no idea where she got it from. Some moments later she pulled it away, and all the boys had turned into priests and clerics.

"Are these priests and clerics mine?" I asked the woman.

"They will be if you train them!" she replied. "If you want to know more, come here." She bade me draw closer to her.

"Tell me, my dear lady," I asked, "what place is this? Where am I?"

She did not reply but motioned to the first crowd of boys to gather about her. They came running and she cried out: *Attention, garçons, silence. Ouvriers, chantez tous ensemble* [Attentions, boys, silence. Sing all together, you workers]. At her signal, the boys broke into a vigorous chorus: "Glory, honor and thanks to the Lord God of Hosts." Their singing was full of

63

harmony, voices ranging from the lowest to the highest register, the lowest notes apparently rising up from the ground and the soprano voices blending into the highest heavens. Their hymn ended with a resounding *Ainsi, soit-il* [Amen]. Then I woke up...

The meaning of Don Bosco's dream was made clear in the proposals which he received from France a few hours later. Events made it certain that there could be no other explanation for it. When Father Lemoyne visited the new house shortly after its opening, he was given the first proof. Walking up from the main floor, where the director's office was located, to the second floor, he entered a room with wall racks and doors leading to other rooms on other floors. He also spotted a small barnyard and a huge, neglected meadow encircled by trees in front of the building. A little farther away was a much larger barnyard where the first boys' home was later built.

The dream came true to its last details. Father Lemoyne, unprepared for such a shock, wrote to Don Bosco immediately, but a still greater surprise awaited Don Bosco himself, when he went there on his second visit. As he was strolling across the property, the boys, headed by one who was holding a bouquet of flowers, ran ahead to meet him.

When he was but a few steps from the boy, Don Bosco blanched, so strong was his emotion, for the boy's build and features fitted the dream exactly. He was Mickey Blain, who became a Salesian and who at this date [1932] resides in our school in Nice. That same evening an assembly was held in Don Bosco's honor. As the choir accompanied Blain's solo, Don Bosco pointed him out to Father [Peter] Perrot, the director, and said, "That boy looks like the boy of my dream."

Don Bosco's dreams often carry prophetic overtones, but one must be cautious of hasty interpretations since often enough predictions may be fulfilled only after a long time. What is a commentator to say if prophets themselves do not always grasp the significance of their own prophecies? Until a few years ago an enigma overshadowed the second group of boys who in the dream were not carrying farm tools and were transformed into priests and clerics. Attempts were made to solve it, one interpretation being that Don Bosco foresaw priestly vocations rising from the pupils of the agriculture school. This explanation, however, was unsatisfactory as being too vague to explain the clear-cut symbolism of the tableau. But when, with total oblivion of the dream, the decision was made to open a house at Navarre for the Sons of Mary—later also a novitiate—the true meaning of that prophecy began to show itself. Father Candela, a councilor of the Superior Chapter, was the first to draw attention to it in the fall of 1929. While preparing to confer the clerical habit on twenty postulants who had been trained there and elsewhere, he marked them out as the ones who fulfilled the transformation which Don Bosco had foreseen fifty years before. (Vol. XIII, pp. 413-417)

SAINT FRANCIS DE SALES

Don Bosco had another dream which he narrated on May 9. In it he saw the fierce battles which faced the men called to his Congregation, and he was given several valuable instructions for all his sons and sound advice for the future.

I saw a hard-fought, long-drawn-out battle between youngsters and a varied array of warriors who were armed with strange weapons. Survivors were few.

A second fiercer and more terrifying battle was being waged by gigantic monsters fully armed, well-trained tall men who unfurled a huge banner, the center of which bore an inscription in gold, "Mary, Help of Christians." The combat was long and bloody, but the soldiers fighting under the banner were protected against hurt and conquered a vast plain. The boys who had survived the previous battle linked forces with them, each combatant holding a crucifix in his right hand and a miniature of the banner in his left. After engaging together in several sallies over that vast plain, they split, some heading eastward, a few to the north, and many for the south. Once they all left, the same skirmishes, maneuvers and leave-takings were repeated by others.

I recognized some boys who fought in the first skirmishes, but none of the others, who nevertheless seemed to know me and asked me many questions.

Shortly afterward I witnessed a shower of flashing, fiery tongues of many colors, followed by thunder and then clear skies. Then I found myself in a charming garden. A man who looked like Saint Francis de Sales silently handed me a booklet. I asked him who he was. "Read the book." was the reply.

I opened it, but had trouble reading, managing only to make out these words:

"For the Novices: Obedience in all things. Through obedience they will deserve God's blessings and the good will of men. Through diligence they will fight and overcome the snares set by the enemies of their souls.

"For the Confreres: Jealously safeguard the virtue of chastity. Love your confreres' good name, promote the honor of the Congregation.

"For the Directors: Take every care, make every effort to observe and promote observance of the rules through which everyone's life is consecrated to God.

"For the Superior: Total self-sacrifice, so as to draw himself and his charges to God."

The book said many other things, but I couldn't read any further, for the paper turned as blue as the ink.

"Who are you?" I again asked the man who serenely gazed at me.

"Good people everywhere know me. I have been sent to tell you of future events."

"What are they?"

"Those you have already seen and those which you will ask about."

"How can I foster vocations?"

"The Salesians will harvest many vocations by their good example, by being endlessly kind toward their pupils, and by urging them constantly to receive Holy Communion often."

"What should we bear in mind when admitting novices?"

"Reject idlers and gluttons."

"And when admitting to vows?"

"Make sure that they are well grounded in chastity."

"How are we to maintain the right spirit in our houses?"

"Let superiors very often write, visit and welcome the confreres, dealing kindly with them."

"What of our foreign missions?"

"Send men of sound morality and recall any who give you serious reason to doubt; look for and foster native vocations."

"Is our Congregation on the right path?"

"Let those who do good keep doing good." (Rv 22:11) "Not to go forward is to go backward." (Saint Gregory the Great) "The man who stands firm to the end will be saved." (cf. Mt 10:22)

"Will the Congregation grow?"

"It will reach out so that no one will be able to check its growth, as long as the superiors meet their obligations."

"Will it have a long life?"

"Yes, but only as long as its members love work and temperance. Should either of these two pillars fall, your entire edifice will collapse and crush superiors, subjects and followers beneath it."

Just then four men showed up bearing a coffin and approaching me.

"Whom is that for?" I asked.

"For you."

"How soon?"

"Do not ask. Just remember that you are mortal."

"What are you trying to tell me with this coffin?"

"That while you are still living you must see to it that your sons practice what they must continue to practice after your death. This is the heritage, the testament you must bequeath to them; but you must work on it and leave it [to your sons] as a well-studied and well-tested legacy."

"Can we expect roses or thorns?"

"Many roses and joys are in store, but very sharp thorns also threaten. They will cause all of you acute distress and sorrow. You must pray much."

"Should we open houses in Rome?"

"Yes, but not hurriedly; proceed with extreme prudence and caution."

"Is the end of my mortal life near at hand?"

"Don't be concerned. You have the rules and other books. Practice what you preach and be vigilant."

I wanted to ask more questions, but muffled thunder rumbled through the air with flashes of lightning. Several men, rather horrid monsters, dashed toward me as if to tear me to pieces. But then a deep darkness enveloped me, shutting everything out. I felt that I must be dead and started to scream frenziedly. I awoke and found I was still alive. It was a quarter to five in the morning.

If we can draw some good from this dream, let us do so. In all things let honor and glory be given to God forever and ever.

(Vol. XIV, pp 88-90)

A SCHOOL FOR BECCHI

On March 1, 1886, Don Bosco narrated the following dream to Father Lemoyne and Brother Festa. It has a prophetic note about it.

Don Bosco dreamed that he was at Becchi. His mother was down by the pump with a bucket in her hand, scooping up dirty water that flowed into a trough. This pump had always given clean water, so Don Bosco wondered how the change had come about.

"*Aquam nostram pretio bibimus,*" Mama Margaret said.

"You and your Latin, mother. That's not scriptural, you know."

"What does that matter? You can supply your own words if you like. The ones I use express my thoughts. Note them well: '*Iniquitates eorum port . . .*' Now add your own."

"*Portavimus? Portamus?*"

"As you wish. Study these words and have your priests study them too. Meditate upon them and you will find out what is going to happen."

Then she brought him behind the pump, and from this higher ground he could see Capriglio and its neighboring hamlets, and even Buttigliera and places beyond it. Mama Margaret pointed this out and asked, "What's the difference between all these hamlets and Patagonia?"

"Oh, I am all for doing good here as well as there."

"Then," Mama Margaret replied, "that is all right." His mother seemed to walk away just then, and he awoke.

After Don Bosco related this dream, he remarked: "The elevated ground where my mother led me is suitable for starting some work of ours, because it is at the center of a circle that takes in quite a number of places that have no church."

Later, a vocational school was built on this spot, thanks to the generosity of Don Bernardo Semeria. The school gets its water supply from the municipality. (Vol. XVIII, p. 27ff)

HELP US ALSO

On the night of July 17, 1885, Don Bosco could not rest. As soon as he closed his eyes, dreams filled his mind until morning. He related the following the next day.

"I do not know whether I was awake or asleep, though I felt that I was still in touch with reality."

Don Bosco seemed to be walking with his mother and brother, Joseph, towards the road called "Dora Grossa"—now the Garibaldi—on his way to pray in St. Philip's. When he came out of the church he met many people, all of whom invited him to visit their homes. He told them that he was not able to accompany them at that time. A workingman came away from the group and said to Don Bosco: "Pay your first visit to me."

Don Bosco agreed, and the whole group started along the road called Po, accompanied by the worker. Near the great square of Victor Emmanuel he saw many little girls playing on an adjoining road. The worker pointed to this place and said: "You must start an Oratory here."

"For heaven's sake, don't say that! We have enough Oratories already; we can hardly provide for the ones we have!"

"An Oratory is needed here for these girls. There are private schools for them, but there is no Oratory where they can gather."

Just as he was passing the square, the little girls left their games and flocked around him, shouting: "Oh, Don Bosco, give us an Oratory for ourselves. We are at the mercy of the devil, who does so much harm among us. Help us. Open a haven of safety for us. Open an Oratory for us."

"My children, I cannot do that. I am at an age when I

cannot see to such things any more. Pray to God and He will provide."

"Yes, yes, we will pray, but you must help us and gather us under the care of Mary Help of Christians."

"All right! Now tell me where you want me to open an Oratory."

"Well, Don Bosco," answered one of them who seemed more talkative than the others, "you see the long stretch of the Po here, don't you? Go closer and you will see the figure "4." There are soldiers there, and a certain man named Burlezza. He owns that land and is willing to give it to you."

"Very well, I'll look into the matter. In the meantime, all of you pray!"

"Certainly we'll pray," they all cried out in unison, "but don't forget us and our needs."

Don Bosco went off to look at the land. He saw the soldiers but did not meet Mr. Burlezza. He returned to the Oratory and awoke.

Don Bosco told Viglietti about the dream and asked him to investigate the piece of property in his dream, the figure "4," and the owner. Father Bonora did the investigation and found things as Don Bosco had described them, but the place was not for sale. (Vol. XVII, p. 486ff)

FIVE HUNDRED AND FOUR

Don Bosco dreamed that he went to gather chestnuts in a spot near Castelnuovo where the nuts were big and plentiful. While busy doing this, he noticed a woman who had just appeared and had begun to gather nuts also and put them into a basket. Don Bosco was a little ruffled at seeing how this woman had taken the liberty of gathering nuts near him.

"Why have you come here?" he asked her. "I don't see how you can presume to gather nuts that belong to me."

"Don't I have the right?"

"Well, they belong to me."

"Then I will gather nuts for you."

The woman spoke in a determined tone of voice, not

pausing in her task even for a moment, and Don Bosco, deciding that it was best not to press the matter, continued gathering nuts.

When each had a basket filled, the woman called to Don Bosco: "Can you guess how many chestnuts I have here?"

"That's a strange question to ask."

"Tell me how many."

"Oh, I wouldn't know. I'm not a fortuneteller!"

"Then I will tell you. There are 504."

"Five hundred and four?"

"Yes, and do you know what they stand for? The houses of the Daughters of Mary Help of Christians."

While they were talking, they heard the noise of an angry or drunken mob. The sounds came from among the trees, so Don Bosco and the woman ran off in the opposite direction until they were stopped by a river. They could not go forward or return the way they had come; they were in a dilemma. Meanwhile, the crowd came nearer, shouting and crushing the nuts beneath their feet.

Don Bosco awoke at the noise, but fell asleep a short time afterwards and continued the dream.

He dreamed that he was sitting on a small hill, and the woman with the basket was sitting nearby. The shouts of the crowd could be heard fading away in the distance. Don Bosco looked at the chestnuts in the woman's basket and thought to himself what excellent quality they were. But on closer examination he noticed that some of the nuts had been attacked by worms.

"Look!" he said to the woman. "What can be done here? These nuts are spoiled."

"We must separate them so that they do not contaminate the others," the woman answered. "Those daughters who are not good and who do not have the spirit of the house should be sent away. The worm of pride or other vices is eating them. This must be done especially in the case of postulants."

Don Bosco began to pick out the spoiled nuts. Seeing that there were not so many, he told this to the woman.

She observed, "Do you think all those that are left are good? Couldn't they have the worm inside them and not show it on the outside?"

"Then how would we know?" asked Don Bosco.

"It's hard. Some people are very clever at deception, and it is difficult to get to know them."

"Well, how then?"

She said, "The only way is to put them to the test and watch them. You can then detect whether they have the spirit of God or not. This test is successful if you are observant."

Don Bosco was thinking about the chestnuts, when he suddenly awoke to the morning light.   (Vol. XV, p. 364ff)

JOURNEY THROUGH SOUTH AMERICA

Don Bosco narrated this dream on September 4, 1883, to the Superior Chapter. Father Lemoyne wrote it down at once, and Don Bosco later went over it.

On the night before the feast of Saint Rose of Lima, August 30, I had a dream. I felt that I was asleep, and yet at the same time I was running swiftly. While I was trying to determine whether the whole matter was real or fantasy, I found myself entering a large hall where people were conversing on a variety of subjects.

One of the conversations was about the many natives in Australia, India, China, Africa and particularly South America, who were sitting in the shadow of death.

"Europe," remarked one of those present, "Christian Europe, that great bastion of civilization and of Catholicism, seems strangely apathetic about the foreign missions. There are very few people who are apostolic enough to brave the long journeys and enter unknown regions to bring salvation to the millions who, like us, have also been redeemed by the Son of God, Jesus Christ."

"What great numbers of idolaters in South America," observed another, "live deprived of the Church and of the knowledge of the Gospel!"

Still another said: "Geographers are mistaken in thinking that the Cordilleras of South America are a kind of wall separating that vast region from the rest of the earth. This is simply not so. Those long chains of high mountains are crisscrossed with valleys that are miles and miles in length. There we would find unexplored forests, as well as species of trees, animals and rocks that are seldom found anywhere else. Coal, oil, lead, copper, iron, silver and gold are all hidden in those mountains, in places where the hand of the beneficent Creator has placed them for the good of mankind. O Cordilleras, O Cordilleras, how rich are your eastern slopes!"

I wanted very much to ask for explanations of many things, to inquire who these people were who were gathered around me, and the name of this place. I glanced around the hall, but I did not know any of them. Just then, noticing me for the first time, the people welcomed me with kindness and invited me to join them.

"Tell me," I said, "Are we in Turin or London or Madrid or Paris? Where is this place? Who are you? With whom do I have the honor of speaking?"

They gave me a vague answer and went on talking about the missions.

Then a young man of about sixteen came along. There was a supernatural beauty about him, and his body shone with sparkling light that was brighter than the sun. His garments were interwoven with heavenly richness, and he wore on his head a cap that looked like a crown studded with flashing gems. He looked at me with great interest, while his smile expressed an affection that was hard to resist.

The young man called me by name, took my hand and spoke about the Salesian Congregation. I was captivated by the sound of his voice. "With whom do I have the good fortune to be speaking? Please tell me your name."

"It's all right," he replied. "You can speak freely, because you are with a friend."

"I would like to know your name."

"I would tell you my name if it were necessary," he answered, laughing, "but it is not necessary, for you should know me."

I looked more intently at that face, brilliant with light. How beautiful it was! Then I recognized him as the son of Count Fiorito Colle of Toulon, one of the most generous benefactors of our house and of our missions in South America. This boy had died some time ago.

"Oh, it's you, Luis!" I exclaimed, calling him by name, "And who are these others around you?"

"They are friends of the Salesians... I want you to do some work for me."

"What work?"

"Stand here near this table and pull this rope."

There was a large table in the middle of the room, and a coil of rope was lying on it. I saw that the rope was marked off like a ruler, with numbers and lines. Later I realized that this room was in South America, right at the equator, and that the numbers marked on the rope were degrees of latitude.

I took hold of the end of the rope and noticed that it bore the figure "0." I laughed.

"This is no time for laughing," the boy said to me. "Look what is written on the rope."

"A zero," I replied.

"Pull the rope."

I did, and the figure 1 came into view.

"Pull again, as you roll it up."

I did so, and there were the numbers 2,3,4, up to 20.

"Enough?" I asked.

"No! Still more! Keep pulling until you come to a knot."

The knot came at number 47. From this point the rope was composed of many strands that pointed right, left and center.

"Now, is that enough?" I asked.

"What's the number?"

"Forty-seven."

"Forty-seven and three make...?" he asked.

"Fifty," I answered.

"Plus five."

"Fifty-five."

"Remember that fifty-five." Then he said, "Pull some more."

"That's the end!" I exclaimed.

"Right! Now turn it around and pull from the other end."

I did so, until I reached the number 10. The youth said, "Pull some more!"

"There's nothing."

"Nothing?" he asked. "Look closely and then tell me."

"There's water," I replied.

I felt that something extraordinary was happening, but I am unable to describe it. There I was in that room, drawing out the rope inch by inch, and as I did so a vast panorama unfolded before me. From 9 to 55, the scene was of an almost limitless country which continued, after a narrow sea, to divide in the distance into hundreds of islands. One island seemed to be much larger than the rest. Here was the explanation for the strands of cord that followed the knot in the rope—every strand touched an island.

Some of these islands were inhabited by fierce men; others were desolate, barren and rocky; still others were covered with snow and ice. To the west there were many islands inhabited by savages.

(Perhaps the knot found at number 47 indicated the departure point of the Salesians, the principal mission from which the missionaries would fan out to Tierra del Fuego and to other parts of South America.)

In the other direction, from 0 to 10, the same land extended outwards until it met the water that I mentioned before. I think this water represents the Antilles Sea, but in my dream it looked so extraordinary that I cannot describe it in words.

When I exclaimed that there was water, the youth answered, "Now put 55 and 10 together, and what do we have?"

"Sixty-five," I said.

"What do you see in this direction?" he asked as he pointed to one area of the panorama.

"There are mountains to the west, and there is water to the east!"

(I must mention that I was seeing in miniature, as it were, what I later saw in its full grandeur. The graded marks on the rope corresponded exactly to degrees of latitude, and so I was able to remember all the places that I visited during the second part of this strange dream.)

My young friend continued. "Good! These mountains form a kind of border or frontier. Here and there, Mass is offered by the Salesians. There are thousands, millions of people waiting for your help, waiting for the Faith."

The mountains were the Cordilleras of South America, and that sea was the Atlantic Ocean.

"How is it possible," I asked, "to bring so many people into the fold of Christ?"

"How can it be done? Look!"

Just then Father Lago arrived, carrying a can of small green figs. He said to me:

"Don Bosco, take these."

"What's this?" I asked him as I eyed the can.

"I have been told to give them to you."

"These figs are not good to eat—they are not ripe."

Then my young friend took the can from Father Lago.

"Here is a gift for you."

"What should I do with it?" I asked.

"These figs," the youth answered, "are not ripe, but they belong to the fig tree of life. You must look for a way to make them ripe."

"How can I do that? If they were only a little bigger! Maybe some straw would ripen them, but they are so small and green . . . It's impossible."

"Well, to get them to ripen you must find some means of attaching them to the stem."

"Incredible! How can that be done?"

"Watch!" He took one of the figs and placed it in a vial of blood, and then immersed it in another vial full of water. He said, "With your sweat and blood, the savages will return to the stem and be once again in the good graces of the Master of life."

I thought to myself, "This will take time." Aloud, I remarked, "I don't know what more to say."

The young man read my thoughts and said, "These things will be accomplished before the end of the second generation."

"When will that be?"

"The present one does not count; it will be the generation after the next."

I was amazed and almost speechless at hearing about the wonderful destiny in store for our Congregation. I asked, "How many years in each generation?"

"Sixty."

"What comes after that?"

"Do you want to see what will happen? Come with me."

Without knowing how, I suddenly realized that we were standing in a railway station where many people were milling about. The young man and I boarded a train. I asked him where we were going, and he replied:

"Take note of this. We are going on a long trip into the Cordilleras. The way is open to the east, right to the sea. This is another of the Lord's gifts."

"When will we get to Boston, since that is where I am going?"

"Everything in its own time."

Saying this, he unfolded a map on which the diocese of Carthage, Columbia, was highlighted.

(I learned later that this was our point of departure.)

As I was looking at the map, the whistle blew and the train moved out of the station. Throughout the trip my friend talked about many things, but because of the noise I could not hear all that he said. However, I did learn some wonderful facts about astronomy, navigation, meterology, mineralogy, flora and fauna, and the topography of these regions—so clear were his explanations. His words were eloquent; at the same time, he spoke with a simplicity and familiarity that showed how fond he was of me. He had taken me by the hand at the start and held it tight to the end of the dream. I put my free hand on top of his, but his hand never seemed to remain there; it seemed to fade away, so that my left hand clasped nothing but my right. The youth smiled at these efforts of mine.

Meanwhile, I looked out of the train windows and saw a passing procession of scenes that were varied and wonderful— forests, mountains, prairies, long and stately rivers, none of which I ever thought existed in a land so far from my own. For more than a thousand miles, the train ran beside virgin forest which had not yet been explored.

My vision for distances seemed to have improved; there was nothing to get in the way. I do not know how to explain this marvel. I was like a man standing on a hill, looking out over a vast expanse of country: If he puts a small strip of paper in front of his eyes, he sees nothing, or very little; but when he removes that paper he sees the whole scene before him. When I fixed my gaze on some object as we were passing by, something like a succession of stage backdrops lifted, revealing miles and miles of terrain. Not only did I see the Cordilleras far away; I could also see, in detail, mountain ranges rising in solitude above immensurable prairies.

(They were the mountains of Panama, Colombia, Ecuador, Venezuela, the three Guianas, Brazil and Bolivia.)

I was able to confirm the truth of what had been said at the beginning of this dream by the people in the large hall.

I looked into gorges in the mountains and vales in the prairies; I marveled at the enormous wealth of those regions, that would one day be discovered. I saw mines of precious metals and inexhaustible deposits of coal and oil that seemed more abundant than on any other place on earth. And that was not all; between 15 and 20 degrees latitude there was a large and expansive valley which rose up from a lake. A voice said to me over and over: "When men begin to dig for the metals hidden in this ground, they will think that they have reached the Promised Land, so unheard of are the riches here."

Still there was more. What surprised me most was the fact that the Cordilleras formed valleys which geographers did not even know existed, because they thought that the mountains in those places were sheer cliffs. Inside these gorges and valleys, some of which were miles and miles long, dwelt tribes of people who had never seen a white man, and whose very existence was not even suspected.

Meanwhile, the train rushed along, here, there and everywhere, until finally it stopped. Many passengers got off and made their way west.

(Don Bosco referred to Bolivia. The station was probably La Paz; a railroad tunnel leads from there to the Pacific shore and also joins Brazil with Lima.)

The train started up again. It traversed forests, sped over gigantic viaducts and through tunnels into the gaping maws of mountains, crossed bridges over lakes and swamps and even mighty rivers, passed through prairies and plains.

We reached the banks of the Uruguay, a very large river. At one point I could also see the river Parana, where it flows near the Uruguay as if to offer it the gift of its waters; but after running parallel for a little while, it veers away. Both of these rivers are immense.

(From this we seem able to conclude that the future railway will reach Santá Cruz from La Paz, making use of the only pass that is in the Cruz de la Sierra mountains, across the river Guapay. It will touch the river Parapiti in the Bolivian region of the Chiquitos and stop just at the northern border of Paraguay; then it will enter the Sao Paulo district in Brazil and go on to Rio de Janeiro. Perhaps a railway line will start from an intermediary station, in the Sao Paulo area, and pass through the country between the Parana and the Uruguay rivers, linking Brazil with the republics of Uruguay and Argentina.)

After traveling a long time, the train once more came to a halt. Another group of passengers got off and headed towards the Cordilleras to the west.

(Don Bosco mentioned the district of Mendoza in the Argentine. The station was probably Mendoza, and the tunnel led to Santiago, the capital of Chile.)

Again the train sped on its way, this time towards the Pampas and Patagonia. Cultivated fields and sparsely scattered houses gave evidence that civilization was finally beginning to creep across those desolate wastes. At the borders of Patagonia we passed over a tributary of the Colorado, the Chubut (or was it the Rio Negro?). I could not see in which direction the waters flowed—towards the Cordilleras or towards the Atlantic. I tried to find the answer but was unable to do so.

At last we reached the coast off the Strait of Magellan. The young man and I disembarked. Punta Arenas was in front of us. I looked around. For miles and miles, the ground was covered with coal heaps, wooden beams and mounds of metal, some being worked and others still in their natural state. When my friend pointed these things out to me, I asked him:

"What do you want to tell me by all this?"

"What is seen now only in imagination will one day be realized. In the future these savages will become so docile that they will come seeking instruction, culture, trade and religion, of their own free will. The things that are now the admiration of the people will reach such proportions that they will be even more amazed."

"I have seen enough," I said. "Take me now to my Salesians in Patagonia."

We went back and got on the train, and after covering a great distance we stopped at a rather large town.

(This was probably the point marked by the 47th degree,

where he had seen the knot in the rope at the beginning of the dream.)

There seemed to be nobody at the station to greet us. As soon as we got off the train, however, we met some Salesians. They showed us a great many Salesian houses, and a vast number of boys. There were also churches, schools, hostels for youths and adults, buildings for the artisans, farm schools, and a convent where numerous domestic arts were taught.

I walked among them; there were so many! But I did not know anyone; not even one of the first Salesians was there. They looked at me in amazement, as though I were some kind of strange creature.

"Don't you know me?" I asked them. "Don't you know Don Bosco?"

"You are Don Bosco? Oh! We know you by reputation, but we have never seen your face except in pictures."

"What about Fathers Fagnano, Costamagna, Lasagna and Milanesio? Where are they?"

"We never knew them, because they were here a long time ago. They were the first Salesians to come here from Europe, but they have been dead many years now!"

I was astonished at this reply and wondered: "Am I dreaming, or is this for real?" I clapped my hands, touched my arms and shook myself; the sound of my hands clapping and the feel of my skin told me that I was not sleeping.

The visit was over in an instant. At the sight of the great progress of the Church, of our Congregation and of civilization in those regions, I thanked Divine Providence that I had been chosen as an instrument for the glory of God and the salvation of so many souls.

Meanwhile, my guide, Luis Colle, indicated to me that it was time to go. I said good-bye to my Salesians and we headed for the station, where the train was ready to depart. We boarded it and were soon on our way north.

I thought to myself that the territory of Patagonia that lies between the Cordilleras and the Atlantic, near the Strait of Magellan, was not as large as geographers commonly supposed. The train sped onwards, and I think it passed through the provinces that had been civilized by Argentina.

After a time the train stopped, and a horrible spectacle

took place before our eyes. A crowd of savages had gathered in a clearing of the forest. Their faces were deformed and frightening, their bodies covered with animal skins; they stood around a man who was bound and lying on a stone slab. The man, who did not belong to that tribe (one could tell by his features), had been captured and fattened by those wild men. They questioned him, and he answered them by telling about his adventures and exploits. Suddenly, a savage jumped up, brandishing a weapon similar to a sword, and with one slash he cut off the head of the prisoner. The cannibals threw themselves upon the body as it lay in a pool of blood and began pulling off bits of the still warm flesh, dropping it into their fires to be roasted and eaten.

The passengers on the train had crowded around the windows and doors, and when they saw this deed they were horrified. Colle himself was watching, but said nothing.

The train had started to move as soon as the victim screamed, and shortly afterwards it had regained its speed.

For hours and hours the train ran alongside a huge river—sometimes on the right bank, sometimes on the left. From the window I could not see the bridges over which we were traveling. Here and there along that river, innumerable tribes of natives appeared, and every time we saw them the young Colle would remark to me, "That's the Salesian harvest!"

We now entered a region that seemed to be infested with wild animals and poisonous reptiles of all shapes and sizes. They swarmed about the foothills and among the valleys, on the ridges of the mountains and the shady hilltops, along the shores of lakes and the banks of rivers, on the slopes and plains, and in the dells.

Some of the animals looked like dogs that had wings and swollen bellies (symbols of greed, pride and luxury). Others were huge toads that ate frogs. I could see some caves in which there were animals that were quite different from those we know. All these were mixed together and growling, as though they would devour their neighbors. There were tigers, hyenas and lions, too, but not the same as those of Africa and Asia.

My companion turned to me, and, pointing to the beasts, said, "The Salesians must tame them."

The train had now arrived back at the place from which we had set out on our journey. Luis Colle took out a finely-detailed map and asked me:
"Would you like to see what places we have visited?"
"Certainly," I replied.
Then he explained the map on which the countries of South America were drawn with excellent precision. I saw there the places and events that were, that had been and that would come to be, and it was all so clear and orderly that I took it in at a glance. I understood it at the time, but, because of the multiplicity of details, the pictures remained clear in my mind for only about half an hour, and then became blurred.

I was waiting for the young man to point out more details on the map, but I seemed to hear the morning Angelus rung by Quirino. I awoke and discovered that the bell of San Benigno was ringing. The dream had lasted the whole night!

Don Bosco concluded his narration:

Through the gentleness of Saint Francis de Sales, the Salesians will draw the teaming thousands of South America to Jesus. Taming the savages will be a hard task, but the children of these savages will be more docile and will obey the words of the missionaries. These young ones will become the nuclei of communities, and civilization will supplant barbarism, so that many of these people will enter the true fold of Christ.
(A few days later, a letter came from Bishop Bernard A. Thiel in Costa Rica, asking Don Bosco to send missionaries to his country. Costa Rica was at degree 10 in the dream!)
The journey I made with Luis Colle (Don Bosco said on February 11, 1884) is being fulfilled as the days go by. It has now become the central focus of our activities. Many things are being written, spoken about and published that bring our plans to realization.
When the vast riches of Patagonia become known (our founder once remarked to Father Lemoyne), an extraordinary development of that country will follow. Hidden in those mountains are veins of precious minerals; between degrees 10 and 20 in the Andes, there are deposits of lead and gold and of things more precious than gold!

To help the reader understand the tremendous significance of this dream, we shall make a few observations:

Don Bosco related to us facts which he could not have heard from travelers or geographers, for at that time no explorations of any sort had been made in those distant latitudes, either by scientific expeditions or with a view to opening them to tourists. Father DeAgostini, Salesian missionary and explorer, gives testimony to the accuracy of Don Bosco's prophecies in the books he has written about his own explorations in those regions. *My Journeys in Tierra del Fuego* is a classic of its genre.

Take Don Bosco's description of the Cordilleras, for example. In his day it was thought that these mountains were like a huge wall, a homogeneous chain extending north and south through more than thirty degrees of latitude. But later explorations and studies of the Andes revealed that, as Don Bosco had dreamed, there were sections where numerous gullies, valleys and indentations existed; these were subdivided and crisscrossed in such a way as to create different geographical and orographical phenomena.

The minute details with which Don Bosco described the Andes, and the fact that his description of future developments proved correct, lead us to conclude that the prophetic vision was supernatural in origin.

Maps from those days convince us that the presence of valleys and winding canyons was unknown. There had been several expeditions to the Cape Horn regions and Chile; for example, those of Parker King and Fitz Roy in their ships the "Adventure" and the "Reagle" in 1826 and 1836, and those of Simpson, Valverde, Rogera and Serrano between 1874 and 1889. In spite of these explorations, the western areas of the Patagonia Cordilleras were unknown. For example, the Baker strait, largest of Patagonia's fiords, runs inland for several hundred miles and breaks into depressions and valleys; yet it was not probed until the year 1898 by John Steffen, explorer and geographer.

Don Bosco described railroads in places that were desolate in his time; today, a network of railways that is a marvel of engineering crisscrosses those regions. Will the day also come, as foreseen by the saint, when North America will be joined by railroad to the Strait of Magellan, right through those very lands of Patagonia? (Vol. XVI, p. 385 ff)

LABOR AND REWARDS

On January 31, 1885, Don Bosco had a dream which he related to Father Lemoyne. The saint had prepared another group of Salesians for the South American missions, but unfortunately could not spend much time with them.

I dreamed that I was with our missionaries as they left us for the missions. They gathered around me asking for advice, and this is what I told them: "Not with knowledge or wealth or riches will you do good and foster the glory of God and the salvation of souls, but with zeal and holiness."

At one moment we were in the Oratory, and then all of a sudden we were in South America. How we got there and by what means I do not know. All I know is that I found myself alone on a vast prairie situated between Chile and Argentina.

The missionaries were scattered about on that unending plain, and as I looked, there seemed to be very few of them. Because of the large number of Salesians I had sent to South America, I expected to see many more than that. Then I realized that they seemed few in number because the field of work was so immense; they were as seeds that needed transplanting in order to germinate and increase.

On this vast plain I could see many long roads, along which numerous houses had been built. The roads were not like those in our country, nor were the houses like any we know; they were mysterious objects. The roads were used by vehicles which were continually taking on diverse shapes and forms, fantastic at times, and amazing. I cannot even describe them.

I noticed with astonishment that the vehicles, when approaching houses, villages or towns, traveled above them, so that anyone in the vehicles looked down upon the rooftops, which, as high as they were, seemed lower than the roads. In the desert places, however, the roads were at ground level, and only when nearing populated areas did they turn into aerial highways that looked like magic bridges. From there you could see people around the houses, the yards and the fields, busy at their various tasks.

Each road began in one of our missions. At the end of one road, which led to Chile, I saw a house with many Salesians in it, who were engaged in works of science, religion, agriculture and professions of various kinds.

Patagonia was to the south. Opposite this I saw, in the twinkling of an eye, all our houses in Argentina come into view. Then I saw the ones in Uruguay, Paysandu, Las Piedras, Villa Colon; and in Brazil, the school of Nicteroy and numerous houses here and there in that great country. Toward the west a new road had been laid; it was very long, and passed over rivers, lakes and other bodies of water until it came to an end in unknown lands. There must have been few Salesians in these areas, for no matter how hard I looked I could make out only two.

Just then I noticed beside me a man of noble bearing; although clean-shaven, he had a look of maturity about him. He was dressed in white and wore a rose-colored cape interwoven with gold around his shoulders. His whole person was shining with light.

"Where are we?" I asked him, pointing to the last country I had seen.

"In Mesopotamia," he replied.

"Mesopotamia?" I exclaimed. "But this is Patagonia!"

"And I tell you, we are in Mesopotamia."

"But ... but ... I am not convinced."

"But it's so!" he answered. "This is M-E-S-O-P-O-T-A-M-I-A."

He spelled the word so I would be all the more impressed. I asked another question:

"Why are there so few Salesians here?"

"What is not now, will be later on," he replied.

As I stood there on that vast plain, I let my gaze follow those endless roads, and I could see, most clearly but unexplainedly, the places where our Salesians work now and where they will be working. What great and wonderful happenings! As though in a flash, I saw the past, the present and the future of our missions. It is almost impossible to give you any idea, even a summary, of it all; it would take a big book just to describe the things I saw in the plains of Chile, Paraguay, Brazil and Argentina, and that would not be a full description.

I saw unending lines of people, stretching from the Pacific coast to the Strait of Magellan, Cape Horn and the Falkland Islands. All this is the harvest destined for our Salesians. The present ones plant the seed, but their successors will do the reaping. Men and women will join our ranks and go out to preach. Even children who give little indication that they will ever be won over to the Faith will nevertheless become evangelizers for their parents and friends.

Our Salesians will do marvelous things, provided they are humble, industrious and temperate. What I have seen pertains to all Salesians, present and future—their regular activity in those lands, their growth and development, the conversion of so many natives and of foreigners who have settled there. Europe will turn to South America. For, from the moment Europe begins to despoil churches, trade will wane. So workers and their families will seek a home in those friendly lands, far from the miseries of their ancient homelands.

After I had seen the fields of labor set aside for the Salesians by the good God, and the glorious future awaiting us, I turned my footsteps toward home. I was carried along, it seemed, with lightning speed over an unknown road that led through the air, and in a flash I was at the Oratory. Turin lay beneath my feet; houses, mansions and steeples looked like small huts, so high was I flying. Below me I could also see streets, gardens, avenues, railroads, the city walls, the fields beyond and the neighboring hills, the towns and villages of the region, the distant range of the Alps capped with snow—the whole panorama a thing of beauty.

From that height, the boys of the Oratory looked like mice, and there were lots of them! Everywhere, priests, seminarians and craftsmasters moved about; many left the Oratory, but many others came to fill the vacant places. The whole movement was a procession in and out. Those who left went to that immense plain between Chile and Argentina, the place from which I had just returned in a twinkling of an eye. I watched them.

A young priest whom I took to be Father Pavia—but he was not—came towards me, smiling affably. He had a face of innocence and candor, and spoke in a genteel manner.

"See the souls and the lands ready for the sons of Saint Francis de Sales."

The crowds that had been there a short time before disappeared gradually into the background; I could not see where they went.

I know very well that my story contains huge gaps. This is because I am not able to pinpoint the exact succession of the wonderful things I saw, or their attendant circumstances. The mind grows weary, the memory flags, and words cannot adequately describe the experience. Besides the mystery inherent in these scenes, the scenes themselves were coming and going, mixing together and often repeating themselves as the missionaries grouped, separated or departed, in relation to the people who had been called to conversion.

Let me say it again: In a single, momentary glance, I saw the past, the present and the future of these missions, with all their successes, failures, dangers, troubles and disappointments. I understood everything at the time, but now I find it almost impossible to disentangle the facts, the ideas and the persons. It would be like someone who tries to understand at one sitting the whole expanse of the heavens and attempts to reduce it all to a unity, while at the same time including the motions and beauty and qualities of all the stars, together with their particular and reciprocal laws! After all, the study of one star is enough to occupy even the most intelligent person. We must also realize that the things I deal with here have no relation with any material objects.

Let me go back to my story.

I have said that I was amazed at the sight of so many people. At that moment, Bishop Cagliero stood beside me, and other missionaries were a little way off. Many others were around me, and among them I noticed several good benefactors of ours; notably, Mgr. Espinosa, Doctor Torrero, Doctor Carranza, and the vicar general of Chile. As we stood talking about the meaning of all I had seen, my interpreter came toward me and gently said:

"Listen and observe."

Suddenly, the plain was transformed into a huge room. I have no words to describe its magnificence and richness, but I shall say this: if anyone tried to describe it, its splendor would far surpass his description and the very flights of his imagination. So immense was the room that you could not see either the far end or the side walls; the height, too, was unattainable, and the ceiling was a series of long and beautiful arches that did not seem to have any visible supports. There were neither pillars nor pilasters. The cupola of that room seemed to be made of the whitest linen, arranged like drapery, and the same can be said of the floor. There were no lights—no sun, moon or stars—and yet there was brilliance all through it. The same linen whiteness lit up the remainder of the place, and brought into relief every detail, every ornament, window, entrance and exit. Everywhere a delightful fragrance lingered, like the mixture of all the sweetest perfumes.

Many tables were arranged in the room, to seat a large number of diners, and these tables radiated from one central point. They were covered with elegant tablecloths, and on them were glass vases holding a lovely array of flowers.

Cagliero was the first to remark:

"The tables are ready, but what about the food?"

As a matter of fact, there was no food or drink anywhere in sight, not even plates or cups or anything else that could contain them.

"The people who come here," observed my interpreter, "will neither thirst nor feel hunger."

At these words, people began to stream into the room, each dressed in white and wearing a rose and gold band, like a collar that encircled the shoulders and neck.

The first to enter was a small group of people who went at once to a table especially prepared for them. They were singing, "Hurrah! Victory!"

After them other groups arrived. They too sang, "Victory!" Then came a crowd of people, different among themselves in stature, age, sex, color, form and character, and all of them were singing "Victory!" as they entered, or "Hurrah!" as they reached their places at table. All these people belonged to nations and tribes whom our missionaries had evangelized.

A glance at the tables told me that our sisters and our confreres were among those seated. They showed no distinctive mark to indicate what they were—priests, sisters or seminarians—but all wore the white garment and the rose-colored scarf.

I was still more amazed when I noticed that among the diners were men of rough appearance who also sang "Hurrah! Victory!"

"Strangers," my interpreter said to me, "and the wild ones of this world who drink the milk of God's word from their instructors will become, in time, heralds of the Gospel."

I noticed also among the rows of people quite a number of strange and crude-looking youngsters.

"Who are these children whose skin looks coarse, like that of a toad, yet they too are so beautiful and resplendent?" I asked.

"They are the sons of Cam who have not yet renounced the heritage of Levi. They will be a good addition to the army of God as a protection for His kingdom, which has finally come among us. They are a small group, but their sons and grandchildren will grow in numbers. Now, listen and take note, though you will not understand the mysteries you see."

Those youngsters belonged to Patagonia and southern Africa.

Now there were so many entering the huge room that there seemed to be no more available chairs. However, the curious thing is that the chair or bench had no one definite form, but took on the shape that its occupant desired; and nobody envied the chair of his or her neighbor.

Now, while all present sang and shouted "Hurrah! Victory!"—another group came in, and with exuberant joy they joined those already at table. They sang "Alleluia! Glory! Victory!"

By now the room was quite full; one could not count those who were in it. A perfect silence fell over all. Then the crowd divided into different sections or choirs, and all began to sing:

(First choir:) "The kingdom of God has come to us; let the heavens be glad and the earth rejoice. The Lord reigns over us. Alleluia!" (cf. Rv 12:10-12)

(Second choir:) "They will conquer; and the Lord Himself will give them to eat of the tree of life, and they will not thirst forever. Alleluia!" (cf. Rv 2:7; 7:16)

(Third choir:) "Praise the Lord, all you nations; praise Him, all you peoples!" (cf. Ps 117:1)

They sang this and other hymns alternately among choirs, and again all fell silent. Now I heard singing that seemed to come from voices unseen and distant, but with such harmony that no one could adequately describe it. The message of their song was: "To God alone be honor and glory forever and ever!" (cf. Rv 4:11) This was answered by other choirs, also unseen and in the distance: "Everlasting gratitude to Him who was, who is and who is to come. To Him be the thanks, to Him alone be the honor eternally." (cf. Rv 4:8)

Those distant choirs now drew near. Among this celestial group I saw Luis Colle. The people in the room joined in the singing; they resembled so many musical instruments having unlimited range. The tune seemed to contain at one and the same time a thousand notes with thousands of variations that formed one harmonious whole. The high voices had so delicate a sound that it is hard for me to tell you what it was like; words fail to describe it.

The whole crowd formed one choir singing in perfect harmony, each section putting so much enthusiasm into it that anyone hearing them would forget everything else.

I dropped to my knees before Cagliero and cried out: "Are we in heaven, John?"

"No, it is not heaven; it is but a faint echo of what awaits us there!"

Again the choirs sang, this time in unison: "To God alone be honor and glory and triumph. Alleluia forever and ever!"

I was completely enraptured.

The next morning (continues Don Bosco), as soon as I awoke I prepared myself and went to say Holy Mass.

The main desire I carried with me, after this dream, was to give Bishop Cagliero and my missionary sons this very important message that would insure the success of their work: "Let Salesians and Daughters of Mary Help of Christians be solicitous in promoting ecclesiastical and religious vocations."

Father Lemoyne observes that when Don Bosco narrated this dream and came to the words "Hurrah! Victory!" his voice would fill with emotion until it trembled. He would have to stop his narration for a moment when mentioning Cagliero, and dab at his tear-filled eyes.

On February 1, 1885, Bishop Cagliero sent the missionaries to Sampierdarena, where he planned to join them later. That same evening he went to say farewell to Don Bosco, who blessed him and said:

"Have a good journey, John, and if we don't meet again in this life we shall meet in heaven."

"Don't speak like that, Don Bosco. After all, I promised that I would be present at your Golden Jubilee!"

"God's will be done; He is the Master. You have much work to do in Argentina and Patagonia, so apply yourself diligently, and our Lady will help you to reap great harvests. Later on you will be called to rule a diocese."

(In 1915, Bishop Cagliero was called to Rome, where he received the cardinal's hat, and five years later he was given the diocese of Tuscola.) (Vol. XVII, p. 299ff)

THE FAR EAST

From time to time, Divine Providence lifted the veil that hides the future and showed Don Bosco the success of Salesian missions in different lands. The following dream is another of these foresights. Don Bosco told it to the Superior Chapter on July 2, 1885.

I dreamed that I stood in front of a very high mountain, on top of which was an angel whose brightness lit up the distance. The angel held a sword in his upraised right hand, and the sword was like a flame of fire. His left hand pointed to the land around. He spoke:

"The angel of Arphaxad calls you to fight the battles of the Lord and to gather peoples into His granaries."

These words were not said as a command (as on other occasions), but rather as a request.

He was surrounded now by a crowd of angels whose names I did not know and could not even remember if they had been told to me. Among them was Luis Colle, and beside him was a host of boys whom he was teaching to sing the praises of God.

Around the foot of the mountain, on its slopes and on its peaks, crowds of people lived. They spoke among themselves, but I could not understand their language. I only knew what the angel said to me. I cannot easily describe the things I saw, because they are difficult to explain.

I saw other objects that completely changed the scene before me. At one time, I thought this was the plains of Mesopotamia; at other times, just a very high mountain. Even the mountain on which the angel stood presented a myriad of forms, like the moving shadows of the people around it.

I would like to record the fact that when I was in front of this mountain, and indeed throughout this journey, I seemed to be viewing everything from a very high elevation, like being above the clouds, with an interminable space around me. How can anyone describe such heights and expanses, such light and brightness? One can enjoy it, but not describe it.

On this, as on other journeys, I was accompanied by people who encouraged me and our Salesians to continue our missionary labors. Among those who were eagerly taking me by the hand and leading me forward was Luis Colle, along with groups of angels who re-echoed the songs of the boys gathered around him.

Suddenly, I seemed to be in Africa, in an immense wasteland; on the ground the word "NEGROES" was traced in very large letters. An angel of Cam stood there, who said:

"Evil will cease... and the blessings of the Creator will descend upon these, His lost children; and the honey and salve will heal the snake wounds they have. Afterwards, the sins of the children of Cam will be covered."

All those people were naked.

Then I seemed to be in Australia.

There was an angel here too, but he had no name. He showed the people the road to the north. This Australia was not a continent but a collection of numerous islands, whose inhabitants differed in character and stature. Crowds of children lived there; they tried to come over to us but were hindered by the distance and the waters that lay between. They held out their hands to Don Bosco and the Salesians and cried:

"Come and help us! Don't you wish to bring to completion the work your confreres have started?"

Many turned back. Others, with great difficulty, passed through wild animals until at last they were able to mix with the Salesians. I did not know any of them. They began to sing: "Blessed is he who comes in the name of the Lord."

Not far away, I could see many islands grouped together, although I was unable to distinguish any of them clearly. It seemed to me that this was an indication that Divine Providence was offering us part of the mission fields to be worked in the future. Our labors would be blessed with fruit, for the Lord would always be with us, provided that we deserved His continuous favors.

If there were only some way of preserving about fifty Salesians of today, they would see, after five hundred years, the marvellous things that Divine Providence has in store for us—if we are faithful. After some one hundred and fifty or two hundred years, Salesians will be masters of the world! Everyone, even the wicked, will regard us with favor, because our special field draws the sympathies of all, good and bad alike. If some madman were to wish us abolished, he would be standing alone, unsupported by others.

All this will come to pass, provided that Salesians do not seek comforts or neglect their work. If we keep to our present mission and do not permit ourselves to fall victim to greed, a long and successful future is assured. Our Congregation will prosper materially if we strive to support and spread the *Bulletin* and the work of the Sons of Mary. How good are these sons of ours! They should be instructed by confreres who are faithful to their own vocation.

These are the three things which Don Bosco saw clearly and could easily recall. He told them in his first account of this dream. But there were other things to be said and remembered, as he told Father Lemoyne. He had seen all the countries where Salesians would work in future days, and had seen them in one swift glance.

In a letter to the father of Luis Colle, Don Bosco wrote: "Our dear friend, Luis, brought me on a tour into the center of Africa, the land of Cam, and into the country of Arphaxad, that is, China."

Here is the summary of Don Bosco's tour as he told

it to Father Lemoyne:

He left Santiago in Chile and saw Buenos Aires, Sao Paulo in Brazil, Rio de Janeiro, Cape of Good Hope, Madagascar, the Persian Gulf, the shores of the Caspian Sea, Sennaar, Mount Ararat, Senegal, Ceylon, Hong Kong, Macao—which stood on the border of an endless sea, near a high mountain on the Chinese mainland. Then he passed through China, Australia and the Diego Ramirez islands, and came to the end of his journey when he returned to Santiago.

Don Bosco could make out islands, lands and people scattered here and there, and many other regions that were little known but densely inhabited. He saw so many things that he found it difficult to be exact in recalling them; for example, he called Macao *Meaco*. Regarding regions of South America, Don Bosco spoke with Captain Bove, but this explorer had not passed through the Megellan Straits, because he had few provisions and was also compelled by certain matters to return home; so he could not help Don Bosco.

Let us say a word about that mysterious *Arphaxad*. Before the dream, Don Bosco did not know what the word meant; after it, he spoke of Arphaxad frequently. He charged the seminarians' Fiesta with the task of looking up Biblical dictionaries, history and geography books and even magazines, to see if they could come across any nation upon earth connected with that personage. Finally, the key was found in the book by Rohrbacher, where it is stated that the Chinese had descended from Arphaxad. The name is also found in the tenth chapter of Genesis, where the sons of Noah are mentioned: "The sons of Sem are Elam and Addur, Arphaxad and Lud and Aram." (cf. Gn 10:22) Like other proper names in the ethnological table, these names indicate the fathers of nations and the lands they dwelt in. So, for example, *Elam*, which means *high country*, points to the Elamite and Susian regions, which later became Persia. *Assur* was the father of the Syrians.

Exegetes are not in agreement about the people with whom the name Arphaxad is connected. Some, like Vigouroux— to mention one of many—assign Mesopotamia to Arphaxad. Be that as it may, Arphaxad is listed as one of the progenitors of the Asian peoples, just after two others who are connected with regions to the east, as written in the Mosaic documents. So it seems that "Arphaxad" indicates a people near to the previously mentioned progenitors. It is not improbable, then, that the angel of Arphaxad means the angel of India and China.

Don Bosco often thought of China, and was heard to say that he felt that within a short time Salesians would be at work in that country. Once, he exclaimed: "If I had twenty Salesians to send to China, I believe they would be well received, in spite of the persecutions now taking place there." He never lost sight of this country, nicknamed "the celestial empire."

Don Bosco spoke often of this dream, with great satisfaction, because he saw in it a confirmation of all his other missionary dreams. (Vol. XVII, p. 643ff)

NICHE IN SAINT PETER'S

Once—we do not know the year—Don Bosco dreamed that he was inside Saint Peter's in Rome. He was standing in a niche! And this niche was located to the right of the central nave, above the bronze statue of the prince of the apostles and the mosaic medallion of Pope Pius IX. Don Bosco did not know how he got up there and was not at all at ease. He looked around to see if he could get down, but there was no way. He cried out, but nobody came to his rescue. Greatly upset, he awoke.

A visitor to the Vatican and Saint Peter's today will see that the niche above the statue of Saint Peter is occupied by the marble statue of a smiling SAINT JOHN BOSCO.

(Vol. XVII, p. 11)

CHAPTER 3

Predictions of Future Events

In the Providence of God, Don Bosco was often able to see into the future. We have already illustrated how he foresaw the establishment and growth of the Society of Saint Francis de Sales. In this chapter we will examine some of his other predictions and demonstrate how they came true in minute detail. Some were relatively unimportant, such as knowing the questions of a test before the teacher gave it; others were of much greater significance, such as his prophecies concerning wars and invasions in France and Italy, and the death of Pope Pius IX. We can only conclude that God revealed these future events to Don Bosco for the good of the Oratory, the Salesian Society and the Church.

THE LATIN TEST

One night John dreamed that his teacher had given a monthly test to determine class rank and that he was doing it. The moment he awoke, he jumped out of bed, wrote out the test, a Latin passage, and began translating it, with the assistance of a priest, a friend of his. Believe it or not, that very morning, the teacher did give a test, and it was the same Latin passage John had dreamed about! Thus quite quickly and without needing a dictionary, he translated it as he had done after awaking from his dream. Of course, the result was excellent. When the teacher questioned him, he candidly told him what had happened, to the teacher's great amazement.

On another occasion John handed in his test so quickly that the teacher seriously doubted that the boy could have

managed all its grammatical problems in such a short time. So he went over the test very carefully. He was amazed to find it totally correct and asked to see his first draft. John gave it to him and again the teacher was speechless. He had prepared the test only the night before. It had turned out rather lengthy and therefore the teacher had dictated only half of it: yet in John's composition book the test was written out in its entirety, to the last word! How could it be explained? John could not have copied it overnight nor could he possibly have broken into the teacher's house, which was a considerable distance from where John lived. What then? He confessed: "I dreamed it." It was for this reason that his schoolmates nicknamed him "the Dreamer."
(Vol. I, pp. 189-190)

A SPIRIT OF PROPHECY

One morning in 1868 two unknown ladies came to the Oratory to see Don Bosco. As they were ushered into his room, he smilingly said to one: "Have no fear of becoming a nun. Be sure that it is God's will."

Shortly afterward the two ladies left, visibly moved. Curious, I asked Don Bosco why they were crying. "You see," he replied, "those two ladies are sisters. One wants to become a nun, and the other opposes her. They agreed to seek my advice."

"Why were they crying?"

"Because I gave them the answer to their question before they could say a word. It really affected them."

"How did you know the problem?"

"You ask too many questions! I had a dream last night and saw those two ladies come to me and ask my opinion on that matter. As soon as they walked in I recognized them and simply repeated the advice I had given them in my dream."

Other similar instances are recorded in our archives. Don Bosco was also endowed with an admirable spirit of prophecy, as we have already narrated. For instance, one evening at supper he told this dream to several at the table with him, including Father Berto.

I saw an Oratory boy lying on the floor in the middle of his dormitory amid blunted knives, pistols, rifles, and several human limbs. He was dying. "What happened?" I asked. "Can't you tell?" he replied. "I committed murder and in a few hours I shall be executed."

I know that boy, Don Bosco went on. I'll strive to straighten him out and make him devout and good-hearted, but his nasty disposition makes me truly fear that he will come to a sad end.

Eventually this boy joined the army, shot an officer, and had to face a firing squad. Fortunately he repented and devoutly received the Last Sacraments.

Don Bosco also predicted several years in advance the suicide of another Oratory boy. He was a good lad, and devout while at the Oratory, but years later he was betrayed and ruined by a vicious companion. Unable to stand the loss of his fortune, family, and reputation, he ended his life with a bullet. The two boys' names are in our archives. Many witnesses—Father Rua among them—can testify to these predictions and their fulfillment. (Vol. IX, pp. 155-156)

POLICE SEARCH

I seemed to see a pack of ruffians break into my room, seize me, and rummage everywhere. While this was going on, one of them kindly said, "Why didn't you remove such and such a document? If those letters of the archbishop were to be found, what would happen to both him and you? And how about these letters from Rome"—he pointed them out—"and those over there? If you had hidden them elsewhere, you would have saved yourself a heap of trouble."

Next morning I jokingly related the dream and shrugged it off as mere fantasy. Nevertheless, I put a few things in order and removed several confidential letters which really had nothing to do with politics or government, but which could be misinterpreted. In those days, any papal or episcopal directive, even if strictly concerned with matters of conscience, could have been considered incriminating. Therefore, by the time the police search did take place, I had already removed all possible evidence. (Vol. VI, p. 312)

STATE FUNERALS

Toward the end of November 1854, Don Bosco had a dream in which he seemed to be standing by the pump near the wall of the Pinardi house—where now the main portico, then only half built, is located. He was surrounded by priests and clerics. Suddenly a red-coated court valet appeared, rushed to Don Bosco, and said aloud,
"News! News!"
"What news?" Don Bosco asked.
"Make this announcement: A state funeral at court!"
Don Bosco was shocked by the sudden apparition and cry. The valet repeated: "A state funeral at court!" Don Bosco wanted more information, but the valet vanished. Don Bosco awoke in distress. Grasping the significance of his dream, he instantly drafted a letter for the king, revealing this dream.

That morning Don Bosco had to go out and returned well past midday. He walked into the dining room quite late for the noon meal, carrying a bundle of letters. Many still recall that it was very cold that day and that Don Bosco wore old, threadbare gloves. As he appeared, Father Victor Alasonatti and many others—for the most part young clerics—crowded around him. Among them were Angelo Savio, [John] Cagliero, [John Baptist] Francesia, John Turchi, [Felix] Reviglio, [Michael] Rua, [John Baptist] Anfossi, [Joseph] Buzzetti, [Peter] Enria, and [Charles] Tomatis. Don Bosco remarked with a smile: "This morning, my dear sons, I wrote to three very important people: the Pope, the king, and the executioner." There was a general burst of laughter on hearing these names lumped together. They were not surprised, however, at the mention of the executioner, for they were aware that Don Bosco was on friendly terms with the prison personnel, and they knew that the man in question was quite religious. In fact, he helped the poor as best he could and even wrote to the king and authorities on behalf of those who could not write. He was also much distressed by his son's having to leave school because his schoolmates kept shunning him on account of his father's occupation.

As for the Pope, the Oratory boys knew that Don Bosco corresponded with him. What really whetted their curiosity was that Don Bosco had written to the king. They knew well enough how he felt about the usurpation of ecclesiastical property. Don Bosco did not keep them in suspense but clearly told them what he had written in order to persuade the king to oppose that infamous law. He then narrated his dream and concluded: "It deeply upset me and left me exhausted." One could see that he was worried. Now and then he would say: "Who knows? ... Who knows? ... Let us pray!"

Dumbfounded, the clerics kept asking each other whether anyone had heard of any important person at the court being ill. Nobody had. In the meantime Don Bosco sent for the cleric Angelo Savio and showed him the draft of the letter to the king. "Copy it," he said, "and send it to the king." Savio did as he was requested. Don Bosco later learned from confidential sources within the royal palace that the king had read the letter.

Five days later, Don Bosco had another dream. He seemed to be writing at his desk when he heard a horse's hoofbeats in the playground. Suddenly the door flew open and again the red-coated valet appeared. He strode into the middle of the room and exclaimed; "Make this announcement: Not *one* state funeral at court, but state *funerals* at court!" He repeated these words twice before withdrawing. Anxious to know more, Don Bosco rushed out to the balcony. The valet was already in the playground, mounting his horse. Don Bosco called out to him, but the valet, once again shouting "State funerals at court!" vanished into the night.

At dawn, Don Bosco personally wrote to the king. He informed him of his second dream and begged him to oppose that bill at all costs and save himself from the threatened punishments ...

Such was the state of affairs when a sorrowful event caused a postponement of the debate. On January 5 [1855], Queen Mother Maria Teresa suddenly fell ill. Throughout the following night she was painfully thirsty, but she steadfastly refused relief so as to be able to receive Holy Communion in the morning, the feast of the Epiphany. From that moment on she was bedridden. At this time King Victor Emmanuel II wrote to General Alfonso La Marmora: "My mother and wife keep telling me that they are dying of distress on my account."

The queen mother died at the age of fifty-four during the early afternoon of January 12. In mourning the Chamber adjourned. Queen Mother Maria Teresa's death was a real loss for Piedmont, a loss felt particularly by the poor, to whom she was very generous. They mourned her, praised her, and blessed her memory.

As she was being laid to rest, a mysterious letter was handed to the king, stating: "A person enlightened from on high warns: 'Beware! There has already been one death. If the law is passed, other misfortunes will befall your family. And this is just the beginning. Evils upon evils will fall upon your house. If you do not turn back you will be opening a bottomless abyss.' "

The king was dumbfounded. His peace of mind was overcome by a sense of terror. Enrico Tavallini hints at this in his book when he writes that the king was "threatened with divine punishment by numerous letters from prelates."

Queen Maria Teresa's solemn funeral took place on the morning of January 16. She was interred at Superga. The extreme cold caused many soldiers and the count of San Giusto, the queen's equerry, to become ill. Hardly had the court returned from paying its last respects to the king's mother when it was again hastily summoned to the bedside of the king's wife. Four days prior to the queen mother's death, Queen Maria Adelaide had happily given birth to a son, but soon complications set in endangering her life. Her sorrow at the loss of one very dear to her further aggravated her condition and made it critical. At about 3 in the afternoon of January 16, Holy Viaticum was brought to her from the royal chapel of the Holy Shroud, while people flocked to church to pray for her recovery. All the realm shared the grief of the royal family, once more proving true an old Piedmontese maxim that the king's sorrows are his people's sorrows. On the morning of January 20 the queen received the Anointing of the Sick, toward noon she was in the throes of death, and at 6 in the evening she breathed her last at the age of thirty-three.

But tragedies were not yet over for the house of Savoy. That same evening, Holy Viaticum was also brought to the king's only brother, Duke Ferdinand of Genoa, whose health had recently been failing. Victor Emmanuel was crushed with sorrow.

On January 21, the day after the queen's death, the Chamber of Deputies met at three in the afternoon to declare a two-week period of mourning and an adjournment of ten days.

The funeral of Queen Maria Adelaide took place on January 24; she, too, was laid to rest at Superga.

The clerics at the Oratory were terrified to see Don Bosco's prophecies so quickly fulfilled, and all the more so since they had attended both funerals. As an interesting sidelight, at the second funeral, also, the cold was so intense that the court master of ceremonies had to let the clergy wear topcoats and hats during the outdoor funeral procession.

For the Oratory, too, these two deaths were a great loss. The clerics kept telling Don Bosco: "Yes, your dream was more than a dream. The court valet was right about state *funerals at court.*"

"Quite true," Don Bosco replied. "The ways of God are really inscrutable. What's worse, we do not even know whether these two funerals will suffice to appease Divine justice."

(Vol. V, pp .115-116, 121-122)

THE TWO PINES

I seemed to be with a few boys in a meadow at Castelnuovo, discussing what gift to send Pope Pius IX on his name day. Suddenly, from the direction of Buttigliera, we saw a gigantic pine, unbelievably large and tall, sail horizontally through the air toward us. Then it straightened itself vertically, reeled, and seemed about to crash on us. In terror, we blessed ourselves and were about to flee for safety when abruptly a withering wind arose, totally disintegrating the tree amid thunder, lightning, and hail.

Shortly afterward, another pine, not quite as large, came

sailing through the air in the same way and from the same direction, until it hovered over us. Then it began to float down. In a state of panic, and fearful of being crushed to death, we dashed off again, repeatedly making the Sign of the Cross. The tree dropped close to the ground and then rested in midair, its branches brushing the ground. As we gazed, a light breeze stirred and dissolved the pine into rain.

Unable to grasp the significance of this, we were all distraught when someone (whose identity I still remember) said: "This is the rain which God will give in due time." Someone else (whose identity I no longer remember) added: "This is the pine which will bring beauty to My dwelling." He even gave the scriptural reference but I can't remember it. (cf. Is 60:13)

I believe that the first pine stood for the persecutions and the storms which afflicted those who were faithful to the Church, whereas the second symbolized the Church herself, which will descend like a refreshing rain upon them.

To our knowledge, Don Bosco did not elaborate on this dream. Without searching for other possible interpretations, we shall venture a comparison. This colossal pine, no less than three hundred and thirty feet in diameter and hovering erect above the earth, recalls to our minds the tree seen by Nabuchadnezzar and described by Daniel. (cf. Dn 4:7-14) Its top reached to the skies, and its far-flung, thickly leaved branches made it look like a forest from a distance. It symbolized overpowering might, proud defiance, rebellion against God, and extermination of His servants. And yet, annihilated by God's wrath, it vanished from the earth. A blistering, violent wind withered its branches, a storm battered it about, and fire consumed it to ashes.

The second pine, lofty and hardy, though not quite as huge as the former, symbolized, perhaps, not so much the Church in general, as some choice segment of the Church, such as a religious congregation—The Society of Saint Francis de Sales, for example. This is suggested by the locale of the dream—Castelnuovo, by the horizontal—rather than vertical—position of the pine, symbolical of humility, and by the scriptural verse: "The glory of Lebanon shall come to you: the cypress, the plane, and the pine, To bring beauty to my sanctuary, and glory to the place where I set My feet." (Is 60:13)   (Vol. VI, pp. 569-571)

THE TWO COLUMNS

On May 26 [1862] Don Bosco had promised the boys that he would tell them something pleasant on the last or second last day of the month, and so at the "Good Night" on May 30 he narrated this parable, or allegory, as he chose to call it:

A few nights ago I had a dream. True, dreams are nothing but dreams, but still I'll tell it to you for your spiritual benefit, just as I would tell you even my sins—only I'm afraid I'd send you scurrying away before the roof fell in. Try to picture yourselves with me on the seashore, or, better still, on an outlying cliff with no other land in sight. The vast expanse of water is covered with a formidable array of ships in battle formation, prows fitted with sharp, spearlike beaks capable of breaking through any defense. All are heavily armed with cannons, incendiary bombs, and firearms of all sorts—even books—and are heading toward one stately ship, mightier than them all. As they close in, they try to ram it, set it afire, and cripple it as much as possible.

This stately vessel is shielded by a flotilla escort. Winds and waves are with the enemy. In the midst of this endless sea, two solid columns, a short distance apart, soar high into the sky: one is surmounted by a statue of the Immaculate Virgin at whose feet a large inscription reads: *Help of Christians*; the other, far loftier and sturdier, supports a Host of proportionate size and bears beneath it the inscription *Salvation of believers*.

The flagship commander—the Roman Pontiff—seeing the enemy's fury and his auxiliary ships' very grave predicament, summons his captains to a conference. However, as they discuss their strategy, a furious storm breaks out and they must return to their ships.

When the storm abates, the Pope again summons his captains as the flagship keeps on its course. But the storm rages again. Standing at the helm, the Pope strains every muscle to steer his ship between the two columns from whose summits hang many anchors and strong hooks linked to chains.

The entire enemy fleet closes in to intercept and sink

the flagship at all costs. They bombard it with everything they have: books and pamphlets, incendiary bombs, firearms, cannons. The battle rages ever more furious. Beaked prows ram the flagship again and again, but to no avail, as, unscathed and undaunted, it keeps on its course. At times a formidable ram splinters a gaping hole into its hull, but, immediately, a breeze from the two columns instantly seals the gash.

Meanwhile, enemy cannons blow up, firearms and beaks fall to pieces, ships crack up and sink to the bottom. In blind fury the enemy takes to hand-to-hand combat, cursing and blaspheming. Suddenly the Pope falls, seriously wounded. He is instantly helped up but, struck down a second time, dies. A shout of victory rises from the enemy and wild rejoicing sweeps their ships. But no sooner is the Pope dead than another takes his place. The captains of the auxiliary ships elected him so quickly that the news of the Pope's death coincides with that of his successor's election. The enemy's self-assurance wanes.

Breaking through all resistance, the new Pope steers his ship safely between the two columns and moors it to the two columns; first, to the one surmounted by the Host, and then to the other, topped by the statue of the Virgin. At this point, something unexpected happens. The enemy ships panic and disperse, colliding with and scuttling each other.

Some auxiliary ships which had gallantly fought alongside their flagship are the first to tie up at the two columns. Many others, which had fearfully kept far away from the fight, stand still, cautiously waiting until the wrecked enemy ships vanish under the waves. Then, they too head for the two columns, tie up at the swinging hooks, and ride safe and tranquil beside their flagship. A great calm now covers the sea.

"And so," Don Bosco at this point asked Father Rua, "what do you make of this?"

"I think," he answered, "that the flagship symbolizes the Church commanded by the Pope; the ships represent mankind; the sea is an image of the world. The flagship's defenders are the laity loyal to the Church; the attackers are her enemies who strive with every weapon to destroy her. The two columns, I'd say, symbolize devotion to Mary and the Blessed Sacrament."

Father Rua did not mention the Pope who fell and died.

Don Bosco, too, kept silent on this point, simply adding: "Very well, Father, except for one thing: the enemy ships symbolize persecutions. Very grave trials await the Church. What we suffered so far is almost nothing compared to what is going to happen. The enemies of the Church are symbolized by the ships which strive their utmost to sink the flagship. Only two things can save us in such a grave hour: devotion to Mary and frequent Communion. Let's do our very best to use these two means and have others use them everywhere. Good night!"

This dream caused the boys no end of wonderment, especially regarding the two popes, but Don Bosco volunteered no further information.

The clerics [John] Boggero, [Secundus] Merlone, and [Dominic] Ruffino, and a layman, Caesar Chiala, wrote down this dream. We still have their manuscripts; two were written on May 31 and two much later. All four narratives agree perfectly except for the omission of some details. We must, nevertheless, remark that in this and similar instances flaws were unavoidable, even though Don Bosco's narration was taken down immediately and as accurately as possible. A talk lasting a half hour or, at times, a whole hour naturally had to be summarized. Some phrase may have gone by unheard or forgotten. Furthermore, as mental fatigue set in, doubts might arise concerning the sequence of events. In such cases, rather than hazard an amplification, the writers preferred to omit what they were not certain of. This of course increased the obscurity of a matter unclear of itself, especially if it concerned the future. Hence, endless arguments and conflicting explanations, as was the case in the dream or parable just described. Some claimed that the popes who successively commanded the flagship were three, not two. This was the opinion of Canon John Maria Bourlot, former pastor of Cambiano (Torino), who in 1862, as a philosophy student, was present at Don Bosco's narration of the dream. In 1886, he visited the Oratory. At dinner, reminiscing with Don Bosco about the old days, he began to narrate the dream of the two columns, stating unequivocally that *two* popes had fallen. He explained that, when the first was struck down, the captains of the other ships exclaimed, "Let's hurry! We can quickly replace him"; whereas when they gathered a second time they did not say that.

While Canon Bourlot was speaking, the author of these *Memoirs* was talking with the one next to him at the table. Noticing this, Don Bosco said to him, "Listen carefully to what Father Bourlot is saying."

When he replied that he was well acquainted with the matter, thanks to the manuscripts in his possession, and that he believed there had been two popes—no more—on the flagship, Don Bosco rejoined, "You know nothing at all!"

On another visit to the Oratory in 1907, Father Bourlot gave another proof of his excellent memory. Forty-eight years after he had first heard that dream he repeated it in its entirety, again maintaining that there had been *three* popes in all and recalling our former argument on his assertion and Don Bosco's statement.

In view of the above, which of the two versions is correct? Events may still resolve the doubt. We shall conclude by saying that Caesar Chiala—as he himself told us—and the three above-mentioned clerics took this dream as a genuine vision and prophecy, even though Don Bosco in telling it seemed to have no other purpose than spurring the boys to pray for the Church and the Pope and fostering their devotion to the Blessed Sacrament and Mary Immaculate. (Vol. VII, pp. 109-110)

THE RED HORSE

On July 6, 1862, Don Bosco narrated a dream he had had the night before.

Last night I had a strange dream. With Marchioness Barolo I seemed to be strolling about a small plaza which opened into a vast plain where the Oratory boys were happily playing. As I respectfully attempted to move to her left, she stopped me, saying, "No, stay where you are." She then began talking about my boys. "It's wonderful that you look after boys," she said. "Let me care for the girls. Leave that to me, so that there'll be no disagreements."

"Well," I replied, "didn't Our Lord come into this world to redeem both boys and girls?"

"Of course," she rejoined.

"Then I must see to it that His Blood be not uselessly shed for either group."

As we were thus talking, an eerie silence suddenly fell over the boys. They stopped playing and, looking very frightened, fled helter-skelter. The marchioness and I stood still for a moment and then rushed to learn what had caused the scare. Suddenly, at the far end of the plain, I saw an enormous horse alight upon the ground. So huge was the animal that my blood ran cold.

"Was the horse as big as this room?" Father Francesia asked.

"Oh, much bigger! It was a truly monstrous thing, three or four times the size of Palazzo Madama. Marchioness Barolo fainted at the sight. I myself was so shaken up that I could barely stand. In my fright I took shelter behind a nearby house, but the owners drove me off. "Go away!" they screamed. "Go away!" Meanwhile I kept thinking, *What can this horse be? I must stop running and try to get a close look at it.* Still quaking with fear, I pulled myself together and, retracing my steps, walked toward the beast. What a horror to see those ears and that frightful snout! At times it seemed to be carrying a load of riders; at other times it seemed to have wings. "It must be a demon!" I exclaimed.

Others were with me. "What kind of monster is this?" I asked one of them.

"The red horse of the Apocalypse," he replied.

At this point I awoke in a cold sweat and found myself in bed.

Throughout the morning, as I said Mass or heard confessions, that beast kept haunting me. Now I would like someone to check if a red horse is really mentioned in the Scripture and find out what it stands for.

[Celestine] Durando was chosen to do the research. Father Rua, though, remarked that a red horse—symbol of bloody persecution against the Church, according to Martini—is indeed mentioned in the Apocalypse [Revelation], Chapter 6, verses 3 and 4: "When the Lamb broke open the second seal, I heard the second living creature cry out, 'Come Forward!' Another horse came forth, a red one. It's rider was given power to rob the earth of peace by allowing men to slaughter one another. For this he was given a huge sword."

Perhaps in Don Bosco's dream the red horse symbolized contemporary [European] godless democracy which, fuming against the Church, was steadily making headway to the detriment of the social order and gaining control over national and local governments, education, and the courts. Its goal was to complete the destruction of the rights of ownership of every religious society and charitable institution, which had been started by conniving national governments. Don Bosco used to remark, "To prevent this calamity, all the faithful, and we too in our small way, must zealously and courageously strive to halt this unbridled monster."

How? By alerting the masses to its false teachings through the practice of charity and wholesome publications and by turning their minds and hearts to Saint Peter's Chair—the unshakable foundation of all God-given authority, the master key of all social order, the immutable charter of man's duties and rights, the divine light which unmasks the deception of evil passions, the faithful and powerful guardian of natural and Christian morality, the irrevocable guarantor of eternal reward and punishment. The Church, Saint Peter's Chair, and the Pope are one and the same thing. That is why Don Bosco wanted an all-out effort to make these truths accepted. His goals were to fully document the incalculable benefits brought by Popes to civil society, to rebut all slanders hurled against them, and to foster gratitude, loyalty, and love for them.

(Vol. VII, pp. 128-130)

THREE PROPHECIES

Sincerely anxious to help all, he [Don Bosco] received singular illustrations to point out the course he should take in alleviating the evils which afflicted the Church and civil society.

The prophetic dream he had had in 1870 is not the only example of its kind. On July 14, 1873, while searching for some papers on Don Bosco's desk, Father Berto found a sheet dated May 24 - June 24, 1873. Later, Don Bosco gave it to him to transcribe along with another document which a messenger delivered to Emperor Franz Joseph I of Austria, king of Hungary and Bohemia, on Don Bosco's behalf.

These last two dreams belong to our narrative, and we shall recount them along with the first, although this has already been published. All three come from a copy made by Father Berto and patiently edited by Don Bosco himself, who also added marginal notes.

This precious document is one of several copies of the "Three Prophecies" which Don Bosco had Father Berto transcribe in 1874 to oblige some devout persons. How had they come to hear of it?

Naturally, to carry out the Lord's directives, Don Bosco had to disclose the three prophecies to those who he thought should be told. In 1870 he revealed the substance of the first vision to Pius IX in a private audience on February 12. He had with him the manuscript but did not dare submit it, and he limited himself to reading an excerpt, which he had transcribed, concerning the Pope himself. We shall identify this excerpt by marking it off with asterisks. At his last audience with Pius IX that year, Don Bosco spoke again of future political events so plainly and in such detail that the latter stopped him in grief and dismay. But after the seizure of Rome, recalling his conversation with Don Bosco, Pius IX sent word to him through a cardinal—who we firmly believe was Joseph Berardi—that he was to speak out "clearly and explicitly, leaving nothing out." Don Bosco, who until then had not inserted into the manuscript the passage he had read to the Pope, added it to the transcript which he had Father Berto make, and sent it to the Pope through the same cardinal. Pius IX kept it among his papers together with the covering letter addressed to the cardinal.

The letter was anonymous. Why? Solely to remain incognito at all costs. But in it he clearly stated that the document "comes from a person who has on other occasions proved that he has been endowed with supernatural gifts" and that there were "other things which cannot be entrusted to writing, but may be said in person with all the secrecy the subject demands... Should anything seem obscure, I will try to make it clearer... You may freely use this document, but I do ask

111

you not to mention my name in any way, for reasons that you will readily appreciate."

Don Bosco also enjoined absolute secrecy on his secretary in regard to this matter. Father Berto jealously saved the original of the second prophecy and the excerpt from the first in an envelope on which he wrote: "Original of an excerpt from a prophecy completing the one sent to the Holy Father on February 12, 1870, which hinted at the above... This excerpt was later inserted in other transcripts made to oblige some devout persons. The original is not here because it was returned to Don Bosco after the first transcript was made from it. He destroyed it himself and pledged me to absolute secrecy on the matter. Until his death I never transgressed his order, despite the insistence and indiscretion of a devout person."

Was that really so?... In a letter to Father Rua dated March 8, 1874, whose original is in our possession, Father Berto wrote from Rome: "Matters are favorable. Pray. God is good to us. I believe he [Don Bosco] will continue to keep the [manuscript of the] prophecy, etc. Carefully scrutinize the passage: 'Before two full moons shall have shone in the month of flowers, the rainbow of peace, etc.' Amazingly, this year the month of flowers [May] has two full moons, respectively on the first and on the last day of the month. On this basis, many are beginning to open their hearts to hope. Let it be so."

What shall we make of this? Was Father Berto perhaps hinting at the two other prophecies? Anyway, during his stay at Rome with Don Bosco, he made several transcripts of the three prophecies, and Don Bosco, as we shall indicate, saw to their delivery to cardinals and prelates, always concealing the fact that they originated from him. Here is the precious document, containing:

1. The prophecy of 1870, generously annotated by Don Bosco and followed by numerous clarifications which he also edited;

2. The prophecy of 1873, with autographed marginal notes, followed by a comment (which he likewise edited) on the person giving those revelations;

3. The letter to the emperor of Austria followed by a postscript also edited by our holy founder.

FIRST PROPHECY

God alone is almighty, all-knowing, all-seeing. God has neither past nor future; everything is present to Him, everything at a single point of time. Nothing eludes God. No person, no place is distant from Him. In His infinite mercy and for His glory He alone can unveil the future to man.

On the vigil of the Epiphany of this year, 1870, all material things in my room disappeared, and I found myself contemplating supernatural matters. It was only a matter of an instant, but I saw a great deal. Although what I witnessed was sensibly present, I find it extremely difficult to communicate it to others intelligibly, as one may realize by what follows. This is the Word of God in human parlance:

"War will come from the south, peace from the north.

"The laws of France no longer recognize the Creator. The Creator will reveal Himself by visiting her three times with the scourge of His wrath. The first time He will destroy her pride by defeat, pillage, and destruction of crops, cattle, and men. On His second visit the great whore of Babylon, which the faithful grievingly call Europe's brothel, shall lose her leader and fall pray to chaos.

"Paris! Paris! Instead of fortifying yourself with the Lord's name, you surround yourself with houses of ill repute. You yourself shall destroy them; your idol, the Pantheon, will be razed to the ground, so that it may truthfully be said that 'iniquity has lied to itself.' Your enemies will plunge you into anguish, famine, terror, and the contempt of nations. But woe unto you if you do not recognize the hand which smites you! I want to punish your immorality, your desertion, your contempt for My law, says the Lord.

"On My third visit, you shall fall under the foreign yoke. From afar your enemies will see your palaces in flames, your homes in ruins, soaked in the blood of your heroes who are no more.

"But behold, a great warrior from the north appears, a banner in his right hand, his arm bearing this inscription: 'Irresistible is the hand of the Lord.' At that moment the Venerable Old Man of Rome went forward to meet him, wielding a flaming torch. The banner then grew larger and its blackness became white as snow; in its center stood out the name of the Almighty in golden letters.

"The warrior *(Don Carlos and the Pope)* and his followers bowed profoundly to the Venerable Old Man and joined hands with him.

* "Now the voice of Heaven is addressed to the Shepherd of Shepherds. *(To Pius IX.)* You are in solemn conference with your co-workers *(the Vatican Council)*, but the enemy of good never stands idle. He cunningly plots and sets all his wiles against you. He will sow discord among your helpers and will rear enemies among My sons. (*The grave frustrations* [suffered by Pius IX] *during the Vatican Council.*) The powers of the world shall vomit fire. They would love to smother my words in the throats of the guardians of My law, but they shall not succeed. *(This has already been attempted and will still be attempted, especially in Prussia.)* They shall do much harm, but only to themselves. Hurry! If knots cannot be untied, sever them. Do not halt in the face of difficulties, but go forth until the hydra of error has been beheaded *(through the proclamation of the dogma of papal infallibility).* At this blow earth and hell shall tremble, but the world will be saved and the faithful shall exult. Gather around you only two co-workers, yet wherever you go, carry on the task entrusted to you and bring it to completion *(the Vatican Council).* Days go by swiftly and your years are reaching their appointed number, but the great Queen shall always assist you, and, as in the past, She shall always be the powerful, prodigious defense of the Church. *

"But you, O Italy, land of blessings, who has plunged you into desolation? Not your enemies, but your own friends. Do you not hear your children begging for the bread of faith, unable to find one to break it for them? What shall I do? I shall strike the shepherds and scatter the sheep so that those who sit upon the chair of Moses may seek better pastures and their flock may gently listen and be fed. *(A seeming allusion to inadequate religious instruction.)*

"But My hand shall be heavy upon both flock and shepherds. Famine, plague, and war shall cause mothers to mourn the blood of their sons and husbands shed on foreign soil. *(A seeming allusion to this year's famine. Pestilence and war shall follow.)*

"What shall befall you, ungrateful, effeminate, proud Rome? You have reached a point when you seek and admire nought in your sovereign but luxury, forgetting that both your glory and his lies on Golgotha. Now he is old, frail, defenseless, and dispossessed. *(Present condition of Pius IX.)* Nevertheless, though captive, his words cause the whole world to tremble.

"O Rome! Four times shall I come to you! The first time I shall smite your regions and its people. The second time I shall bring slaughter and destruction to your very gates. Should not that make you open your eyes? A third time shall I come, and I will demolish your defenses and defenders. *(The present state of Rome.)* At My Father's command, terror, dismay, and desolation will reign.

"My wise followers flee *(many live away from Rome, many are obliged to disperse)*, but My law is still trod underfoot. Therefore, I shall come a fourth time. Woe to you if My law again shall go unheeded. There shall be defections among both learned and ignorant. *(This has happened and is still happening.)* Your blood and that of your children shall wipe out your transgressions. *(A seeming allusion to some future disaster.)*

"War, plague, and famine are the scourges to smite human pride and malice. *(This summarizes the above-mentioned punishments.)* Where are your magnificent villas and palaces, you people of wealth? *(We shall see!)* They have become the litter of squares and streets!

"And you priests, why are you not prostrate between the vestibule and the altar, weeping and praying that the scourge may cease? Why do you not take up the shield of faith and preach My Word from the rooftops, in the houses, streets, and squares, and even in inaccessible places? Do you not know that this is the terrible two-edged sword which smites My enemies and placates the wrath of God and man?

"These things shall inexorably come to pass, all in succession.

"Things follow too slowly upon each other, but the great Queen of Heaven is at hand; the Lord's power is Hers. Like mist She shall scatter Her enemies. She shall vest the Venerable Old Man with all his former garments.

"There shall yet come a violent hurricane. Iniquity is at an end, sin shall cease, and before two full moons shall have shone in the month of flowers, the rainbow of peace shall appear on the earth.

"The great Minister shall see the Bride of his King clothed in glory.

"Throughout the world a sun so bright shall shine as was never seen since the flames of the Cenacle until today, nor shall it be seen again until the end of time."

Clarifications

"War will come from the south...." From France, which declared war on Prussia.

"... peace from the north." From the north of Spain where the present war began. Furthermore, Don Carlos resided in Vienna, which is north of Italy.

"The Pantheon will be razed to the ground!" Contemporary newspapers reported that it was damaged by several bombs. But what concerns France has not yet fully taken place.

"But, behold, a great warrior from the north appears...." Don Carlos from northern Spain.

"The Venerable Old Man of Rome went forward to meet him, wielding a flaming torch." Faith in God which guides and upholds the great warrior in his undertakings.

"The banner then grew larger and its blackness became white as snow...." The massacre ceased. Blackness—symbol of death or persecution, such as the *Kulturkampf.*

"... in its center stood out the name of the Almighty in golden letters." According to press reports, Don Carlos' banner bears on one side a picture of the Heart of Jesus and on the reverse that of the Immaculate Conception.

"... wherever you go...." Seemingly an allusion to the Pope's exile. See the second prophecy.

"... war shall cause mothers to mourn the blood of their sons ... shed on foreign soil." This has still to come.

"... I shall come a fourth time." This visit to Rome has still to take place.

"There shall yet come a violent hurricane." See the next prophecy where the hurricane is fully described.

"... before two full moons shall have shone in the month

of flowers...." This year, 1874, the month of May has two full moons, one on the 1st and the other on the 31st.

"... the rainbow of peace...." A hope which seemingly is rising in Spain today, March, 1, 1874.

"Throughout the world a sun so bright shall shine...." Triumph and growth of Christianity.

"... his (the warrior's) arm bearing this inscription, 'Irresistible is the hand of the Lord!' " Newspapers say that Don Carlos apparently began his exploits without weapons, money or victuals, and only with fourteen men. Yet today, April 1, 1874, he has an army over 100,000 strong. There is no report as yet that he has lost a single battle.

SECOND PROPHECY

It was a dark night *(error)*, and men could no longer find their way back to their own countries. Suddenly a most brilliant light *(faith in God and in His power)* shone in the sky, illuminating their way as at high noon. At that moment from the Vatican came forth, as in procession, a multitude of men and women, young children, monks, nuns, and priests, and at their head was the Pope. *(It seems to allude to the suppression of monasteries and schools run by religious and to the Pope's exile.)*

But a furious storm then broke out, somewhat dimming that light, as if light and darkness were locked in battle. *(Perhaps this means a battle between truth and error, or else a bloody war.)* Meanwhile the long procession reached a small square littered with dead and wounded, many of whom cried for help.

The ranks of the procession thinned considerably. After a two-hundred-day march, all realized that they were no longer in Rome. In dismay they swarmed about the Pontiff to protect him and minister to him in his needs.

At that moment two angels appeared, bearing a banner which they presented to the Supreme Pontiff, saying: "Take the banner of Her who battles and routs the most powerful armies on earth. Your enemies have vanished; with tears and sighs your children plead for your return."

One side of the banner bore the inscription: "Queen conceived without sin" and the other side read: "Help of Christians."

The Pontiff accepted the banner gladly, but he became very distressed to see how few were his followers.

But the two angels went on: "Go now, comfort your children. Write to your brothers scattered throughout the world that men must reform their lives. This cannot be achieved unless the bread of the Divine Word is broken among the peoples. Teach children their catechism and preach detachment from earthly things. The time has come," the two angels concluded, "when the poor will evangelize the world. Priests shall be sought among those who wield the hoe, the spade, and the hammer, as David prophesied: "He raises up the lowly from the dust; from the dunghill he lifts up the poor. To seat them with princes, with the princes of his own people." (Ps 113:7-8)

On hearing this, the Pontiff moved on, and the ranks began to swell. Upon reaching the Holy City, the Pontiff wept at the sight of its desolate citizens, for many of them were no longer. He then entered Saint Peter's and intoned the *Te Deum*, to which a chorus of angels responded, singing: "Glory to God in the highest, and peace on earth to men of good will."

When the song was over, all darkness vanished and a blazing sun shone. The population had declined greatly in the cities and in the countryside; the land was mangled as if by a hurricane and hailstorm, and people sought each other, deeply moved, and saying: "There is a God in Israel."

From the start of the exile until the intoning of the *Te Deum*, the sun rose two hundred times. All the events described covered a period of four hundred days.

Note

The person reporting these things is the same who unerringly predicted what happened to France a year before it took place. These predictions were widely known and were fulfilled day by day, as if a script were being followed.

According to this same person, France, Spain, Austria and a German power would be the instruments of Divine Providence in preventing the collapse of civil society and restoring peace to the Church which for so long and in so many ways has been fought against. These events would start in the spring of 1874 and would be completed within a year and a few months, unless new iniquities should be perpetrated against God's will.

THIRD PROPHECY

Thus says the Lord to the emperor of Austria: "Be of good cheer and look after My faithful servants and yourself. My wrath is now spilling over all the nations because they want to make people forget My laws, glorifying those who defile them and oppressing My faithful adherents. Will you be the rod of My power? Will you carry out My inscrutable designs and become a benefactor of the world? Rely on the Northern Powers, but not on Prussia. Enter into relations with Russia, but form no alliance. Join forces with Catholic France; after France, you shall have Spain. All together, become one in will and action.

"Observe absolute secrecy with the enemies of My holy name. Prudence and vigor will make you and your allies invincible. Do not believe the lies of whoever tells you otherwise. Abhor the enemies of the Cross. Put your hope and trust in Me. I make armies victorious. I am the Savior of nations and sovereigns. Amen. Amen."

Note: This letter was sent to the emperor of Austria in July 1873 through a trusted person who delivered it to him in person. He read it attentively and sent his hearty thanks to the sender, saying that he would avail himself of it.

... The marginal notes and the clarifications and comments in the text and footnotes make additional remarks superfluous, except for one observation which we think is highly interesting.

The first prophecy has these words for the Pope: "Wherever you go...." It was, indeed, generally taken for granted that the Pope would leave Rome. He did not, however, and this was due precisely to this message from Don Bosco: "Let the sentry, the angel of Israel, remain at his post and guard God's stronghold and His holy ark." The solemn tone of these words clearly reveals their source.

Nor did the Pope ever forget them! While even Catholics continued to believe that his departure from Rome was imminent, Don Bosco, to the astonishment of all, hastened to defend the rights of the Church and of the Supreme Pontiff so effectively that the latter was able to appoint bishops for more than a hundred vacant Italian dioceses without governmental interference. At the same time, with the Holy Father's approval, he began negotiations [with the government] concerning the bishops' revenues. He did this on two trips he made to Rome in 1871. Then, as soon as he began convalescing from the serious illness that struck him at Varazze, he wrote to Premier [John] Lanza on February 12 and April 8 [1872], expressing his pleasure at the reverent and warm welcome that the new bishops were receiving in the various dioceses. He also informed the Holy Father of this. The latter replied in his own hand on May 1, confiding his full trust in God's goodness and the enduring protection He had promised to His Church.

We believe that at this time too these confidential exchanges between Don Bosco and Pius IX strengthened the Pope in his resolve not to leave Rome.

And so, the sentry of Israel remained at his post, guarding God's rock. On his part, until the end of his days, Don Bosco kept hoping and working zealously for a reconciliation of Italy and the Church. "We are both of the same age," he wrote to a fellow priest. "When we were born, Europe was settling down to peace after long years of war. May we dare hope to see peace in the world and the Church's triumph before the end of our lives? We could then sing our *Nunc dimittis.* However, may God's will be done in all things. The triumph of the Church is certain; if we do not see it here below, we shall witness it, I hope, from heaven."

He did indeed see it from heaven [in 1929] when the Lateran Treaty was signed. [As Piux XI declared] it gave "God back to Italy, and Italy back to God." The signing took place just a month before Pius XI's proclamation of the acceptance of the miracles which had been submitted for Don Bosco's beatification.

In pointing out the "charming, admirable and striking coincidence," the Pope characterized Don Bosco as a "great, faithful and truly clear-sighted servant of the Church and of the Holy See. . . . " Such indeed he always was! Pius XI then went on to state that he had learned "from Don Bosco himself" how much "a solution of this deplorable dissension was truly uppermost in his thoughts and desires . . . a solution that would, above all, guarantee the honor of God and of the Church, and the welfare of souls." (Vol. X, pp. 49-59)

THE DEATH OF POPE PIUS IX

Two days after his return to the Oratory, Don Bosco found himself back in Rome in a dream. It was a prophetic dream which he privately narrated to the directors gathered for their annual conference. We transcribe the narrative as it was immediately recorded by Father Barberis and Father Lemoyne. It is necessary to know, first, that Raphael Cardinal Monaco La Valletta, the Holy Father's vicar after the death of [Constantine] Cardinal Patrizi, had asked Don Bosco to send Salesians to direct the Hospital of Our Lady of Consolation, just a stone's throw from the Roman Forum. Personnel was scarce, but since this was the first request of the new cardinal vicar to the Salesian Congregation, Don Bosco was very anxious to oblige. On the night of February 7, he went to bed preoccupied with this thought and dreamed that he was back in Rome.

I seemed to be in Rome again. I went at once to the Vatican, unconscious of the fact that it was the dinner hour and that I needed an appointment, or of anything else. I was in one of the halls when Pius IX walked in and informally sat down in an armchair of some sort near to me. Greatly astonished, I tried to rise and pay my respects, but he would not let me. Indeed he insisted solicitously that I sit by his side, and then he began a conversation which substantially ran as follows:

"It isn't long since we last met," he remarked.

"Yes, it was only a few days ago," I replied.

"From now on we must see each other more often because we have to discuss many things. Meanwhile, tell me what you have been doing since you left Rome."

"There wasn't time for much. I settled a few matters which awaited my return and then I set to thinking what could be done for the Conceptionists, when suddenly I received a request from the cardinal vicar that we assume the direction of the Hospital of Our Lady of Consolation. This is the cardinal's first request of us and we would like to oblige, but at this time we are handicapped by lack of personnel."

"How many priests have you already sent to the Conceptionists?" (Meanwhile he took my hand and, holding it, had me pace the hall with him.)

"We sent only one. We were seriously considering sending more, but we are in a bind because we have no one."

"Well, first provide for the Santo Spirito Hospital."

(Moments later, the Holy Father stood erect, his countenance raised and almost beaming with light, and he gazed upon me.)

"Oh, Holy Father, if our boys could only see your face now, I am sure that they would be beside themselves with joy. They love you so much."

"It is not impossible. . . .Who knows but that they may see their wish fulfilled?"

Then, as if suffering from a sudden dizzy spell, leaning here and there, he tottered over to a sofa and, sitting down, he stretched out upon it full-length. Thinking that he was tired and was trying to get some rest, I attempted to slip a cushion under his head, but he refused. Stretching out his legs, he said, "I need a white sheet to cover me from head to toe."

Frightened and dumbfounded I stared at him, not knowing what to say or do. I could make no sense of what was happening.

At that moment the Holy Father arose and said, "Let's go." We walked into a hall full of prelates and the Holy Father went straight toward a closed door. No one seemed to pay attention to him. I quickly opened the door for him as he got close to it so that he could go through. Seeing this, one of the prelates shook his head, murmuring, "That's none of Don Bosco's business. There are people who are charged with doing that."

I apologized as best I could, remarking that I claimed no privilege but had opened the door only because no one else had moved to do so and because I feared that the Holy Father might be inconvenienced or might stumble. The Pope overheard this and, turning back, said smilingly, "Leave him alone. I am the one who wants him to do this." He then went through the door and did not come back.

So there I stood all alone, no longer knowing where I was.

As I turned here and there to orient myself, I saw Buzzetti. His presence made me feel much better. I was about to tell him something when he came over to me and said, "Look, your shoes are worn out and messy."

"I know, but what can I do? These poor shoes have done a lot of walking. They are still the ones I was wearing when I went to Lanzo. They have twice traveled to Rome. They have already gone to France and now they are back here. Obviously they have to be worn out by now."

"You can't wear them any longer. Can't you see that the soles are all gone and your feet are resting on the ground?"

"You are quite right, but now tell me: Do you know where we are, or what we are doing here? Do you know why I am here?"

"Sure I do."

"Then tell me. Am I dreaming or is all this that I am seeing something real? Say something."

"Be at ease. You are not dreaming. All you see is real. We are in Rome at the Vatican. The Pope is dead. And all of this is so real that, if you were to try to leave, you would have a hard time and would not even be able to find the staircase."

I went to the doors and windows. Everywhere I saw buildings in ruins and rubble, and the staircases in shambles.

"Now I really know that I am dreaming." I said. "Just a little while ago I was in the Vatican with the Pope, and there was nothing of this sort."

"The ruins you now see are the effect of a sudden earthquake which will occur at the Pope's death, since the whole Church will be fearfully shaken by his demise."

I did not know what to do or say. At any cost I wanted to get away from where I was. I tried to go downstairs, but I was afraid of plunging into some deep pit.

Even so I did try, but many people were holding me back, some by my arms, some by my cassock. One even grabbed me by the hair and would not let go on any account. I began to scream, "You are hurting me!" So intense was the pain that I awoke and found myself in bed in my own room.

Although Don Bosco did not think he should keep this unusual dream to himself, he still forbade the directors to mention it to anyone, saying that, for the time being at least, there was no need to make much of it. That this was no ordinary dream became evident exactly a year later when, in the early hours between February 6 and 7 [1878], the great Pontiff Pius IX surrendered his beautiful soul to God after a brief illness. (Vol. XIII, pp. 25-27)

Chapter 4

Dreams About the Boys of the Oratory

Many of the dreams of Don Bosco concerned the Oratory. In these dreams, Don Bosco would see himself with Oratory boys and their supervisors, many of whom he recognized. At times he predicted the deaths of boys, often months in advance, down to the very day and the circumstances. Most of the dreams in this chapter are highly symbolic, employing monsters or other strange animals to represent evil spirits or to illustrate the state of soul of individual members of the Oratory. These dreams also reflect the Theology of the day, with the emphasis on staying in the state of grace, preserving the virtue of purity, and saving one's soul. We who live in a post Vatican II Church should not look down on the views or the spirituality of those who went before us; their grasp of the truths of faith was incomplete, as is our own. The dreams and visions of Don Bosco were undoubtedly supernatural in character; yet they are a product of the times in which he lived. We should interpret these dreams with this in mind.

GIFTS FOR MARY

Don Bosco found consolation in acts of devotion to Mary Help of Christians, whom the whole Oratory honored particularly in the month of May. Of his "Good Nights" the chronicle records but one—a most precious one—which he gave on the 30th:

I dreamed that you boys were heading in procession toward a lofty, richly decorated altar of Our Lady. You were all singing the same hymns to Her but not in the same way: many sang beautifully, others rather poorly and some totally out of tune. I saw too that some kept silent, strayed from the ranks, yawned or kept disturbing others.

Everyone carried gifts, mostly flowers, to Our Lady. The bouquets differed in size and kind. There were bouquets of roses, carnations, violets and so on. Some boys carried very odd presents, such as pigs' heads, cats, slimy toads, rabbits, lambs and so on. A handsome youth stood by the altar. A close look would show that he had wings. He may have been the Oratory's guardian angel. As you boys presented your gifts, he took each and placed it on the altar.

The first to reach the altar offered gorgeous bouquets which the angel silently placed on it. From other bouquets, instead, he had to remove decayed or scentless flowers, such as dahlias, camelias and the like, because Mary is not satisfied with mere looks. Some bouquets even had thorns and nails which, of course, were promptly plucked out and thrown away.

When a boy carrying a pig's head came up, the angel said to him, "How dare you offer this to Our Lady? Don't you know that this animal symbolizes the ugly vice of impurity? Mary Most Pure cannot tolerate such a sin. Step aside. You are not worthy to stand in Her presence."

To those who offered a cat the angel said, "Don't you know better? A cat represents theft, and you dare present it to Mary? Those who take what does not belong to them, those who steal food from the house, tear their clothes out of spite or waste their parents' money by not studying as they ought, are nothing but thieves!" These too the angel ordered to withdraw. He was equally indignant with boys offering toads. "Toads symbolize the shameful sin of scandal, and dare you offer them to Our Lady? Step aside. Join the unworthy ones." These boys too shamefully withdrew.

Some lads came up with a knife stuck in their hearts, a symbol of sacrilege. "Don't you realize that there is death in your soul?" the angel asked them. "If it weren't for God's mercy, you would be lost forever. For heaven's sake, have that knife removed from your heart!"

Eventually the rest of the boys reached the altar and presented their gifts—lambs, rabbits, fish, nuts, grapes and so on. The angel took them and placed them before Our Lady. Then he lined up all the boys whose gifts had been accepted in front of the altar. I noticed to my deep regret that those who had been made to step aside were much more numerous than I had thought.

Two other angels now appeared at each side of the altar carrying ornate baskets filled with gorgeous, exceedingly beautiful crowns of roses. They were not earthly roses, but heaven-grown, symbolizing immortality. With these the guardian angel crowned all the boys ranged before Our Lady's altar. I noticed among them many whom I had never seen before. Another remarkable thing is this: some of the most beautiful crowns went to boys who were so ugly as to be almost repulsive. Obviously, the virtue of holy purity which they eminently possessed amply made up for their unattractive appearance. Many other boys possessed this virtue too, though not to the same degree. Youngsters excelling in obedience, humility, or love of God were also crowned according to their deserts.

The angel then addressed all the boys as follows: "It was Our Lady's wish that you should be crowned today with these beautiful roses. See to it that they may never be taken from you. Humility, obedience and chastity will safeguard them for you. With these three virtues you will always find favor with Mary and one day receive a crown infinitely more beautiful than that you wear today."

All of you then sang the first stanza of the *Ave Maris Stella*. Afterward you turned around and filed away as you had come, singing the hymn *Lodate Maria* so full-heartedly that I was really amazed. I followed you for a while; then I went back to take a look at the boys whom the angel had pushed aside, but they were no longer there.

My dear children, I know who was crowned and who was turned down. The latter I will warn privately so that they may strive to bring gifts pleasing to Our Lady.

Now let me make a few observations:

1. All you were carrying a variety of flowers, but unfailingly every bouquet had its share of thorns—some more, some less. After much thinking I came to the conclusion that these thorns symbolized acts of disobedience, such as keeping money instead of depositing it with Father Prefect, asking leave to go

to one place and then going to another, being late to school, eating on the sly, going to other boys' dormitories although knowing that this is always strictly forbidden, lingering in bed after rising time, neglecting prescribed practices of piety, talking during times of silence, buying books and not submitting them for approval, sending or receiving letters on the sneak, and buying and selling things among yourselves. This is what the thorns stand for.

"Is it a sin to break the house rules?" many will ask.

After seriously considering this question, my answer is a firm "yes." I will not say whether it is mortal or venial. Circumstances will determine that, but it certainly is a sin.

Some might counter that the Ten Commandments say nothing about obeying house rules. Well, the Fourth Commandment says: "Honor thy father and thy mother." Do you know what "father" and "mother" stand for? Not only parents, but also those who take their place. Besides, doesn't Holy Scripture say: "Obey your leaders"? (Heb 13:17) If you must obey them, it follows that they have the power to command. This is why we have rules, and these must be obeyed.

2. Some bouquets had nails among the flowers, the nails which crucified Jesus. How could that be? As usual, one starts with little things and goes on to more serious ones... He allows himself undue liberties and falls into mortal sin. This is how nails managed to find their way into those bouquets, how they again crucified Jesus, as Saint Paul says: "... crucifying the Son of God." (Heb 6:6)

3. Many bouquets contained rotten or scentless flowers, symbols of good works done in the state of mortal sin—and therefore unmeritorious—or from human motives such as ambition, or solely to please teachers and superiors. That's why the angel, after scolding those boys for daring to offer such things to Our Lady, sent them back to trim their bouquets. Only after they had done this did the angel accept them and place them on the altar. In returning to the altar, these boys did not follow any order, but went up to the angel as soon as they had trimmed their bouquets and then joined those to be crowned.

In this dream I saw both your past and your future. I have already spoken of it to many of you. I shall likewise tell the rest. Meanwhile, my children, see to it that the Blessed Virgin may always receive gifts from you which She will not have to refuse. (Vol. VIII, pp. 73-76)

FOUR KINDS OF BREAD

Don Bosco was often favored with heavenly warnings and admonitions during the spiritual retreats or novenas in honor of Our Lady at the Oratory. We have the following report from Father Dominic Bongiovanni, Father [Michael] Rua, and Bishop [John] Cagliero:

One evening Don Bosco publicly said that in a dream he had seen all the Oratory boys divided into four groups, each holding a different kind of bread. One group had tasty rolls of the purest flour; another had ordinary white bread, the third had coarse bread, while the last group fed on stale, moldy bread. To the first group belonged those who had never committed a mortal sin; to the second, those who had regained God's grace; to the third, those in mortal sin at that moment; the last group represented those who lived in habitual mortal sin with no effort to change their lives. After explaining the dream, Don Bosco said that he remembered perfectly what kind of bread each of us was eating, and that he would tell us if we asked him. Many did. To each he revealed what he had seen and with such a wealth of details regarding the state of his conscience that all were convinced his dream could not be dismissed as a mere dream or an attempt at guessing. Their innermost secrets, unconfessed sins, dishonest intentions, moral blunders, virtuous deeds, state of grace, and vocation—in a word, whatever pertained to their spiritual lives—all was clearly exposed, described, or foretold. After talking to Don Bosco, the boys were dumbfounded and made their own the Samaritan woman's comment: "He told me everything I ever did." (Jn 4:39) We heard this story repeated over and over during the course of many years.

Sometimes the boys would confide what Don Bosco had told them to some trusted companions. On his part, Don Bosco never revealed these secrets to anyone except the individuals he had seen in his dreams. These dreams—like the one just mentioned which repeated itself in several other forms—while saddening him in part, also assured him that most of his boys lived habitually in the grace of God. (Vol. V, pp. 478-479)

THE HANDKERCHIEF OF PURITY

On the night of June 14 I had no sooner fallen asleep than I was startled by a heavy blow on the bedstead, as if someone had struck it with a board. I jumped up and immediately thought that it was lightning. I looked about but found nothing unusual. Convinced that I had most likely been dreaming, I again tried to sleep. Hardly had I begun to doze when a second blow startled me again. This time I got out of bed and searched everywhere—under the bed, under the desk, and in the corners of the room—but I found nothing amiss. Commending myself to God's safekeeping, I blessed myself with holy water and slipped into bed. It was then that my mind began to wander and I saw what I am going to tell you.

I seemed to be in our church pulpit, about to start a sermon. All the boys were seated at their usual places, looking up and waiting, but I had no idea what to preach about. My mind was a complete blank. For a while I stood there dumbfounded and dismayed. Never had anything like this happened to me in all my years of ministry. Then suddenly the walls and boys disappeared, and the church turned into an immense valley. I was beside myself and could not believe my eyes. "What's this?" I questioned. "A moment ago I was in the pulpit in church and now I am in a valley? Am I dreaming? What's happening to me?"

I decided then to get going, hoping to meet someone and find out where I was. After a while, I came to a stately palace. Its many balconies and broad terraces beautifully harmonized with the building and landscape. In front of the palace there was a large plaza. In a corner, at the right, a large number of boys were crowding around a lady who was handing out handkerchiefs, one to each boy. On taking theirs, the boys walked up to the terrace and ranged themselves along the parapet. Drawing close to the lady, I heard her say to each lad as she gave him a handkerchief, "Do not unfold it when it's windy, but if you are surprised by a wind, turn at once to the right, never to the left."

I kept looking at those boys, but then and there I did not recognize any of them. When all the handkerchiefs had been distributed, the boys were all lined up on the terrace in complete silence. As I watched, one boy took out his handkerchief and unfolded it. Others followed his example and soon all had them out. The handkerchiefs were very large and exquisitely embroidered in gold. On each, lengthwise, there was written in gold: "Queen of virtues."

Suddenly a soft breeze came out of the north—that is, from the left; gradually it grew stronger, then it became a wind. Immediately some boys folded their handkerchiefs and hid them, while others turned quickly to the right. Others, instead, left them exposed and flapping in the wind. Meanwhile the disturbance gained force while ominous clouds gathered overhead and darkened the sky. Lightning flashed as thunderous, frightening rumbles rolled across the heavens, followed by hail, rain, and snow. Unbelievably, many boys still kept their handkerchiefs flapping in the storm. The hail, rain, and snow battered them mercilessly. In no time they were riddled with holes, torn beyond recognition.

I was stunned, not knowing what to make of it. However, I was in for a still greater shock. As I got closer to those boys for a better look, I recognized every one of them. They were my own Oratory boys. I hurried up to one and asked, "What in the world are you doing here? Aren't you so-and-so?"

"Yes," he replied, "I am." And then, pointing to several others, he added, "So-and-so and so-and-so are here too!"

I then went over to the lady who had distributed the handkerchiefs. Several men were around her.

"What does all this mean?" I asked them.

The lady herself [hearing my question] turned to me. "Didn't you see the inscription on those handkerchiefs?" she asked.

"Why yes, my lady," I replied. "Queen of virtues."

"Do you understand now?"

"Yes, I do!"

All those boys exposed their purity to the wind of temptation. Some, on realizing the danger, immediately fled. Those are the boys who folded and hid their handkerchiefs. Others, taken by surprise and unable to fold their handkerchiefs, turned to the right. These are the boys who promptly have recourse to prayer when in danger and turn their backs upon the enemy. Others, instead, kept their handkerchiefs open to the full blast of temptation and fell into sin.

Saddened by this sight and the realization that so very few of my boys had kept themselves pure, I nearly lost heart and burst into tears. When I was able to control myself again, I asked, "Why did even raindrops and snowflakes riddle the handkerchiefs? Aren't they symbols of venial sins?"

One of the men replied: "Don't you know that where purity is concerned there is no matter that is not considered to be grave? Nevertheless, don't be downhearted. Come and see."

He moved to the balcony and, signaling to the boys with his hand, shouted, "Right about face!" Nearly all obeyed, but a few did not budge. Their handkerchiefs were torn to shreds. I noticed, too, that the handkerchiefs of those who had turned to the right had shrunk and were covered with patches. They had no holes but were pitifully shapeless.

"These boys," the lady explained, "had the misfortune of losing purity, but they regained God's grace through confession. Those few who did not stir are those who persist in sin and perhaps will go to perdition." Finally, she said to me: "Tell no one in particular, but give only a general warning."

(Vol. VI, pp. 582-584)

TABLETS, COOKIES AND BISCUITS

For three consecutive nights I found myself in the countryside of Rivalta with Father [Joseph] Cafasso, Silvio Pellico, and Count [Charles] Cays. The first night we discussed current religious topics; the second night we debated and solved moral cases relevant to the spiritual direction of young people. After having the same dream twice, I decided I would tell you about it, if it came to me again. Sure enough, on the night of December 30 I found myself once more with the same people in the same place. Putting other matters aside, I recalled that the following night, the last of the year, I would have to give you the customary *strenna* [word of advice] for the New Year.

Therefore, I turned to Father Cafasso and said, "Father, since you are such a dear friend of mine, please give me the *strenna* for my boys."

"On one condition," he replied. "First you must tell them to put their accounts in order."

We were standing in a large room with a table in the center. Father Cafasso, Silvio Pellico, and Count Cays sat themselves at the table. As I had been requested by Father Cafasso, I went out to get my boys. They were all busy adding up figures on a tablet. As I called them one by one, they presented their papers to the above-named gentlemen, who checked the sums and either approved or rejected them. Quite a few boys were turned back, sad and worried. Those whose totals had been found correct were quite happy and ran out to play. Since the line of boys was long, the examination took some time, but eventually it came to an end, or so it seemed to me until I noticed that some boys were still standing outside and were not coming in.

"Why don't they come in?" I asked Father Cafasso.

"Their tablets are perfect blanks," he replied. "They have no totals to show us. This is a question of summing up all that one has done. Let them add up whatever they have done and we'll verify the totals."

After all the accounts had been checked, I went outside with the three gentlemen. All the boys whose totals had been found correct were running about having a joyful time, as happy as could be. You cannot imagine how that sight cheered me. Some boys, though, just stood apart, wistfully watching the games. Some were blindfolded; others had a mist about their eyes or a dark cloud around their heads. Smoke came from the heads of some; others had a head full of clay, or empty of the things of God. I recognized each boy. So clear is the picture in my mind now that I can name each one. I soon realized too that many boys were missing. "Where can those boys be who had blank tablets?" I wondered. I looked for them [but in vain]. Finally I spotted some boys in a distant corner of the playground. What a wretched sight they were! One lad was stretched out on the ground with the pallor of death; others were seated on a low, filthy bench; still others were resting on dirty straw mattresses or on the hard, bare ground. These were the boys whose totals had not been approved. They had various diseases: their tongues, ears, and eyes were swarming with worms that ate into them. One boy had a rotting tongue; another's mouth was crammed with mud; a third's breath was foul with pestilence. Other diseases afflicted the rest. One boy's heart was moth-eaten; another's was rotted away; others had all kinds of sores. One lad's heart seemed to be all chewed up. The whole scene was a veritable hospital.

The sight shocked me, and I could not believe my eyes. "How can this be?" I kept asking myself. I went up to one boy and asked, "Are you really so and so?"

"Yes," he replied, "that's me."

"What happened to you?"

"It's my own doing, flour from my own grist. I reaped what I planted!"

I questioned another and got the same reply. I felt terribly hurt, but was soon to be comforted by what I am about to tell you.

Meanwhile, pitying these boys, I turned to Father Cafasso and begged for a remedy. "You know what must be done just as well as I," he replied. "Figure it out for yourself."

"At least give me a *strenna* for the healthy ones," I insisted humbly but trustfully.

Beckoning me to follow, he went back to the mansion and opened a door leading into a spectacular hall which was richly draped, glittering with gold and silver. Dazzling chandeliers of a thousand lights flooded it with blinding radiance. As far as the eye could see, it stretched endlessly in length and width. In its center stood a giant table laden with all kinds of sweets, oversized bitter-sweet cookies, and biscuits. Any one delicacy alone would have satisfied a person. At the sight, I impulsively made as if to run and call my boys to enjoy this bonanza, but Father Cafasso stopped me. "Wait!" he said. "Not everyone may enjoy these sweets, but only those whose totals were approved."

Even so, the hall was quickly filled with boys. I started breaking up and handing out the cookies and biscuits, but again Father Cafasso objected. "Not everyone here may have those," he said. "Not all deserve them." And he pointed some boys out to me: those whose totals had been approved but who had a mist over their eyes or clay in their hearts or whose hearts were empty of the things of God. These too were excluded, just as those with sores who had not been allowed into the hall.

I immediately begged Father Cafasso to let me give them some of the sweets too. "They also are my dear children," I said, "and besides, there is plenty."

"No," he repeated firmly. "Only the healthy ones can savor these sweets. The others have no taste for these delicacies. They would only get sick."

I said no more and began serving those who had been pointed out to me. When I was through, I gave out another generous helping to all of them. I must say that I really enjoyed seeing the boys eat with such relish. Joy shone on their faces and so transfigured them that they did not look like the same boys anymore.

The lads in the hall who had not been allowed to have any sweets stood in a corner, sad and mortified. I felt so sorry for them that again I begged Father Cafasso to let me give them some also.

"No," he replied. "Not yet. Make them get well first." I kept looking at them, as well as at the many others outside. I knew them all. I also noticed that, to make matters worse, some had moth-eaten hearts. Turning to Father Cafasso, I said, "Won't you please tell me what medicine to give them?" Again he replied: "Figure it out for yourself. You know what to do!"

Again I asked him for a *strenna* to give to all the boys.

"Very well," he answered. "I'll give you one." Turning about as if to leave, he exclaimed three times, each time in a louder voice: "Watch out! Watch out! Watch out!" With these words he and his companions vanished. I woke up and found myself sitting in bed. My shoulders were as cold as ice.

That's my dream. Make of it what you like. It's just a dream, but if anything in it is good for our souls, let's take it. However, I wouldn't want you to talk about it with outsiders. I told it to you because you are my children. I positively don't want you to tell it to others.

Meanwhile, I assure you, I have you all present in my mind as I saw you in the dream, and I can tell who was diseased and who was not, who was eating [those sweets] and who was not. I am not going to disclose each boy's condition here, but I will do so privately.

Now here is the *strenna* for the New Year: "Frequent and sincere confession, frequent and devout Communion."

We will make three comments. The first one is in the very words of the chronicler, Father Ruffino:

In telling his dreams, Don Bosco gives only a summary of what exclusively concerns the boys. Had he desired or been free to tell them in their entirety, each account might have filled a whole volume. Every time we had a chance to question him at leisure about the dreams, his answers disclosed so many new angles and details as to double and triple his previous narration. Many times, even on his own, he hinted at having received knowledge of future events—often, though, in a veiled way—events which he either was not free to manifest or could not explain.

Father Ruffino made the above comment on January 30, 1861. We must therefore infer that Don Bosco had already told other dreams of which we have no record, or, at least, that with great wealth of details, reflections, and warnings he narrated those dreams which we scarcely mentioned in the preceding volumes. Whatever the case, we cannot help but concur with Father Ruffino's statement because, after hearing these narratives from Don Bosco's own lips, we came to the same conclusions.

The second comment is from Father Rua and concerns the authenticity of the knowledge Don Bosco received from the dreams of the boys' spiritual condition. Father Rua declared:

Someone may think that, in manifesting his pupils' conduct and personal secrets, Don Bosco was availing himself of information he had received from the boys themselves or from the young clerics supervising them. I can state with absolute certainty that, throughout the many years I lived with him, neither I nor any of my companions ever noticed any such thing. Furthermore, boys can hardly keep a secret, and since all of us were then young and always with them, we would easily have found out whether he had received private information. The belief that Don Bosco could read our sins on our foreheads was so common that, when anyone committed a sin, he shied away from Don Bosco until he had gone to confession. This happened particularly whenever Don Bosco narrated a dream. This conviction arose in the pupils especially when they saw that in confession—even when they were perfect strangers to him—he told them sins they had forgotten or were trying to conceal.

Besides showing them their state of conscience as he had seen it in his dreams, Don Bosco used to announce things one could not humanly know, such as future deaths and other events. The more I consider these facts and revelations of Don Bosco as I grow older, the more deeply am I convinced that God had endowed him with the gift of prophecy.

The third comment is strictly our own. From this dream we may see that Father Cafasso was the judge in matters of piety and moral conduct, Silvio Pellico in what concerned diligence in studies and work, and Count Cays in matters of obedience and discipline. The sweets perhaps symbolize the food of those who are only beginners in God's service, and the bitter-sweet cookies the more substantial nourishment of those who have already progressed in God's service. To all, however, we can truthfully apply the words of the Psalmist: "While Israel I would feed with the best of wheat, and with honey from the rock I would fill them." (Ps 81:17)   (Vol. VI, pp. 478-483)

A MYSTERIOUS VINE

On [Wednesday] April 29 [1868], Don Bosco made this announcement to the Oratory students: "Tomorrow night, Friday night, and Sunday night I'll have something special to tell you. If I were to neglect this, I believe that I would have to die before my time. What I must say is far from pleasant. I wish the artisans to be present too."

Accordingly, on the following night the artisans came from their portico, where Father Rua or Father Francesia usually addressed them after night prayers, and joined the students. Don Bosco addressed the assemblage:

My dear boys, last night I said that I had something unpleasant to tell you. It's a dream I had. I wasn't going to talk about it because I thought it was nothing but a dream and because, whenever I have narrated my dreams, remarks and objections have been made. Now, however, a second dream forces me to reveal the first, and all the more so considering that for the past few nights—particularly the last three nights—I have been repeatedly troubled by nightmares. You know that I went to Lanzo for a little rest. Well, on my last night there, no sooner had I fallen asleep than I dreamed that I saw a most loathsome toad, huge as an ox, enter my room and squat at the foot of my bed. I stared breathlessly as its legs, body, and head swelled and grew more and more repugnant, its green body, fiery eyes, red-lined mouth and throat, and small bony ears presenting a terrifying sight. Staring wildly, I kept muttering to myself: *But a toad has no ears.* I also noticed two horns jutting from its snout and two greenish wings sprouting from its sides. Its legs looked like those of a lion, and its long tail ended in a forked tip.

At the moment I seemed not a bit afraid, but when that monster began edging closer to me, opening its huge, tooth-studded jaws, I really became terribly frightened. I thought it was a demon from hell because it looked like one. I made the Sign of the Cross, but nothing happened. I rang the bell, but no one responded. I shouted, but in vain. The monster would not retreat. "What do you want of me, you ugly devil?" I asked. As if in answer, it just crept forward, ears fully stretched out and pointing upward. Then, resting its front paws on the top of the bedstead and raising itself on its hind legs, it paused momentarily, looked at me, and crawled forward on my bed until its snout was close to my face. I felt such revulsion that I tried to jump out of bed, but just then the monster opened its jaws wide. I wanted to defend myself and shove the monster back, but it was so hideous that even in my predicament I did not dare to touch it. I screamed and frenziedly reached behind me for the small holy water stoup, but I only hit the wall. Meanwhile the monstrous toad had managed to mouth my head so that half of my body was inside its foul jaws. "In the name of God," I shouted, "why are you doing this to me?" At these words, the toad drew back and let my head free. Again I made the Sign of the Cross, and since I had now dipped my hand in the holy water stoup, I flung a few drops of water at the monster. With a frightening shriek it fell backward and vanished, while a mysterious voice from on high clearly said: "Why don't you tell them?"

The director of Lanzo, Father Lemoyne, awakened by my prolonged screams, heard me pounding on the wall. "Don Bosco," he asked me in the morning, "were you having nightmares last night?"

"Why do you ask?"

"Because I heard your screams."

I realized that God willed I should reveal what I had seen. For this reason, and to rid myself of these nightmares, I have decided to tell you everything. Let us thank the Lord for His mercy. Meanwhile, let us strive to carry out His admonitions, no matter what way He may choose to make them know to us, and let us use the means He sends to enable us to save our souls. Through these dreams I have come to know the state of conscience of each of you.

I wish, though, that you keep within these walls what I am going to disclose to you. I beg you not to write about it or talk about it outside the house because such things are not to be ridiculed, as some people might do, and also because I want to avoid possible unpleasant complications. I tell you these things confidentially as a father to his beloved sons, and you should listen as though it were your own father telling them to you. Well then, here are the dreams which I would rather forget but must reveal.

I began to have these dreams on [Sunday] April 5, at the very beginning of Holy Week, and this went on for several miserable nights. These dreams so exhausted me that in the morning I felt more done in than if I had been working all night. They also alarmed and upset me very much. The first night I dreamed that I was dead: the second, that I was standing at God's judgment seat to settle my accounts. Each time I awoke to realize that I was alive and had time to prepare better for a holy death. The third night I dreamed that I was in heaven. I surely enjoyed that, but it all vanished when I woke up the next morning. I nevertheless felt determined, no matter what the cost, to gain that eternal kingdom which I had glimpsed. So far these dreams did not concern you in the least and would have meant nothing to you. When one falls asleep with something on his mind, his imagination goes to work and he dreams about it.

Anyway, I had another dream, and this is the one I must tell you. The night of Holy Thursday (April 9) I had hardly dozed off when I dreamed I was standing in these porticoes with our priests, clerics, and boys around me. Then all of you vanished, and I seemed to step into the playground with only Father Rua, Father Cagliero, Father Francesia, Father Savio, and young Preti. A little distance away stood Joseph Buzzetti and Father Stephen Rumi, a good friend of ours from the Genoa seminary. Suddenly the Oratory, as we now know it, changed its appearance and looked as it had been in its very beginning, when only those just mentioned were there. At that time our playground adjoined vast, untilled fields stretching up to the citadel meadows where our boys often strayed in their games.

We sat near the present cabinet shop under my bedroom window, where once we had a vegetable garden, and began talking about the house and the boys. Suddenly a gorgeous vine—the very one that used to be there—sprouted out of the ground in front of this pillar supporting the water fountain near the entrance of the old Pinardi shed. (The platform on which Don Bosco was standing was backed against this pillar.) We were astonished at the appearance of the vine after so many years, and we wondered how it could have happened. Meanwhile, the vine kept growing to about a man's height, spreading countless shoots and tendrils into all directions until it covered the entire playground and stretched beyond it. Oddly, its shoots did not grow upward, but spread out parallel to the ground like a very vast arbor with no visible support. Its budding leaves were a deep green, and its shoots were astonishingly healthy and strong. Soon handsome clusters of grapes broke out, grew in size, and took on a purplish-red color.

"How can this vine have grown so quickly?" we asked each other in amazement. "What does it all mean?"

"Let's wait and see," I replied.

I kept watching the vine most carefully, when suddenly all the grapes fell to the ground and turned into a crowd of lively, cheerful boys. In no time the whole playground and the area covered by the vine were filled with boys who were jumping about, playing, and having a grand time. It was a sight to behold.

There under that unusual arbor I could see all the boys who ever have been, are, or will be at the Oratory and in other Salesian schools. Very many were unknown to me.

You know that a guide always shows up in my dreams. Well, at this point a stranger appeared at my side and stood watching the boys with me. Then a mysterious curtain abruptly appeared before us, blotting out this joyous scene.

No higher than the vine itself, this curtain in its entire width seemed to be hanging from the shoots of the vine like a stage curtain. All we could see now was the upper part of the vine stretched out like an enormous green carpet. In the meantime the boys' cheerful hubbub had quickly turned into gloomy silence.

"Look!" the guide told me, pointing to the vine.

I got closer. The lovely grape-laden vine had now nothing but leaves, bearing this inscription: "[He] found nothing there except leaves." (Mt 21:19) Puzzled as to its significance, I asked my guide, "Who are you? What does this vine symbolize?"

In answer, he parted the curtain. Only a portion of the great many boys I had seen before were there now, most of them unknown to me.

"These boys," he explained, "have plenty of opportunities for doing good, but they do not aim at pleasing God. They make believe they are doing good to keep up appearances, painstakingly obey house rules to avoid reprimands or loss to esteem, and are respectful towards superiors, but they do not profit by their teachings, exhortations, or efforts. All these boys strive for is some prominent, money-making position in the world. With no concern to discover their vocation, they readily reject the Lord's call while they keep disguising their intentions lest they lose any advantage. I short, they are those who do things out of necessity and derive no good for eternity."

How disappointed I was to see in that group several boys whom I believed to be very good, affectionate, and sincere!

"Unfortunately this is not all," my guide continued, letting go of the curtain. "Look up there now." And he pointed to the upper part of the arbor.

Among the leaves I could see clusters of grapes that looked very tasty. Happily I got closer and noticed that the grapes were pockmarked, overripe, moldy, wormy, pecked, rotten or

141

shriveled—a total disaster. Their stench fouled the air.

Again the stranger lifted the curtain. "Look," he said. I saw another throng of boys, but not the countless number as at the beginning of the dream. Formerly very handsome, they now appeared ugly, sullen, and covered with hideous sores, and they walked about with great melancholy as if stooped or wasted by age. No one spoke. All were past, present, and future pupils of ours. The last mentioned were the most numerous. They all looked dejected and did not dare raise their eyes.

My companions and I were dismayed and speechless. "What happened?" I finally asked my guide. "These boys, once so handsome and joyful—why are they now so ugly and melancholy?"

"Because of their sins," was the answer, and as these boys were meanwhile walking past me, he added, "Take a good look at them."

I noticed then that their foreheads and hands bore the name of each boy's sin. To my great surprise, I recognized several boys. I had always believed them to be very virtuous; now I was discovering that hideous sores were festering in their souls.

As they filed past, I could read on their foreheads: Immodesty, Scandal, Malevolence, Pride, Idleness, Gluttony, Envy, Anger, Vindictiveness, Blasphemy, Impiety, Disobedience, Sacrilege, Theft.

"Not all the boys are as you see them now." my guide remarked, "but they will be so one day if they do not change their ways. Many of these sins are not serious in themselves, but they will lead to serious falls and eternal perdition. Gluttony breeds impurity, contempt for superiors leads to contempt for priests and the Church, and so on!

Downhearted at such a sight, I took my notebook and pencil to jot down the names of the boys I knew and their sins, or at least their predominant sin, so that I might warn and correct them. But the guide held my arm. "What are you trying to do?" he asked.

"I want to jot down what's written on their foreheads in order to warn them so that they may amend their lives."

"You may not do that."

"Why not?"

"They have all they need to go through life unscathed. They have house rules; let them observe them. They have superiors; let them obey them. They have the sacraments; let them receive them. They have Penance; let them not profane it by concealing different sins. They have the Holy Eucharist; let them not partake of it in the state of mortal sin. Let them check their eyes, avoid bad companions, bad books, foul conversations, and so on. Keeping the house rules will save them. Let them promptly obey the bell; let them stop trying to fool their teachers so as to idle away their time. Let them willingly obey their superiors instead of looking upon them as boresome watchdogs, self-interested counselors, or even enemies. Let them not consider it a great victory when they succeed in concealing their wrongdoings and escaping punishment. Let them be reverent in church and pray willingly and devoutly without disturbing others or chattering. Let them study when it's time to study, work when it's time to work, and behave at all times. Study, work, and prayer are the things that will keep them good."

Notwithstanding his prohibition, I kept pestering my guide to let me write down the boys' names. At this, he snatched my notebook and threw it on the ground, saying, "For the last time, I say there is no need to write down their names. God's grace and the voice of conscience will tell your boys what to do and what not to do."

"Does this mean," I asked, "that I cannot tell my dear boys anything of what I have seen? Have you any suggestions for them?"

"You may tell them whatever you will remember," he replied.

He again let the curtain drop and once more we saw the vine. Its nearly leafless shoots held handsome clusters of ruddy, full-grown grapes. I went closer and found them to be as good as they looked. Their delightful sight and pleasant smell made my mouth water.

Again my guide lifted the curtain. Under that arbor I once more saw many boys—our present, past, and future pupils. They were handsome beyond compare and radiant with joy.

"These," the stranger explained, "are the boys who, thanks to your care, are yielding or will yield good fruit. They are those who practice virtue and will greatly console you."

Delighted though I was, I somehow also felt grieved that their number was not as great as I had hoped. As I stood watching them, the bell rang and the boys left. The clerics who were with me went to their tasks. I looked about me and found myself alone. The vine was gone and my guide had vanished. At this point I woke up and was able to get a little rest.

On Friday, May 1, Don Bosco continued his narrative:

As I told you last night, I awoke thinking I had heard the bell ring, but then I returned to sleep. Suddenly somebody shook me. I found myself in my room, answering my mail. Afterward, I walked to the balcony, gazed for a moment at the majestic dome of our new church, and then went downstairs and stepped into the porticoes. At short intervals, priests and clerics came from their various assignments and crowded around me, among them Father Rua, Father Cagliero, Father Franscesia, and Father Savio. As I stood chatting with them, the Church of Mary, Help of Christians, and all our present buildings abruptly disappeared, and we found ourselves in front of the old Pinardi shed. [As in the previous dream] a vine sprouted up in exactly the same place, as if from the same roots, grew to the same height, and then spread its shoots horizontally throughout a very vast area. The shoots in turn sprouted leaves; then there came clusters of grapes that ripened under my very eyes. But no boys were to be seen. The bunches of grapes were truly enormous, like those of the Promised Land. One of them would have taxed the strength of a man. The perfectly ripe, golden grapes were oblong and extraordinarily large so that a single one would have been quite a mouthful. Briefly, they looked so good as to make one's mouth water. "Eat me," they seemed to say.

Father Cagliero and the other priests marveled, while I kept exclaiming, "How gorgeous they are!"

Unceremoniously Father Cagliero plucked a few grapes and put one in his mouth. No sooner did he sink his teeth into it than he spat it out so forcefully that we thought he was vomiting. The grape had the taste of a rotten egg. "Goodness gracious!" he exclaimed after much spitting. "What stuff! It's enough to kill a man!"

We all stood speechless. At this moment, a serious-looking man came out of the sacristy of the old chapel and determinedly strode up to me.

"How can such beautiful grapes taste so rotten?" I asked him. As if in answer, he gravely fetched a bundle of sticks, picked a well-knotted one, and offered it to Father Savio, saying, "Take this and thrash these shoots!" Father Savio refused and stepped back. The man then approached Father Francesia, but he too declined. The stranger then turned to Father Cagliero and, taking him by the arm, tried to press the stick in his hand. "Take it and strike!" he said. "Thrash and knock down." So saying, he pointed to a certain spot. Startled, Father Cagliero stepped back. "Are you joking?" he exclaimed, striking his fist into his other hand. But the stranger insisted, "Take it and strike!" "Not I!" Father Cagliero shot back. Then he hid behind me in fright.

Foiled but unperturbed, the stranger turned to Father Rua who, like Father Cagliero, took refuge behind me. The man then came up to me. "Take this stick and strike those shoots," he commanded. I made a great effort to see whether I was dreaming or awake, but it all seemed very real to me.

"Who are you?" I asked. "Why must I knock these shoots to the ground? Am I dreaming? Am I imagining things? Are you speaking to me in God's name?"

"Draw closer to the vine," he answered, "and see what's written on those leaves!" I complied and read: "Why should it clutter up the ground?" (Lk 13:7)

"That's from the Gospel," my guide exclaimed.

"Yes," I remarked, "but remember that in the Gospel we also read that Our Lord allowed the vinedresser to dig around it and manure it, putting off its destruction until every attempt had been made to help it bear good fruit."

"All right. We will postpone the punishment. Meanwhile, take a look." So saying, he pointed to the vine. I looked but could not understand what he was driving at.

"Come here," he said, "and read what's written on the grapes."

I noticed then that they bore the name of each pupil and his predominant sin. I was aghast at what I saw. I was particularly frightened by such inscriptions: "Proud, Unfaithful to His Promises, Unchaste, Two-Faced, Neglectful of His Duties, Calumniator, Vindictive, Heartless, Sacrilegious, Contemptuous of Authority, Stumbling Block, Follower of False Doctrines. I saw the names of those "whose god is their belly"; of those who "are bloated by knowledge"; of those who "seek their own interest, not Our Lord's"; of those who scheme against their superiors and the house rules. Those names identified past, present, and future pupils of ours. The last mentioned—quite a number of them—were unknown to me.

"This is the fruit we get from this vineyard," the man said gravely— "bitter, bad, and harmful to eternal salvation."

I immediately tried to jot down some names in my notebook, but again my guide stopped me. "What are you up to?" he asked.

"Please let me take down the names of those I know so that I may warn them privately and correct them," I pleaded.

It was no use. He would not consent.

"If I tell my boys the pitiful state they are in, they will amend their lives," I insisted.

"If they do not believe the Gospel," he replied, "they won't believe you either."

I kept insisting that I wanted to take some notes for the future, but, ignoring me, he walked up to Father Rua with the bundle of sticks. "Take one," he told him, "and strike the vine." Crossing his arms, Father Rua bowed his head and, murmuring "Patience," glanced at me. I nodded approval. Father Rua then grabbed a stick, got close to the vine, and began to beat it at the spot indicated. He had hardly dealt a blow when the guide motioned him to stop and shouted to all of us to step back.

We all withdrew a certain distance. From where we stood we could see the grapes swell up and, though retaining their golden color and oblong shape, become hideous masses resembling shell-less snails. Again the guide shouted: "Watch now: the Lord takes His vengeance!" Immediately the sky darkened and a dense fog covered the vine entirely from our sight. Through the darkness lightning flashed, thunder roared, and dreadful thunderbolts struck everywhere over the playground. The vine shoots bent under the furious wind and all the leaves were stripped away. Finally a hailstorm hit the vine. I tried to flee, but my guide held me back. "Look at the hail!" he said.

I noticed that the hailstones, big as eggs, were either black or red, each pointed at one end and flat at the other, like a mallet. Those nearest to me were black but beyond I could see the red ones.

"It's weird!" I exclaimed. "I never saw hailstones like these."

"Get closer," the stranger said, "and you will see something else."

I complied, but an awful stench made me draw back immediately. At the man's insistence, I picked one up to examine it, but, unable to stomach the smell, I dropped it instantly. "I couldn't see anything," I said.

"Try again," he replied.

Overcoming my revulsion, I took up a black hailstone and read on it: "Immodesty." Then I walked over to the red hailstones. Though ice-cold, they started fires wherever they fell. I picked one up. It still smelled very badly, but I found it easier to read on it: "Pride." Somewhat embarrassed by these findings, I asked, "Are these then the two main vices threatening this house?"

"These are the two main vices that ruin most souls not only in your house but all over the world. In due time, you will see how many will plunge into hell because of them."

"Then what must I tell my sons to make them abhor them?"

"You will soon find out," he said and moved away from me. Meanwhile hailstones kept pelting the vine furiously amid thunder and lightning. The grapes were now a mess, looking as if they had been thoroughly crushed by vintners' feet in a vat. The juice fouled the air with such a sickening stench that it was hardly possible to breathe. Each grape gave out a foul smell of its own, each more repelling than the other, depending on the number and kind of sin. Unable to stand it, I put my handkerchief to my nose and turned to go to my room. I realized then that I was utterly alone. Father Francesia, Father Rua, Father Cagliero, and all the others had fled. In that silence and solitude I became so frightened that I broke into a run and woke up.

As you see, this was a very nasty dream, but what happened the following night was much worse. I'll tell you about it soon. What these dreams imply are at present beyond your understanding. I shall explain them in due time. It is late now, and so I'll let you go to bed.

We must bear in mind that the grave faults revealed to Don Bosco did not all refer to that specific year but to future years as well. He not only saw all his past and present Oratory pupils but countless others, unknown to him, who would attend his schools throughout the world. Similarly, the parable of the fruitless vine in the Book of Isaiah spans several centuries.

Furthermore, we should not forget for a moment what the guide said: "Not all the boys are now as you see them, but they will be so one day unless they mend their ways." The path of evil leads to the abyss.

We also wish to point out that after the appearance of the vine a stranger came upon the scene who, though not immediately recognized by Don Bosco, later acted as his guide and interpreter. In narrating these and other dreams, Don Bosco occasionally called him "a stranger" in order to play down what was most striking about his dreams and—let us say it—what too clearly indicated a supernatural intervention.

Taking advantage of the intimacy with which he honored us, we often asked him about this "stranger." Though we did not get a clear-cut answer, we became convinced through other clues that the guide was not always the same. In turn, he may have been an angel, a deceased pupil, Saint Francis de Sales, Saint Joseph, or some other saint. On certain occasions, as Don Bosco explicitly stated, Louis Comollo, Dominic Savio, and Luis Colle had acted as guides. Sometimes, too, other personages appeared along with them. (Vol. IX, pp. 75-84)

AN ENORMOUS ELEPHANT

Every year around Christmas, I regularly beg God to suggest a *strenna* that may benefit you all. In view of your increased number, I doubled my prayers this year. The last day of the year [Wednesday] came and went, and so did Thursday and

Friday, but nothing came to me. On Friday night [January 2] I went to bed exhausted, but could not fall asleep. The next morning I got up, worn out and almost half dead, but I did not feel upset over it. Rather, I was elated, knowing from past experience that a very bad night is usually a forewarning that Our Lord is about to reveal something to me. That day I went on with my work at Borgo Cornalese; the next day by [early] evening I arrived back here. After hearing confessions, I went to bed. Tired from my work at Borgo and from not sleeping the night before, I soon dozed off. Now began the dream which will give you your *strenna*.

My dear boys, I dreamed that it was a feast day afternoon and that you were all busy playing, while I was in my room with Professor [Thomas] Vallauri discussing literature and religion. Suddenly there was a knock at my door. I rose quickly and opened it. My mother—dead now for six years—was standing there. Breathlessly she gasped, "Come and see! Come and see!"

"What happened?" I asked.

"Come! Come!" she replied.

I dashed to the balcony. Down in the playground, surrounded by a crowd of boys, stood an enormous elephant.

"How did this happen?" I exclaimed. "Let's go down!"

Professor Vallauri and I looked at each other in surprise and alarm and then raced downstairs.

As was only natural, many of you had run up to the elephant. It seemed meek and tame. Playfully it lumbered about, nuzzling the boys with its trunk and cleverly obeying their orders, as though it had been born and raised at the Oratory. Very many of you kept following it about and petting it, but not all. In fact, most of you were scared and fled from it to safety. Finally, you hid in the church. I, too, tried to get in through the side door which opens into the playground, but as I passed Our Lady's statue beside the drinking fountain and touched the hem of Her mantle for protection, She raised Her right arm. Vallauri did likewise on the other side of the statue, and the Virgin raised Her left arm. I was amazed, not knowing what to think of such an extraordinary thing.

When the bell rang for church services, you all trooped in. I followed and saw the elephant standing at the rear by the main entrance. After Vespers and the sermon, I went to the altar, assisted by Father Alasonatti and Father Savio, to give Benediction. At that solemn moment when you all deeply bowed to adore the Blessed Sacrament, the elephant—still standing at the end of the middle aisle—knelt down too, but with its back to the altar.

Once services were over, I tried to dash out to the playground and see what would happen, but I was detained by someone. A while later, I went out the side door which opens into the porticoes and saw you at your usual games. The elephant too had come out of the church and had idled over to the second playground where the new wing is under construction. Mark this well, because this is precisely the place where the grisly scene I am going to describe occurred.

At that moment, at the far end of the playground I saw a banner followed processionally by boys. It bore in huge letters the inscription "Holy Mary, help Your forlorn children!" To everybody's surprise, that monstrous beast, once so tame, suddenly ran amuck. Trumpeting furiously, it lunged forward, seized the nearest boys with its trunk, hurled them into the air or flung them to the ground, and then trampled them underfoot. Though horribly mauled, the victims were still alive. Everybody ran for dear life. Screams and shouts and pleas for help rose from the wounded. Worse—would you believe it?— some boys spared by the elephant, rather than aid their wounded companions, joined the monstrous brute to find new victims.

As all this was happening (I was standing by the second arch of the portico, near the drinking fountain) the little statue that you see there (*and he pointed to the statue of the Blessed Virgin*) became alive and grew to life-size. Then, as Our Lady raised Her arms, Her mantle spread open to display magnificently embroidered inscriptions. Unbelievably it stretched far and wide to shelter all those who gathered beneath it. The best boys were the first to run to it for safety. Seeing that many were in no hurry to run to Her, Our Lady called aloud, "Come all to Me!" Her call was heeded, and as the crowd of boys under the mantle increased, so did the mantle spread wider. However, a few youngsters kept running about and were wounded before they could reach safety. Flushed and breathless, the Blessed Virgin continued to plead, but fewer and fewer were the boys who ran to Her. The elephant, meanwhile, continued its slaughter, aided by several lads who dashed about, wielding one sword or two and preventing their companions from running to Mary. The elephant never even touched these helpers.

Meanwhile, prompted by the Blessed Virgin, some boys left the safety of Her mantle in quick sorties to rescue some victims. No sooner did the wounded get beneath Our Lady's mantle than they were instantly cured. Again and again several of those brave boys, armed with cudgels, went out and risking their lives, shielded the victims from the elephant and its accomplices until nearly all were rescued.

The playground was now deserted, except for a few youngsters lying about almost dead. At one end by the portico, a crowd of boys stood safe under the Virgin's mantle. At the other stood the elephant with some ten or twelve lads who had helped it wreak such havoc and who still insolently brandished swords.

Suddenly rearing up on its hind legs, the elephant changed into a horrible, long-horned specter and cast a black net over its wretched accomplices. Then, as the beast roared, a thick cloud of smoke enveloped them, and the earth suddenly gaped beneath them and swallowed them up.

I looked for my mother and Professor Vallauri to speak to them but could not spot them anywhere. Then I turned to look at the inscriptions on Mary's mantle and noticed that several were actual quotations or adaptations of Scriptural texts. I read a few of them:

"They that explain Me, shall have life everlasting." (Sir 24:31)

"He who finds Me, finds life...." (Prv 8:35)

"Let whoever is simple turn in here...." (Prv 9:4)

"Refuge of sinners."

"Salvation of believers."

"Full of piety, meekness and mercy."

"Blessed are they that keep My ways."

All was quiet now. After a brief silence, the Virgin, seemingly exhausted by so much pleading, soothingly comforted and heartened the boys and, quoting the inscription I had seen inscribed at the base of the niche, She went on:

"You heeded My call and were spared the slaughter wrought by the devil on your companions. Do you want to know what caused their ruin? Foul talk and foul deeds. You also saw your companions wielding swords. They are those who seek your eternal damnation by enticing you from Me, just as they did with many schoolmates of yours.

"Those for whom God keeps waiting, He punishes more severely. The infernal demon enmeshed and dragged them to eternal perdition. Now, go in peace, but remember My words: 'Flee from companions who befriended Satan, avoid foul conversation, have boundless trust in Me. My mantle will always be your safe refuge.' "

Our Lady then vanished; only our beloved statuette remained. My deceased mother reappeared. Again the banner with the inscription "Holy Mary, help your forlorn children" was unfurled. Marching processionally behind, the boys sang "Praise Mary, ye faithful tongues." Shortly afterward, the singing waned and the whole scene faded away. I awoke in a sweat. Such was my dream.

My sons, now it's up to you to draw your own *strenna*. Examine your conscience. You'll know if you were safe under Mary's mantle, or if the elephant flung you into the air, or if you were wielding a sword. I can only repeat what the Virgin said. Turn to Her; call on Her in any danger. I can assure you that your prayers will be heard. Those who were so badly mauled by the elephant are to learn to avoid foul talk and bad companions; those who strive to entice their companions from Mary must either change their ways or leave this house immediately. If anyone wants to know the role he played, let him come to my room and I'll tell him. But I repeat: Satan's accomplices must either mend their ways or go! Good night!

Don Bosco had spoken with such fervor and emotion that for a whole week afterward the boys kept discussing that dream and would not leave him in peace. Every morning they crowded his confessional; every afternoon they pestered him to find out what part they had played in that mysterious dream.

That this was no dream but a vision, Don Bosco had himself indirectly admitted when he had said: "I regularly beg God to suggest . . . A very bad night is usually a forewarning that Our Lord is about to reveal something to me." Furthermore, he forbade anyone to make light of what he had narrated.

But there is more. On this occasion he made a list of the wounded and of those who wielded one or two swords. He gave it to Celestine Durando, instructing him to watch them. The cleric handed this list over to us, and it is still in our possession. The wounded were thirteen—probably those who had not been rescued and sheltered beneath Our Lady's mantle. Seventeen lads wielded one sword; only three had two. Scattered marginal notes next to a boy's name indicate an amendment of life. Also, we must bear in mind that the dream, as we shall see, referred also to the future.

That it mirrored the true state of things was admitted by the boys themselves. "I had no idea that Don Bosco knew me so well," one of them stated. "He revealed my spiritual condition and my temptations so exactly that I could find nothing to add."

Two other boys were told that they were wielding swords. "It's quite true," each admitted. "I knew it all along." They mended their ways.

One afternoon, while talking of this dream and remarking that some boys had already left the Oratory and others would soon follow lest they harm their companions, he came to mention his own "wizardry," as he called it. In this connection he told the following incident:

> Some time ago, a boy wrote home and falsely accused priests and superiors of this house of grave wrongdoings. Fearing that Don Bosco might see his letter, he held on to it till he could secretly mail it. That same day, right after dinner, I sent for him. In my room I told him of his misdeed and asked why he had told such lies. Brazenly he denied everything. I let him talk and then, word for word, I repeated the contents of the letter to him. Embarrassed and frightened, he knelt at my feet in tears. "Was my letter intercepted?" he asked.
>
> "No," I replied. "Your family has probably received it by now, and it's up to you to put matters right."

The boys around him asked how he had found that out. "Oh, it's my wizardry," he answered with a laugh. This wizardry and his dream, which revealed not only the boys' present spiritual condition but their future as well, must have been one and the same thing. Many years later, a boy who had been quite close to Father Rua wrote him a long letter, giving his full name and Turin address. We report it here:

Turin, February 25, 1891

Dear Father Rua:

... Among other things I recall a vision of Don Bosco in 1863, when I was at the Oratory. He saw the future of all the boarders. He himself told us about it after night prayers. It was the dream about the elephant. (*After describing the dream, he went on:*) At the end, Don Bosco told us, "If you want to know what part you played, come to my room and I will tell you.

I too went. "You," he told me, "were one of those trailing after the elephant both before and after church services. Naturally you became a victim. The elephant flung you high into the air with its trunk. When you tumbled down, you were so badly hurt that you could not make it to safety, though you tried hard. A companion of yours, a priest, unrecognized by you, grabbed your arm and dragged you under the Madonna's mantle."

This was not a dream, as Don Bosco called it, but a genuine revelation of my future which Our Lord made to His servant during my second year at the Oratory, when I was a model of conduct and piety. Yet Don Bosco saw me in that condition.

When the summer vacation of 1863 came around, I went home because of health and I did not return to the Oratory. I was then thirteen. The following year, my father apprenticed me to a shoemaker, and two years later (1866) I went to France to complete my training. There I associated with anticlericals, gradually stopped going to church and the sacraments, began to read irreligious books, and even grew to loathe and hate the Catholic faith. Two years later I returned to Italy but kept reading impious books, drawing further and further away from the true Church.

Yet all this time I constantly prayed to God in the name of Jesus to enlighten me and lead me to the true faith. This struggle lasted thirteen years. I strove continually to raise myself up, but I was wounded. I had fallen prey to the elephant and was powerless.

Toward the end of 1878, during a mission which drew great crowds, I went to hear those good preachers. I was delighted by the incontestable truths they expounded. The very last sermon was on the Blessed Sacrament, about which I still had grave doubts. (In fact I no longer believed in the real or even spiritual presence of Jesus in the Blessed Sacrament.) The preacher presented the truth so clearly and so convincingly that, touched by God's grace, I decided to go to confession and place myself under the Blessed Virgin's mantle. Since then I have never ceased to thank God and Our Blessed Mother for this grace.

Please note that, as Don Bosco had seen in his dream, I later found out that the missionary had been a schoolmate of mine at the Oratory.

Dominic N . . .

P.S. Should you see fit to publish this letter, I also authorize you to edit it, short of substantial changes, because what I wrote is genuinely true. I kiss your hand respectfully, dear Father Rua, and by this act I intend to pay homage to our beloved Don Bosco.

Certainly, this dream must also have enlightened Don Bosco in appraising priestly and religious vocations and the applicants' inclinations to good so well displayed by those brave boys who had confronted the elephant and his accomplices, had wrested their wounded companions from their clutches, and had carried them to safety under the Madonna's mantle. He therefore continued to accept applicants to the Salesian Society and to admit to triennial vows those who had satisfactorily completed their probationary period. The mere fact that he accepted them will be their imperishable honor. Some did not take vows or left after their expiration, but nearly all, as diocesan priests or as public school teachers, persevered in their mission of saving and educating the young. Their names are recorded in the minutes of three chapter meetings of the Salesian Society.

(Vol. VII, pp. 213-219)

THE SNAKE AND THE ROSARY

I want to tell you a dream I had some nights ago, most probably on the eve of the Assumption. I dreamed that I was at my brother's home at Castelnuovo d'Asti with all my boys. While they were at play, a total stranger came up to me and asked me to go with him. He took me to a meadow alongside the playground and pointed to a huge, ugly snake, over twenty feet long, coiled in the grass. Frightened, I wanted to run off, but the stranger held me back. "Get closer and take a good look," he said.

"What?" I gasped. "Don't you realize that monster could spring on me and gobble me up in no time?"

"Don't be afraid! Nothing of the sort will happen. Just come with me."

"Nothing doing! I'm not crazy!"

"Then stay where you are," the stranger replied. And he went to fetch a rope.

"Take this end," he said on his return, "and grip it tightly with both hands. I'll hold the other, and we'll let it dangle over the snake."

"And then?"

"Then we'll snap it across its back."

"You must be crazy! The snake will leap up and tear us to pieces."

"No, it won't. Leave that to me."

"Count me out! I have no intention to risk my life for a thrill of this kind!"

Again I tried to run away, but the stranger once more assured me that I had nothing to fear because the snake would do me no harm. He talked so persuasively that I stayed on and agreed to his plan. He went around to the other side of the monster. We stretched the rope and then snapped it across the snake's back. The monster immediately sprang up and struck at the rope, but, as it did so, it ensnared itself as in a noose.

"Hold on!" the stranger shouted. "Don't let go!" He ran to a nearby pear tree and tied his end of the rope to it. Then he came to me and tied my end to the iron grating of a window in the house. The snake kept furiously struggling to free itself, writhing, thrashing, and flailing about. In its fury it tore itself to pieces, scattering its flesh over the area, till it was slashed to a mere skeleton.

The stranger then untied the rope and coiled it up. "Now watch very carefully!" he said as he put it into a box and closed it. By this time the boys had swarmed about me. Within a few moments he opened the box. We looked in and were astounded to see the rope shaped into the words *Ave Maria*.

"How did that happen?" I asked.

"The snake," the man replied, "is a symbol of the devil, whereas the rope stands for *Ave Maria* or, rather, the rosary, a succession of Hail Marys with which we can strike, conquer, and destroy all of hell's demons."

What I've told you so far—Don Bosco concluded—is the first part of the dream. What followed is even stranger and more amazing, but it's too late to tell you now. I'll leave it for tomorrow. In the meantime let us give thought to what that stranger said about the Hail Mary and the rosary. Let us devoutly say a Hail Mary whenever we are tempted, and we'll be sure to win. Good night.

On August 21 [1862], after night prayers, we were all anxious to hear the second part of the dream which Don Bosco had described as strange and interesting, but we were disappointed. "Last night," Don Bosco said, "I stated that I would tell you the second part of the dream but, regretfully, I do not think it opportune to keep my promise."

A general murmur of regret and disappointment greeted these words. When it subsided, Don Bosco went on: "What can I say? I thought it over last night and again today, and I decided I had better not disclose the dream's second part because of some things I do not wish known outside this house. Therefore, be satisfied with making the best of what I have already told you."

The following day, August 22, we again pestered him to tell us, at least privately, the part of the dream he had not revealed. He did not want to change his mind, but after much insistence on our part, he finally relented and promised that he would tell us more that evening. At the "Good Night" he spoke as follows:

Yielding to your repeated entreaties, I shall tell you the second part of the dream or at least what little I can. First, I must make it clear that no one is to write or talk about it outside this house. Discuss it among yourselves, laugh at it, do as you wish, but only among yourselves.

Now, while talking with that stranger about the rope, the snake, and what they symbolized, I turned around and saw boys picking up scraps of snake meat and eating them. "What are you doing?" I shouted. "Are you mad? That meat is poisonous!"

"It's delicious!" they replied.

And yet, no sooner had they swallowed it than they would crumple to the ground and their bodies would swell and harden like stone. I was helpless because, despite this, more and more boys kept eating that meat. I shouted and yelled at them, and even slapped and punched them to keep them from eating, but in vain. For every one who crumpled to the ground, another took his place. Then I called the clerics and told them to go among the boys and do all they could to make them stop eating that meat. My order was ineffective; worse yet, some clerics themselves began to eat it and they too fell to the ground.

Nearly out of my mind at seeing so many boys lying about me in such a pitiful state, I turned to the stranger. "What does this mean?" I asked. "These boys know that this meat will kill them, yet they eat it, Why?"

"Because 'the sensual man does not perceive the things that are of God.' That's why!" he answered.

"But isn't there some way of saving these boys?"

"Yes, there is."

"What?"

"Anvil and hammer."

"Anvil and hammer? What for?"

"To put the boys back in shape!"

"You mean I am to put them on an anvil and strike them with a hammer?"

"Look," the stranger said "this whole thing is a symbol. The hammer symbolizes confession, and the anvil symbolizes Holy Communion. These are the remedies you must use." I went to work and found the treatment very effective, but not for all. While most boys were restored to life and recovered, a few did not because their confessions were bad.

After the boys had retired to their dormitories. I (Provera) asked Don Bosco privately why his order to the clerics had proved ineffective. "Because not all obeyed," he replied. "Worse yet, some even ate that meat."

On the whole, these dreams represent real life. Along with Don Bosco's words and deeds, they reveal the state of things in any average community where the most outstanding virtues are matched by deplorable weaknesses. This comes as no surprise, because evil unfortunately tends to spread far more readily than virtue. (Vol. VII, pp. 143-144, 146-147)

FAITH, OUR SHIELD AND OUR VICTORY

I seemed to be at the Oratory in the midst of my boys, my glory and crown. It was evening. Dusk was just setting, so one could see but dimly. As I was walking from this portico toward the main gate, an unbelievably huge crowd of boys closed in about me, as you do because we are friends. Some had come to say hello, others to tell me something. Saying a word here and there, I slowly made my way to the center of the playground. Suddenly I heard drawn out moans and sobs followed by a resounding roar with intermingling boyish screams and wild shrieks which seemed to come from the main entrance. The students ran there to see what was happening, but almost immediately they ran back madly to us along with the terrified artisans. Many artisans had already fled from the gate to the other end of the playground.

As the cries and howls of pain and hopelessness kept increasing, I anxiously asked what was happening and tried to shove forward to help, but the boys about me wouldn't let me.

"Let me go," I cried. "Let me see what is happening to frighten everyone so."

"No, no, please don't go!" they shouted. "Stay away. There's a monster which will swallow you up. Run away with us! Don't go there!"

But I wanted to see and, shaking off the boys, I got close to the artisans' playground.

"Look out!" the boys screamed. "Look out!"

"What's wrong?"

"Look! Back there!"

I turned in the direction indicated and saw a horrid animal. At first I thought that it was a giant lion, but it was nothing like an earthly lion. I gazed intently at it. It was monstrous; it looked like a bear, but seemed more ferocious and was far more terrifying. It had an undersized rump but enormous shoulders and a huge belly. Overly large too was its head, with grotesquely cavernous jaws, open wide, ready to swallow a person at one bite. Its mouth sprouted two thick, long, pointed tusks shaped like sharp swords.

I stepped back among the boys, who kept asking what they were to do, but I was frightened too and at a loss. "I wish I could tell you," I replied, "but I don't know myself. Just now let's stay together under the porticoes."

No sooner had I said this than the bear stalked into the second playground and made its way toward us with a slow heavy tread as though assured of its prey. We drew back in terror until we stood here under this portico, the boys clinging fast to me and all eyes centered on me. "Don Bosco, what should we do?" they pleaded. I kept looking at them in silence, not knowing what action to take. Finally I exclaimed, "Let's turn back to the farther end of the portico, where Our Lady's statue stands. Let's kneel and pray more fervently than usual so that She may tell us what to do and what kind of a monster this is, and so that She may rescue us. If it is just a wild animal of some kind, we shall manage to kill it somehow; if it is a demon, Mary will come to our aid. Don't be afraid. Our heavenly Mother will see to our safety."

Meanwhile the beast kept up its slow approach, belly close to the ground, crouching and preparing to spring and seize us.

We fell to our knees in prayer. It was a moment of utter helplessness. The huge monster had gotten so close that in one leap it could be upon us. Then, all at once—I don't know how or when—we found ourselves on the other side of the wall in the clerics' dining room.

In the center I could see Our Lady. I am not sure, but She looked like the statue we have here in the portico or the one in the dining room itself, or maybe like the statue atop the dome or the one inside the church. But, be it as it may, there She shone like the sun at midday, thronged by saints and angels. The dining room seemed like heaven. Her lips moved as though She wished to say something to us.

We were a countless crowd in that dining hall. Astonishment had replaced terror in our hearts. The eyes of all were upon the Madonna. "Do not be afraid," She reassured us in the gentlest of tones. "My divine Son is just testing you."

I looked carefully at the persons brilliant in glory who surrounded the Blessed Virgin and recognized Father Alasonatti, Father Ruffino, a certain Brother Michael of the Christian Schools, whom some of you knew, and my own brother Joseph. I saw others too who had once attended our Oratory or belonged to our Congregation and are now in heaven. In their company I also saw several others who are living today.

Suddenly, one of those about the Blessed Virgin loudly announced, "Let us rise!"

Since we were already standing, we could not understand his command.

"Why 'Let us rise?' We are already on our feet."

"Let us rise!" he repeated in stentorian tones. The boys looked at me, thoroughly surprised and still, waiting for directions because they had no idea of what to do. I turned toward the one who had given the command and asked, "What do you want us to do? What does [it] mean, since we are already on our feet?"

"Let us rise!" he again ordered in a stronger tone. The order made no sense to me; it was incomprehensible.

As I was standing on a table for better control of the crowd, one of those who thronged around the Blessed Virgin addressed me in a wondrously powerful voice. The boys listened intently as he said to me, "You are a priest and should understand what this means. When you offer Holy Mass, do you not say "lift up your hearts" every day? Are you speaking about the physical act of standing up? Don't you mean instead the uplifting of the heart's love to God?"

Turning to the boys I instantly shouted, "Up, up with your hearts, my sons! Let us strengthen our faith and raise our hearts to God. Let us make an act of love and repentance. Let us earnestly strive to pray with lively fervor. Let us trust in God." I gave a sign and we all knelt down.

Moments later, as we softly prayed in an outburst of confidence, we again heard a voice ordering, "Rise!" Leaping to our feet, we all felt that we were being lifted from the ground by some kind of supernatural power—how high I cannot say, but I know that we were all raised quite a distance above the ground. I have no idea what supported us. I do recall that I held fast to the sill or frame of a window. All the boys were clinging to windows or doors—one gripping here and one there, some holding on to iron bars or stout spikes, some others to the cornices of the ceiling. We were all hanging in the air, and I wondered that none of us fell to the floor.

Then, behold, the monster we had seen in the playground stormed into the dining room, followed by a vast herd of other wild animals. They stamped about the dining hall growling frightfully, straining for combat and ready to pounce upon us at any moment. But, though they kept eying us, staring with bloodshot eyes and tossing their heads, they did not immediately attack us. We looked down on them from above. Clinging for life to that window, I thought, *Were I to fall, how horribly they would tear me to shreds!*

Caught as we were in these strange positions, we heard Our Lady sing out the words of St. Paul: "In all circumstances hold faith up before you as your shield..." (Eph 6:16) So harmonious was the sound, so full, so sublimely melodious, that we listened ecstatically. Every note could be heard from the lowest to highest, and we thought that a hundred voices had blended into one.

Intent upon this heavenly song, we noticed a number of graceful young lads, who had descended from heaven on wings, leave Our Lady's side and draw near to us. They bore shields in their hands and put one up against the heart of each boy. They were large shields, sparkling in beauty and reflecting the light which shone from the Madonna. It was a heavenly sight. Each shield seemed to have a steel center, surrounded by a large ring of diamonds, and the whole shield was edged in purest gold. It was all one could hope for in beauty, sweetness, and melody.

As I gazed about me, lost in the music, I was startled by a booming voice which cried: "To arms!" Then the wild beasts began stamping about furiously.

In a flash we all found ourselves on the floor, each on his feet, each engaged in deadly combat with those monsters, protected only by our divine shields. I can't say whether the struggle took place inside the dining hall or out in the playground. The heavenly choir did not interrupt its singing. The monsters rushed at us as smoke streamed from their gaping mouths along with leaden balls, spears, arrows, and weapons of all kinds. But these weapons either missed us or hit our shields and bounced off. Our adversaries were bent on wounding and slaughtering us, and they kept hurling themselves against us, but all in vain. Meeting us head on, they smashed their fangs and were forced to flee. In waves these hordes of frightful monsters assailed us, but all met with the same fate.

It was a lengthy battle, but finally we heard Our Lady saying: "... the power that has overcome the world is this faith of ours." (1 Jn 5:4)

At Her voice, the entire herd of frightened beasts balked and, dashing headlong, disappeared, leaving us safe, free, victorious in that immense dining hall, still ablaze with the brilliance emanating from the Madonna.

Then I carefully studied the faces of those who bore the shields. They were an immense number. Among others I could see Father Alasonatti, Father Ruffino, my brother Joseph, and the Christian Brother who had fought by our side.

But the boys could not take their eyes away from the Blessed Virgin. She was chanting a canticle of thanksgiving which gladdened us with a new joy and an ecstasy beyond words. I doubt that a lovelier canticle can be heard in heaven itself.

Suddenly our happiness was rudely broken by bloodcurdling shrieks and cries intermingled with bellowing roars. Were some of our boys being torn to pieces by the wild beasts which had fled the scene but moments before? I immediately tried to rush out and help these sons, but I could not because the boys kept restraining me and firmly refused to let me out of the room. I struggled to free myself. "Let me go to help those poor boys," I begged. "I want to see them. If they are hurt or killed, I want to die with them. I must go, even if it costs me my life." Tearing myself from those who were holding me, I dashed out to the portico. Oh, what horror! The playground was strewn with the dead, the dying and the wounded.

Boys, panicking with fear, tried to flee in all directions, only to be pursued by those monsters which pounced on them, sinking their fangs into their arms and legs, tearing them to pieces. Every second some boys fell to the ground and died amid horrifying screams.

But the beast that wrought the most fearful slaughter of all was the bear which had first appeared in the artisans' playground. With its sword-sharp tusks it pierced the boys' chests first from the right side to the left, and then from left to right. The victims fell tragically dead with a double mortal wound through the heart.

With determination I shouted, "Courage, my dear sons!" Immediately many lads ran to me for protection, but they were pursued by the bear. Summoning up my courage, I stepped forward in its path, joined by some of the boys who had already conquered the beasts in the dining room. That prince of darkness flung itself upon us but could not hurt us because of our shields. In fact, it could not even touch us because the very sight of the shields forced it to back away in terror and even homage. Then it was that, as I fixed my gaze on the two long sword-sharp tusks, I noticed one word on each in big letters: *Idleness* on one, *Gluttony* on the other. In utter surprise I kept asking myself: Is it possible that here where everyone is so busy and we do not know where to begin doing all the work we have to do, there is still someone who idles away his time? As for the boys, I think they keep busy with their work, study and play. It made no sense to me.

Then someone said: "And yet how many half-hours they waste!"

"But gluttony too?" I asked. "Here at the Oratory one could not indulge in gluttony if he wanted to. There is hardly ever a chance. Our food is most ordinary and so is what we drink. We barely have just what we need. How could one be so intemperate as to endanger his eternal salvation?"

Again came the reply: "Oh, you priest! You think you are well versed in moral theology and quite experienced, but on this point you know nothing. You are a babe in arms. Do you not know that one may sin by gluttony and intemperance even when drinking water?"

I wasn't convinced at all, and I wanted a better explanation. While the dining hall was still bright with the Blessed Virgin's presence, I went very sadly to Brother Michael to clear up my doubts. "My friend," he answered, "you are still a novice in these things. I will teach you.

"As regards gluttony, you must learn that one can be intemperate by eating, drinking or sleeping more than one needs, and by pampering the body in other ways. As for idleness, you must know that it does not just mean being lazy. It also means letting one's fantasy run on to dangerous thoughts. One can also be idle during study periods by fooling around and disturbing others, by wasting time in silly reading, or by being slothful, especially in church. Idleness is the father, the font and source of many temptations and of all evils. You who are these boys' director must safeguard them from these two sins by striving to strengthen their faith. If you can manage to make your boys temperate in the little things I have mentioned, they will always overcome the devil. Through temperance they will grow in humility, chastity, and other virtues as well. If they will properly use their time, they will never fall into the clutches of the infernal enemy but will live and die as saintly Christians."

I thanked him for his instructions and then, wanting to verify the reality of all this, lest it be a mere dream, I tried to grasp his hand but touched nothing. Again and again I tried but failed. I grasped nothing but air. Yet I could see those people. They were talking and seemed real. I approached Father Alasonatti, Father Ruffino, and my brother, but once more I grasped nothing.

Beside myself, I cried out, "Is this all true or not? Aren't these all real people? Didn't I hear them talk?"

Brother Michael replied, "After all your studies, you should know that as long as my soul is separated from my body, it is useless to try to touch me. You cannot touch a pure spirit. We take on our former likeness only to enable mortal eyes to see us. But when we shall all have risen at the Last Judgement, then we shall put on our bodies, immortal and spiritualized."

Then I tried to draw close to Our Lady who seemed to have something to tell me. I was almost beside Her when I heard a new uproar and more shrieks from outside. I immediately dashed out of the dining hall again, but as I did so, I awoke.

To conclude his account, Don Bosco added these reflections and suggestions:

Whatever this mixed-up dream may mean, it does restate and explain Saint Paul's words. However, I was so worn out and exhausted by the strain of this dream that I begged the Lord never to send me any more dreams like that. But—wouldn't you know it?—the following night that very same dream came back, only this time I had to see it to the end, something I was spared the night before. I was so frightened that I screamed. Father Berto heard me and in the morning he asked me why I had shrieked and if I had passed a sleepless night. These dreams drain me far more than if I were to spend the night at my desk.

As I said, this is only a dream. I do not want you to give it any more importance. Think of it only as a dream, no more. I would not like you to write home about it or tell outsiders who know nothing of the Oratory, lest they say, as they have already, that Don Bosco fills his boys with dreams. I don't really mind, though. Let them say what they will, but let each of us draw from this dream whatever applies. Just now I will not give you any explanations because all of you can easily understand the dream. I only recommend very strongly that you revive your faith, which is safeguarded particularly by being temperate and avoiding idleness. Let temperance be a friend and sloth an enemy. Some other evening I will return to this subject. For now, good night. (Vol. XII, pp. 249-255)

THE GLOBE

At the "Good Night" on November 29, 1873, after returning to the Oratory from a visit to the Salesian schools at Sampierdarena, Varazze and Alassio, Don Bosco narrated another dream. Father Berto jotted it down and then wrote out this detailed description:

These past few days, while I was away, I had a very frightening dream. I went to bed one evening, thinking about the stranger who—as I told you a few nights ago—had taken me in a dream through the dormitories and with a lamp had shown me the boys' sins on their foreheads. While I was wondering whether he was a human like us or a spirit in human form, I fell asleep and immediately seemed to be carried back to the Oratory. To my surprise, it was no longer here in Valdocco, but at the entrance of a valley long and wide, hemmed in between two lovely hills.

I was with you, but you were all silent and tense. Suddenly the sun broke out, shining so strongly that we were forced to lower our heads. We remained in that position for some time until the blinding light dimmed almost to absolute darkness, making it difficult for us to see or recognize even those closest to us.

The sudden change was very frightening. As I tried to figure out what to do, a greenish light flashed at one corner of the valley and, streaming across it, formed a graceful rainbow between the two hills. The darkness receded, and from the rainbow—very similar to a rainbow after a heavy rainfall or the aurora borealis—multi-colored beams of light streamed into the valley.

While we were all intent on admiring and enjoying this charming spectacle, I noticed a phenomenon even more astounding at the far end of the valley—a gigantic electric globe hanging in midair, darting blinding flashes in all directions so that no one could look at it without the risk of falling to the ground in a daze. The globe kept floating down toward us, illuminating the valley more brilliantly than ten of our suns could have done at full noon. As it drew nearer and nearer, the boys, blinded by its glare, dropped face to the ground, as if struck by lightning.

At first I too was terrified, but then, getting hold of myself, I forced my eyes to gaze boldly upon the globe, following its movement until it stopped some three hundred meters above our heads. Then I decided that I must see what sort of phenomenon this was.

I scanned it thoroughly and, distant though it was, I could

see that its summit had the shape of a large sphere and bore a huge inscription: "The Almighty." The whole globe was ringed by several tiers of balconies, crowded with joyful, jubilant people: men and women, young and old, dressed in sparkling, indescribably beautiful garments of many colors. Their warm smiles and friendliness seemed to invite us to share their joy and triumph.

From the center of this heavenly globe countless shafts of light radiated, flashing so blindingly that any boys looking at them were stunned, staggered a moment, and then fell face down to the ground. I too, unable to endure such brilliance any longer, exclaimed, "Oh Lord, I beg You, either let this divine sight vanish or let me die, for I can no longer withstand such extraordinary beauty!" Then I felt faint, and I too dropped to the ground, with the cry, "Let us invoke God's mercy!"

Coming to myself again, I stood up moments later and decided to tour the valley and see what had happened to the boys. To my great surprise and wonder, I saw that all were prostrate and motionless in prayer. In order to find out whether they were dead or alive, I prodded several with my foot, asking, "What's the matter? Are you alive or dead?" All gave me the same answer: "I am imploring God's mercy."

Then, to my deep sorrow, I came upon several, their faces as black as coal, who kept gazing defiantly upon the globe, almost as if challenging God. I went up and called them by name, but they gave no sign of life. Paralyzed by the rays of light darting from the globe because of their obstinate refusal to fall prostrate and implore God's mercy with their companions, they had become as cold as ice. What grieved me even more was that they were so numerous.

Just then an abnormally huge, indescribably horrid monster rose up at the far end of the valley. Never had I seen anything as frightening as that! It strode toward us. I told all the boys to stand up, and they too were terrorized by the horrible sight. Gasping in anguish, I searched frantically for some Salesian to help me get the boys up the nearest hill for safety, but I could find no one.

Meanwhile the monster kept getting closer and closer. When it was about to overtake us, the brilliant globe, which until then had hovered over our heads, quickly dropped almost to the ground, shielding us from the monster, and at that moment a voice thundered through the valley. "What accord is there between Christ and Belial . . ." (2 Cor. 6: 15), between the children of light and the children of darkness, that is, between the good and the bad whom Holy Scripture calls the children of Belial.

At these words I awoke in a cold sweat. Although it was only midnight, I could not fall asleep again or feel warm the rest of the night. I was amply consoled at having seen almost all our boys humbly seek God's mercy and faithfully respond to His favors, but I must admit my profound grief at the goodly number of proud, hard-hearted lads who rejected God's loving invitation and drew His chastisements upon themselves.

I already summoned a few of these boys last night and others today so that they may soon make their peace with God and stop abusing His mercy and scandalizing their companions. There can be no alliance between God's children and the devil's followers. This is their last warning.

As you see, my dear boys, what I have told you is but a dream like all the others. Still, let us thank God for using this means to show us our spiritual condition. How generously He enlightens and favors those who humbly implore His help and assistance in material and spiritual need. "God is stern with the arrogant but to the humble he shows kindness." (1 Pt 5:5)

According to Father Berto, Don Bosco did not further elaborate on the details of the dream, but we can easily grasp the message. As long as we are in this valley of tears, God permits periods of light and darkness in our spiritual life, just as day alternates with night. Those who withstand the darkness and apparent abandonment humbly and trustingly soon see light return more brilliant than ever with a new, magnificent rainbow. And if they faithfully and most humbly keep their thoughts centered on God, they come to understand ever more clearly their own nothingness in face of God's sublime majesty and the ineffable beauty of the reward He has prepared for us. Furthermore, they shall always feel that they must remain prostrate before Him and implore His infinite mercy.

Those instead who, full of themselves, neglect their spiritual life and are concerned only with earthly matters soon lose

God's grace and repeatedly fall prey to the infernal monster who, like a roaring lion, endlessly roams about seeking to wrest souls from God.

Those who are habitually united with God remain unshaken even when subjected to the most harrowing trials because God is their shield. They can count on His help here below while ensuring heaven for themselves. Humility, then, is the path to heaven. Humility and greatness go hand in hand, Saint Augustine said, because the humble man is united with God. Humility does not consist in shabbiness of dress, speech or demeanor, but in lying prostrate—mind, heart and soul totally centered on God—with full awareness of one's nothingness, in an endless plea for His mercy.

Don Bosco constantly fought against all error and sin, but he thought so highly of God's mercy that he openly proclaimed his hope that even Voltaire had obtained God's pardon in his last moments. This indicates how horrible seemed to him the fate of those who died unreconciled with God.

(Vol. X, pp. 63-66)

RAGING TORRENT

Don Bosco told this dream to the director [Father John Baptist Lemoyne] on April 17, the morning of his departure, asking him to narrate it to the community. Father Lemoyne accompanied him to Turin because he had to go to Mirabello to preach the spiritual retreat, and from Turin he wrote the following letter to his boys at Lanzo to acquaint them with Don Bosco's message:

April 18, 1868

My dear sons,

My hurried departure prevented me from saying good-bye to you as I had wished, but now, while in Turin, I send you in writing what I wanted to tell you. Listen carefully because it is the Lord speaking to you through Don Bosco.

The last night of Don Bosco's stay in Lanzo was a very bad

one. As you know, my room is next to his. Well, that night I was startled out of my sleep twice by what I thought were prolonged, frightening screams. I sat up in bed and listened carefully. I was sure the screams were coming from Don Bosco's room. The next morning I mulled over what I had heard and decided to mention it to Don Bosco. "It's quite true," he replied. "Last night I had dreams which truly grieved me. I seemed to be on the bank of a torrent, not too wide, but turbulent with muddy, frothy waters. All the Lanzo boys were with me, trying to jump to the other side. Many took a running leap and landed safely on the opposite bank. They were good athletes. However, others did not do so well. Some barely hit the bank, fell backward, and were swept away by the current; others toppled into the middle of the torrent and vanished; still others struck rocks jutting out of the water, fracturing their skulls or suffering other injuries. This went on for a considerable time while Don Bosco fruitlessly kept shouting to them to be more careful. The torrent was now strewn with bodies which, tumbling through the rapids, were finally dashed against a boulder set in a bend of the torrent where the water was deepest, and were sucked into a whirlpool.

How many of my poor sons now listening to the reading of this letter are now in those depths and in danger of being eternally lost! But why did boys [like you]—so lively, cheerful, and nimble—fail to land safely on the opposite bank? It was because wretched companions tripped them or held them back by their coats or shoved them as they jumped. These unhappy scoundrels (a few, mind you), who are in league with the devil and try to ruin their companions, are also listening to the reading of this letter. Let me ask them in Don Bosco's own words: "Why, by your evil conversation, do you want to kindle in your companions' hearts the flame of passions that will consume them for all eternity? Why do you teach evil to some who may still be innocent? Why crack certain jokes and make certain deals which keep you away from the sacraments? Why won't you listen to one who can put you on the path to heaven? All you gain is God's curse."

Never forget Our Lord's frightful threats that I have so often repeated. My dear sons, listen: you are a cause of evil to others, but you are still dear sons of mine and you have a special place in my heart because you need me more than all the others do. Give up sin; save your souls. If I were to know that even one of you were to be lost, I would never have a moment's peace in my life again! Your eternal salvation is my sole thought, my sole desire, my sole worry. All I want is to make good Christians out of you and help you reach heaven. You will listen to me, won't you?

The dream needs no explanation. You already know its meaning. The bank on which Don Bosco stood is our present life. The opposite bank represents eternity, heaven. The torrent which swept the boys away is sin which drags people to hell.

Stricken in anguish by such a sight, Don Bosco tried to save you with shouted warnings. He awoke and said to himself, *Oh! How I wish I could warn the boys I recognized, but tomorrow I have to leave.*

Then he fell asleep again. He seemed to find himself in a vast meadow where you were playing and running. To his horrow he also saw in your midst all kinds of wild animals—fiery-eyed lions, tigers clawing the earth, wolves crouching about you, grimacing bears squatting on their haunches and stretching out their front paws to hug you. Such a horrible company! And, worse, you were at the mercy of these ferocious animals which furiously kept lunging at you.

Some of you were lying on the ground, covered by beasts which tore you to pieces with their claws and fangs; others were being pursued and were fleeing in terror to Don Bosco. At this sight the wild animals retreated. There were also boys who strove to defend themselves singlehandedly, but, overcome by the beasts' superior strength, they were torn to pieces. Then—you wouldn't believe it—there were youngsters who, instead of running to safety, stood there smiling at those monsters and petting them, as if they enjoyed being smothered by them. Don Bosco kept running here and there, shouting and trying to summon you to him, but no matter how much he shouted, some would not listen. The meadow was now strewn with dead and wounded. Groans and whimpers strangely mingled with the snorting and roaring of wild animals and Don Bosco's cries. It was then that he awoke a second time.

This was the dream, and you know the dreams Don Bosco has! You may imagine my heartbreak on hearing it. If, formerly, the mere thought of being momentarily away from you weighed heavily upon me, you can be certain that after hearing the dream I would have returned to you instantly had not my duty of obedience kept me where I was. I wouldn't worry so much if you weren't so dear to me.

What do these lions, tigers, and bears represent, if not the devil and his temptations? Some boys overcome them because they run to their guide for help; others fall victims because they yield to temptation; still others love sin and the devil and freely run into his clutches. My sons, will you be brave? Will you always keep in mind that you have a soul to save?

Later, Don Bosco told me, "I saw all these boys. I came to know the sly foxes among them! But I shall keep this secret to myself. As soon as I will be able to come back to Lanzo, I shall tell each one what concerns him. This time my toothache prevented me from talking to all, but in my next visit I shall warn those who need it."

So I know nothing, my dear sons, because Don Bosco told me nothing, but a day will come—Judgement Day—when I shall know everything. How sad I shall be if, after having spent my best years working hard for you, loving you with my whole heart, I should have to be separated from some of you for all eternity! If you do not begin to love God now, you will not love Him in your later years. "Train a boy in the way he should go; even when he is old, he will not swerve from it." (Prv 22:6)

My sons, my children, do not belittle my words, for they are the words of our beloved Don Bosco. Spend the few days of your life trying to earn paradise. Pray that my spiritual retreat may proceed well and that my sermons may bear fruit.

Yours affectionately in Jesus Christ,
Father J. B. Lemoyne
(Vol. IX, pp. 68-70)

A LIFE-SAVING RAFT

I seemed to be near a village that looked like Castelnuovo d'Asti, but was not. You boys were joyfully playing about in a vast, open prairie, when suddenly water surged from the far end of the plain and we found ourselves surrounded by a flood that grew more threatening as it kept rushing toward us. The Po River had overflowed and was spawning raging torrents.

Very much frightened, we ran as fast as we could toward a thick-walled, isolated grist mill and did not stop until we got to its courtyard. The surging flood, however, soon reached us, forcing us to seek safety in the upper floors, wherefrom we could gauge the wide sweep of the disaster. The whole Po valley from the Superga hills to the Alps had become an immense lake engulfing meadows, fields, orchards, woods, hamlets, villages and towns.

The water kept rising and so we had to climb to the top floor. Realizing that our situation was desperate, I urged you to put all your trust in God and in Our Blessed Mother. As the water neared the top floor and chilled our hearts with terror, a huge raft suddenly materialized in front of us. It was our only chance for safety. Breathless with fear, everyone wanted to jump on it, but no one dared because a wall juttting out of the water kept the raft away from the building. The only way to get across the water was by treading a long, narrow tree trunk connecting the raft with the mill. But this was risky because one end of the trunk rested on the raft and kept bobbing up and down. Bracing myself, I was the first to cross over. To make it easier for you and encourage you, I appointed priests and clerics to help you at both ends of the makeshift bridge. Oddly enough, they tired very fast and became so exhausted that they had to lie down and rest. The same happened to those who relieved them. Wondering what the matter might be, I tried it myself. In no time I too felt exhausted.

Meanwhile, many boys were growing impatient. Spotting a long, wide plank floating by, they seized it and maneuvered it into position to us as a gangplank to the raft. Then, either out of panic or recklessness, they rushed onto it without waiting for help.

"Wait, wait!" I shouted. They paid no attention to me. Bumping into each other or otherwise losing their balance, many fell off and were swallowed up by the murky, putrid waters. Eventually, the unsteady catwalk overturned. All in all, one-fourth of you boys were lost.

Up to this point I had been steadying my end of the tree trunk while you were crossing. Noticing that the water level was now above the wall, I managed to push the raft flush against the mill where Father Cagliero, one foot on a windowsill, the other on the raft's edge, helped the still stranded boys safely aboard. Some, however, had climbed up to the roof and were huddled on the ridge. The ever-rising flood, meanwhile, had submerged the eaves and part of the rafters, but had also raised the raft. Seeing those boys in their predicament, I shouted to them to pray with all their hearts and not to panic. Then I told them to link their arms and step down to the raft which was now poised at the eaves' level. They followed my instructions and with their companions' help boarded the raft. On it a very generous quantity of bread was safely stored in many baskets. When all of you were safely aboard I took command, though still jittery. "Mary is the Star of the Sea," I said. "She never forsakes those who trust in Her, so let us get under Her protecting mantle. She will lead us out of danger and guide us safely to port."

Then we let the raft go to the mercy of the waves, and it began to float away. The wind-swept waters propelled it so swiftly that we had to hold fast to each other for dear life and form one body, lest we be swept away.

In no time we had traveled a great distance, but abruptly the raft came to a stop and then spun round and round with such speed that we thought we were surely being sucked into a whirlpool. Fortunately a mighty gust of wind pulled us out of it in the nick of time. We then sailed on at a more moderate speed. We had to contend with a few more small whirlpools, but finally we came to a full stop near a beautiful, vast shore, perfectly dry, sloping upward like a hill rising from the middle of the sea.

Entised by it, many of you immediately shouted that God had placed men on land and not on water, and, urging others to follow, jumped ashore without permission.

Alas, their joy was short-lived. A sudden storm again swelled the waters and dashed them against the bank. Submerged to the waist and screaming in terror, those boys were finally swallowed up by the waves.

"How true indeed," I exclaimed brokenheartedly, "that he

from the flood. Still others deceived themselves into thinking that the land was not far off or were afraid that soon food would run out. The upshot was that they wrangled among themselves and refused to obey. I tried to reason with them but in vain.

At this moment, other rafts came into sight, apparently on a course different from ours. Following their own whims, the dissenters decided to leave me. They threw some planks into the water and, jumping on them and on others even wider which were floating nearby, they steered toward the other rafts. I can't tell you how greatly pained I was to see these unfortunate sons of mine rush headlong to their ruin. The wind blew and the waves kept rising. Some boys were swallowed up by the raging billows, others were caught in whirlpools, and still others rammed into floating debris and sadly drowned. A few managed to board the rafts, but, soon after, the rafts broke apart. As night fell, we could hear the victims' heartrending cries. At this spectacle, these words came to my mind: *In the sea of this world all shall perish who are not aboard this ship—Our Lady's ship.*

The number of my dear boys was now considerably reduced, but we kept up our trust in Our Heavenly Mother as we moved on throughout the dark night. At daybreak, our raft entered a very narrow strait between two muddy banks lined with brush, boulders, rocks, logs, branches, broken planks, masts and oars. Our raft was surrounded by tarantulas, toads, snakes, dragons, crocodiles, sharks, vipers and other hideous animals. Overhanging willows harbored strange-looking, oversized cats which devoured human flesh, while huge monkeys, swinging from the branches, attempted to snatch boys who in their fear squatted low to escape their clutches.

Here, to our surprise and horror, we saw again those unfortunate boys who had drowned. The waves had finally cast them up to this shore, shattered to pieces upon the rocks or partially buried in mud; hair, arms, torsos and heads were visible here and there. A few corpses were also floating about. Suddenly a boy cried out from the raft: "Look! A monster is devouring so-and-so!" Repeatedly calling the lad by name, he pointed him out to his terrified companions. Something worse yet—a mammoth blazing furnace with people in it—was coming into view not too far from where we stood. Feet, legs, arms, hands and heads were bubbling up and down like beans in a boiling pot. With dismay we recognized many of our pupils. The lid over the furnace bore a large inscription: "Sixth and Seventh Commandments."

Nearby rose a lofty hill dotted here and there with trees. A large number of boys who had fallen off the raft or left it of their own accord wandered about on it. Heedless of danger, I jumped off the raft and dashed up to them. As I got close, I noticed that their eyes, ears and hair and even their hearts were covered with vermin that most viciously gnawed at them. One lad seemed to be in greater pain than the rest. I tried to get closer to him, but he ran away and hid behind a clump of trees. I saw others loosening their clothes to get some relief, exposing at the same time their waists girded with snakes or vipers clinging to their chests. To all I pointed out a gushing mineral spring. Whoever washed in its cool waters was instantly cured and could return to the raft. Most of the boys followed my suggestion, but some refused. Delaying no further, I beckoned to those who had been cured to follow me, and they did so without fear because the monsters had now vanished.

As soon as we were abroad the raft, the wind rose again and out we glided through the rest of the strait into the limitless ocean.

Sorrowing over the sad lot of those left behind, but grateful for Our Lady's protection, we thanked Her by singing "O Praise Her! O Bless Her." Instantly, as if by Mary's command, the wind abated and the raft began to glide rapidly and smoothly, as though propelled by the playful, backward push of the boys' hands on the water. Then a rainbow appeared in the sky, more marvelous and colorful than the northern lights. Inscribed on it was a mysterious word "MEDOUM." Though we had no idea what it meant, it seemed to me that its letters could stand for "Mary, Mother and Mistress of the Whole Universe."

After a long time we sighted land, and as we drew nearer, we felt an inexpressible thrill in our hearts. Before our eyes was the delightful sight of enchanting meadows dotted with trees of every kind, radiant with light as if the sun were rising behind the background of hills—a light whose soft brilliance, like that of a glorious summer evening, instilled a feeling of rest and peace.

Our raft finally came to shore, slid on the sand and stopped at the foot of a luscious vineyard. Of this raft we may well say, "O God, You gave us a bridge to enable us to cross the groundswells of this world and to reach Your safe harbor."

You were all very anxious to get into the vineyard, and a few of you, more eager than the rest, jumped off at once. But after only a few steps, remembering what had happened to their companions when the raft was going through the strait, those boys quickly ran back. All eyes were turned on me with the silent question: "May we?"

"Yes," I said after a moment's reflection. "It's safe."

Shouting with joy, you all ran out into those neatly arranged rows of vines and trees. From the vines hung clusters of grapes like those of the Promised Land, and the trees were laden with the choicest and most delicious fruit.

In the center of that very vast vineyard stood an imposing castle that was encircled by a most beautiful garden enclosed within massive walls. We headed for it and were allowed in. Tired and hungry, we reached a large, richly decorated dining hall. A long table held all kinds of food we could eat to our hearts' content. Toward the end of our meal, a richly clad, indescribably handsome young man came into the hall and warmly greeted each of us by name. Noticing our bewilderment and wonder at his beauty and the many splendid things we had seen, he remarked, "Friends, this is nothing! Come and see!"

We followed him. From the balconies he showed us the gardens, telling us that they were for our recreation. He then led us on a tour of the whole building and through halls ever more breath-taking for their architectural beauty. Finally, opening a door leading into a church, he invited us to step in. The church looked small from outside, but as soon as we walked in, we realized how wrong we were. It was so vast that we could hardly see the other end. The floor, the walls and the ceiling were exquisitely ornamented with marble, silver, gold, and precious stones. "How heavenly!" I exclaimed, bewildered. "I wouldn't mind staying here forever!"

At the center of this majestic temple, on a rich pedestal, stood a huge, magnificent statue of Mary Help of Christians. By now many of you had scattered about to admire the church's beauty. Calling you together, I asked you to gather in front of

Our Lady to thank Her for the many favors She had bestowed on us. I realized then how vast the church was! There were thousands of you, but it looked as if you were but a small group.

While we stood admiring the statue's heavenly beauty, to our great wonderment it suddenly seemed to come alive and smile.

"Her eyes are moving!" several cried out. Clearly, Our Lady was turning Her eyes with unspeakable motherly affection on all of you.

"Our Lady is moving Her hands!" you all exclaimed moments later. Indeed She was slowly opening Her arms and spreading Her mantle to gather us all under it. Tears of emotion ran down our checks.

"Her lips are moving," whispered a few. A profound silence fell over us.

"If you will be loving children to Me, I will be a loving mother to you!" Our Lady spoke.

At these words we all fell to our knees and broke into the song, "O Praise Her! O Bless Her!"

The singing was so heartfelt and sweet that I awoke, overwhelmed by it.

As you see, my dear children, we can recognize in this dream the stormy sea of this world. If you will readily obey me instead of listening to evil counselors, at the end of our lives, after struggling to do good and to avoid evil by overcoming our bad inclinations, we shall reach safe harbor. There we shall be met by Our Lady's messenger who, in God's name, will usher us into His most consoling presence to rest from our toils.

But if you disregard my advice and follow your own whims, you will be miserably shipwrecked.

Later on, privately, Don Bosco gave more detailed explanations of this dream, which seemingly concerned not only the Oratory but the Salesian Congregation as well:

The prairie is the world. The all-engulfing flood is its vices, irreligious maxims and persecution of the faithful. The grist mill, set apart in peace but equally threatened, is the House of Bread, the Catholic Church. The bread in the baskets is the

Holy Eucharist, the food for the voyagers. The raft is the Oratory. The tree trunk linking the mill to the raft is the Cross, symbolizing one's immolation to God through Christian mortification. The plank, placed by the boys as an easier bridge to the raft, is the transgression of the rule. Many boarded the raft for selfish, base motives: self-advancement, money, honors, comfort, higher status and so on. These were the ones who did not pray and even mocked those who did. The priests and clerics symbolize obedience and show the wonders of salvation that may be achieved by it. The whirlpools represent frightful past and future persecutions. The boys who set foot on the island that was flooded soon after are those who, despising their vocation, leave the Oratory to go back to the world. The same must be said of those who sought refuge on other rafts. Those who fell into the water, but held out their hands to their companions on the raft and, with their help, scrambled on it again, are the boys who, on unfortunately falling into sin, regain God's grace through sincere sorrow. The strait, the big cats, monkeys and other monsters signify the disturbances, enticements and allurements of sin. The vermin on the eyes, tongue, and heart symbolize immodest looks, foul talk and disorderly affections. The spring of healing water stands for confession and Communion. The miry swamp and the fire signify places of sin and damnation.

This does not mean, though, that all those who fell into the mud or into the fiery furnace are destined for hell. God forbid! It means that at that time they were in the state of mortal sin, and had they died then and there, they would certainly have been eternally lost. The verdant island and the church represent the Salesian Society solidly established and triumphant. The handsome youth welcoming the boys and leading them on a tour of the palace and of the church seemingly is a deceased pupil already in heaven—perhaps Dominic Savio.

This last explanation suggests that in this, as in other dreams of Don Bosco, there was a hidden meaning referring mainly to the Salesian Society. We must further remark that [in Don Bosco's dreams] every segment was supplemented by other simultaneous manifestations that completed and clarified it. Don Bosco did not deem it opportune to speak of these. We are led to this conclusion also from what Don Bosco told Father Julius Barberis in 1879—that in this dream of the flood and the raft, he had seen Father Cagliero crossing vast expanses of water and helping others to do the same, and that he and his companions had made ten stops. He was then foreseeing their journeys in [South] America. Likewise, in 1885, he declared that he had understood that this dream was related to the one he had had in 1854 foreshadowing Father Cagliero's episcopal consecration.

On the morning of January 2 [1866], the boys, anxious to know the state of their conscience, hastened to make their confessions to him in the sacristy. To one lad who confessed his sins, and then asked where and how Don Bosco had seen him in that mysterious dream, Don Bosco replied, "You were on the raft. As you were fishing, you fell into the water several times, but I pulled you back onto the raft each time."

"And did you see me also in the church?"

"Yes, yes," he replied smilingly.

To a seminarian from Vercelli who had stopped him in the playground to ask him about himself, he answered, "You were among those who hindered the rescuers."

And to a priest, "I saw you apart from the others busily readying fishing lines for the rescuers." He added a few more things which wondrously came to pass twenty years later but need not be mentioned here.   (Vol. VIII, pp. 143-150)

THERE ARE TEN OF US

From the 3rd to the 7th of July the Oratory pupils made a spiritual retreat preached by Father Lemoyne and Father Corsi. After praying to God to know how fruitfully the retreat had been made, Don Bosco had this dream which he later narrated to the community:

I seemed to be in a playground far larger than ours at the Oratory, totally surrounded by houses, trees and thickets. Scattered throughout trees and thickets were nests full of fledglings about to fly off to other places. While I was delightedly listening to their chirping, a little nightingale dropped in front of me. *Oh,* I exclaimed, *you fell! Your wings can't hold you yet and I'll catch you!* I stepped forward and reached out to pick it up. As I caught hold of its wings, the little bird shook itself free and flew to the center of the playground. *Poor little thing,* I thought to myself, *your efforts are vain. You won't be able to get away because I'll run after you and catch you.* And so I did, but again the bird fooled me the same way and flew off quite a distance. *Oh, so you want to match wits with me,* I said. *Well, we will see who is the winner!* I went after it a third time, but as though it purposely was trying to make a fool of me, it slipped out of my hands as soon as I caught hold of it and flew far off.

I was following its course, astonished at its daring, when suddenly a large hawk swooped upon it and, clutching it in its hooked talons, carrried it off as prey. I shivered to see it. Bewailing the foolishness of the incautious little bird, I kept following it with my eyes. *I wanted to save you,* I said to myself, *but you would not let me take hold of you. You even tricked me three times in a row, and now you are paying for your stubbornness.* Turning toward me, the nightingale feebly chirped three times. "There are ten of us...ten of us...." Startled, I woke up and naturally thought of the dream and of those mysterious words, but I could not make head or tail of them.

The following night the dream returned. I seemed to be in the same playground, fenced in by the same houses, trees and thickets. The same hawk with its grim expression and bloodshot eyes was near me. Blasting it for its cruelty to that poor little bird, I threatened it with my fist. It flew away in fright, dropping a note at my feet. Uneasily I picked it up and read the names of ten boys here present. I quickly grasped the full meaning. These were the boys who had no regard at all for the spiritual retreat, who had not set their consciences straight, and who, rather than return to God through Don Bosco, had preferred to yield to the devil.

I knelt down and thanked Mary Help of Christians for so graciously and singularly showing me those boys who had strayed from my side, and I promised Her that I would never cease to do my utmost to reclaim those lost sheep.

This report was by Father Berto and edited by Father Lemoyne. Father Berto presented it also during the Informative Process for the cause of our beloved father's beatification and canonization with this remark: "I recall that Don Bosco saw to it that those boys should be privately warned, and that one of them, who refused to change his conduct, was dismissed from the Oratory." (Vol. X, pp. 42-43)

FIRST DEATH AT THE ORATORY

One day in March, 1854, after Vespers, Don Bosco gathered all the boarders in a room behind the sacristy and told them that he wanted to tell them a dream. [John] Cagliero, [John] Turchi, [John Baptist] Anfossi, and the clerics [Felix] Reviglio and [Joseph] Buzzetti were among those present; our narration is based on their accounts. All of them believed that Don Bosco's dreams were true supernatural revelations. Don Bosco spoke as follows:

I was with you in the playground, delighted to see all of you so lively and happy, jumping, shouting, and running about. Suddenly, however, one of you came out of the building wearing some sort of top hat and began strolling around in the playground. The transparent headgear was lit from the inside and revealed the picture of a moon with the number '22' in its center. Amazed, I was about to walk up to the boy and tell him to cut off that nonsense when suddenly all of you stopped playing as if the bell had rung and lined up as usual on the porch by classes. It was now semidark. While all of you looked frightened, nearly a dozen of you were deathly pale. I passed in front of these pale ones for a closer look, and among them I saw the boy with the top hat. He was even paler than the rest, and a black drape—like those used at funerals—was hanging from his shoulders. I was about to ask him what his strange garb meant when a grave and dignified-looking stranger stopped me and said: "Wait! Know that this boy has only twenty-two moons to live. Before these are over, he will die. Take care of him and prepare him!" I wanted some explanation of this message and his sudden appearance, but the stranger had already vanished. My dear boys, I know who that lad is. He is right here among you.

Terror gripped all of the boys. This was the very first time that Don Bosco had ever predicted the death of anyone in the house publicly and so solemnly. He could not help noticing their fear, and so he continued: "Don't be afraid! True, I know that boy, and he is here now, but this is a dream, as I have said, and you know that dreams are only dreams. One thing is certain, though—we must always be prepared, just as Our Divine Savior has warned us in the Gospel, and never commit sin. If we follow this rule, death will not frighten us. Put your conscience in order, therefore, and resolve not to offend God anymore. On my part, I shall look after the boy of the twenty-two moons. These moons signify twenty-two months. I hope that he will die a good death."

Understandably, this announcement frightened the boys, but in the long run it did them good because their attention was focused on death as they kept themselves in God's grace and counted the months. Now and then when Don Bosco would ask: "How many more moons?" they would reply "Twenty" or "Eighteen" or "Fifteen" and so on. Sometimes those who paid the closest attention to everything he said would tell him that so many moons had already gone by, attempting at the same time to make their own predictions or guesses, but Don Bosco would say nothing. When [John Baptist] Piano entered the Oratory as a young student in November, 1854, he heard his companions say that nine moons had already passed. He then found out about Don Bosco's prediction and he too began keeping track of the moons.

The year 1854 went by, and so did many months of 1855, and then came October, the twentieth month. At this time the cleric [John] Cagliero was in charge of three adjoining rooms in the old Pinardi house. They served as a dormitory for several boys, including Secundus Gurgo a handsome, healthy, seventeen-year-old from Pettinengo (Biella) who seemed destined to live to a ripe old age. His father had asked Don Bosco to take him in as a boarder. The youth, an excellent pianist and organist, studied music assiduously and earned good money by giving lessons in town. From time to time during the course of the year Don Bosco had asked Cagliero about the conduct of his charges with more than routine interest. In October he called him and asked: "Where do you sleep?"

"In the last room," Cagliero answered. "From there I can keep an eye on the other two."

"Wouldn't it be better if you moved your bed into the middle room?"

"If you say so, but I think I'd better tell you that it is rather damp because one of its walls is actually the wall of the church tower, which is still very porous. Winter is coming and I might get sick. Besides, I can watch all the boys in the dormitory quite well from where I am!"

"I know you can," Don Bosco replied, "but it would be better if you moved into the middle room." Cagliero complied, but after a while he asked Don Bosco's permission to move his bed back to the last room. Don Bosco did not let him do so. "Stay where you are and don't worry," he told him. "You won't get sick!"

Cagliero felt at ease again. A few days later Don Bosco summoned him again. "How many sleep in your room?"

"There are three of us: Gurgo, Garovaglia, and myself—four, if you include the piano!"

"Good," Don Bosco said. "You are all musicians and Gurgo can teach you to play the piano. Make sure that you look after him well." That was all he said, but Cagliero's curiosity was aroused. Suspecting something, he tried to question Don Bosco, but he cut him short, saying: "You'll know in due time." The secret, of course, was that the boy of the twenty-two moons was in that room.

One evening, at the beginning of December, after night prayers, Don Bosco mounted the podium as usual to give the "Good Night" and announced that one of the boys would die before Christmas. We must note that no one at the Oratory was sick at that time. Naturally this announcement, coupled with the fact that the twenty-two moons would soon be over, made everyone jittery. There was much talk about what he had said as well as fear that it would come true.

During these days Don Bosco once more sent for the cleric Cagliero. He asked him how Gurgo was behaving and whether he returned to the Oratory punctually after giving his music lessons in town. Cagliero replied that the boy was doing fine, as were the other boys. "Good," Don Bosco said. "See that they keep it up, and let me know if anything goes wrong."

About the middle of December Gurgo had a sudden attack of abdominal pains so violent that the doctor, who had been summoned at once, recommended that the boy receive the *Last Sacraments.* The pains continued for eight days, but, thanks to Dr. Debernardi's care, they at last began to subside and Gurgo was able to get up again. The trouble apparently vanished, but—in the doctor's opinion—the boy had had a narrow escape. Meanwhile, his father had been informed. No one had, as yet, died at the Oratory, and Don Bosco wanted to spare the boys the sight of a funeral. The Christmas novena had begun and Gurgo—now almost completely recovered—was planning to go home for Christmas. Nevertheless, Don Bosco seemed to doubt the good news of the boy's recovery. His father arrived and, finding his son in good condition, asked permission to take him home for some further convalescence. He then went to book two seats on the stagecoach, intending to leave on the next day for Novara and Pettinengo. It was Sunday, December 23 [1855]. That evening Gurgo felt a craving for meat, although the doctor had forbidden it. Thinking that it would help to build his strength, his father went out to buy some and cooked it in a little pot. The boy drank the broth and ate the half-cooked meat—perhaps to excess. At bedtime his father retired for the night while Cagliero and the infirmarian remained with the boy. Sometime during the night Gurgo sufferered another very severe attack of colic. "Cagliero, Cagliero!" he gasped. "I'm through giving you piano lessons."

"Come now, don't say that!" Cagliero protested.

"I'll never see home again. Pray for me. Oh, what pains.... Pray to Our Lady for me."

"Of course I'll pray, and you do likewise."

Cagliero began praying but, overcome by fatigue, he soon fell asleep. He was suddenly awakened by the infirmarian who pointed to Gurgo and ran out to call Father Alasonatti whose room was next door. He came immediately, but within minutes Gurgo was dead. That morning Cagliero met Don Bosco as he was coming down the stairs on his way to say Mass. He had who clings to his own way pays with his own coin!" The raft too, tossed by the billows, threatened to sink. As you all turned to me pale and trembling, I tried to bolster you up.

"Take courage, sons," I shouted. "Mary will not forsake us!"

Then, one in heart and voice, we recited the acts of faith, hope, charity and contrition, several Our Fathers and Hail Marys and the Hail, Holy Queen. Finally, still kneeling and holding one another by the hand, we said a few more prayers privately.

Some foolish fellows however, ignoring the danger, stood up and began walking about as if nothing had happened, loudly laughing among themselves and almost making fun of their praying companions. Abruptly the raft stopped and swiftly spun round and round, while a furious wind swept all thirty of them into the deep, slimy water. In no time they disappeared. At this sight, more fervently than ever we invoked the protection of the Star of the Sea by singing the *Salve, Regina.* Soon the storm abated, but the raft kept going as if self-propelled—whither we did not know.

Meanwhile relentless rescue activity was going on, both to prevent boys from accidentally falling into the water and to pull them out promptly. Indeed, there were some who foolishly leaned over and lost their balance; then there were others who cruelly and unashamedly enticed companions to the raft's edge and pushed them over. For this reason, several priests were busy readying sturdy fishing poles and giving them out, while others were already at their rescue stations. As soon as a boy fell in, a pole would be lowered and the poor fellow would either grasp it or get hooked by his clothes and rescued. But even among the rescuers there were some who were more of a hindrance then a help. The young clerics meanwhile were kept busy holding back the boys, who, thank God, were still a great multitude.

I stood at the foot of a lofty mast in the center of the raft, surrounded by very many boys, clerics and priests ready to carry out my orders. As long as they followed my instructions, everything went on smoothly and we felt tranquilly happy and safe. But soon several began to complain that the raft was uncomfortable and the voyage too long, arduous and dangerous. Others argued about our destination or the means of escaping been informed of the death and looked very, very sad.

The whole Oratory was stunned. The twenty-second moon was not yet over. By dying shortly before dawn on December 24 Gurgo had also fulfilled Don Bosco's second prediction—namely that one of the boys would die before Christmas.

After lunch, the boys and the clerics silently gathered around Don Bosco. The cleric John Turchi asked him point-blank whether Gurgo had been the boy of the moons. "Yes," Don Bosco replied, "it was he; he was the one I saw in my dream." Then he added: "You may have noticed that some time ago I had him sleep in a special room. Into that same room I also moved one of the best clerics, John Cagliero, so that he could look after him constantly." As he said this, he turned to Cagliero and said: "The next time you'll know better than object to Don Bosco's arrangements. Do you understand now why I did not allow you to leave that room? I did not let you have your way because I wanted Gurgo to have someone to look after him. If he were still alive, he could tell you how often I spoke to him of death in a roundabout way and prepared him for it."

"I understood then," Bishop Cagliero later wrote, "why Don Bosco had given me those instructions. I learned to appreciate more and more his words and fatherly advice."

"I still remember," Peter Enria stated, "that on the evening of that day—Christmas Eve—at the "Good Night" Don Bosco was looking about as though searching for someone. After a while he said: 'Gurgo is the first boy to die here at the Oratory. He was well prepared and we hope he is now in heaven. I exhort you to be ever ready. . . .' He could say no more, so great was his grief at the loss of one of his boys."

(Vol. V, pp. 243-247)

DEATH'S MESSENGER

I must tell you a dream. Try to picture to yourselves the Oratory at recreation time loud with happy, boisterous youngsters. I seemed to be leaning out of the window of my room, watching boys joyfully playing their games, running, and dashing about the playground. Suddenly I heard a loud disturbance at the main entrance. I looked and saw a tall old man; he had a wide forehead, oddly sunken eyes, a long white beard, and white locks thinly falling about his shoulders. He was draped in a winding sheet which he clutched tightly in his left hand, while in his right he held a dark blue flaming torch. He advanced slowly and gravely, halting at times to search stoopingly about, as if trying to find a lost object. Unseen, he wandered about the entire playground several times, while the boys went on with their games.

Dumbfounded and puzzled, I kept watching him. He went up to the carpenter shop, halted before a boy who was playing *barra rotta* [a sort of cops-and-robbers game] and, extending a lanky arm, held the torch up to the lad's face. "He's the one, I'm sure," he muttered and brusquely nodded two or three times. Then abruptly he cornered the boy and handed him a note from the folds of his winding sheet. Taking it, the boy unfolded it and visibly paled as he read it.

"When?" he asked. "Soon?"
"Now," was the ghastly reply.
"Can't I finish the game?"
"You may be caught while you're playing."

It meant a sudden death. Trembling, the boy tried to say something, to plead, but somehow couldn't. Unclutching his robe, the stranger then pointed to the portico with his left hand: "Look," he said. "Do you see that coffin? It's for you! Quick, let's go!" In the center of the passageway leading into the orchard lay a coffin.

"I'm not ready.... I'm still too young to die!" the boy screamed. Silently the stranger quickly strode away.

As I tried to learn who he was, I woke up. From what I have said you may well understand that one of you must prepare himself because the Lord will soon call him into eternity. I know who he is because I saw the whole thing. I know the boy to whom the stranger handed the note. He is here now, listening to me, but I shall tell no one till after his death. However, I'll do all I can to prepare him for a happy death. Let each of you look after himself, for while he wonders who it is, he himself may be just the one. I have told you this because if I failed to do so, the Lord would ask me, "Why don't you speak up at the proper time?" So, let each one correct himself, especially during these last three days of the novena before the feast of the Annunciation. Pray especially for this purpose and, during these three days, say at least one Hail, Holy Queen to the Blessed Virgin for the boy who has to die. When he departs from this life, our several hundred prayers will greatly help him.

The Bonetti chronicle continues:

When Don Bosco stepped down, some asked him privately to tell them at least if that boy would die soon. He replied that this would unfailingly happen before two feast days beginning with the letter "P" and perhaps even before the first of those feasts; it might be two or three weeks.

This dream caused shudders; everyone feared he might be the one. As on previous similar occasions, it did a lot of good. Each one took heed of his spiritual welfare, and on the following day the boys went to confession in greater numbers than usual.

For several days many lads personally tried to get Don Bosco to tell them their fate, but they kept asking in vain. Two things stood out very clearly in their minds: death would be sudden and it would occur before two solemn feast days beginning with the letter "P"—obviously *Pasqua* [Easter] and *Pentecoste* [Pentecost]. The first fell on April 20. The Bonetti chronicle goes on:

There was a great hubbub at the Oratory on April 16 [1862] when a twelve-year-old boy, Louis Fornasio of Borgaro Torinese, died at home. There are several things to be said about him. When Don Bosco announced that one of the boys was to die, this lad, though by no means bad, began to be a model of good behavior. The first few days after the announcement he pestered Don Bosco to let him make a general confession. Reluctant at first, because the youngster had already made one before, Don Bosco finally relented as a special favor and heard his confession in two or three different sessions. Moreover, on the same day that he had asked for this favor, or on the day when he started his confession, the youngster began to feel slightly sick, and this condition persisted for the next few days. At this juncture, two of his brothers came to visit him and, seeing that he was ill, got Don Bosco's permission to take him home for a while. On this very day—or the day before—Fornasio had finished his general confession and had also received Communion. He went home with them, was on his feet for a few days, but then had to take to bed. His illness soon took a turn for the worse, affecting his brain and depriving him of speech and at times his consciousness. Of course, he could not make his confession or receive Communion. When Don Bosco, a good father, paid him a visit, Fornasio recognized him and tried to say something, but after vain efforts he broke into sobs while his whole family wept with him. He died the following day.

When this news reached the Oratory, several clerics asked Don Bosco whether Fornasio was the boy of the dream. Don Bosco gave them to understand that he was not. Nevertheless several believed that this boy's death had fulfilled the prediction. [At the "Good Night"] that same evening (April 16), Don Bosco announced Fornasio's death, remarking that it taught them all an important lesson. "Make hay while the sun shines," he said. "Let us not allow the devil to delude us into thinking we may put our conscience in order at the moment of death." When someone publicly asked him whether Fornasio was the boy destined to die, he replied that he would say nothing for the moment. He added, though, that it was usual at the Oratory for boys to die in pairs—one calling another—and that, therefore, we should still be on guard and heed Our Lord's advice: "You must be prepared in the same way. The Son of Man is coming at the time you least expect." (Mt. 24: 44)

When he descended from the platform, he said quite plainly to a few priests and clerics that Fornasio was not the boy of the dream.

On April 17, during after-dinner recreation, a crowd of boys kept pestering Don Bosco, "Tell us the name of the boy who is to die!" Smilingly, Don Bosco kept shaking his head, but they insisted, "If you don't want to tell us, then tell at least Father Rua." Don Bosco continued to shake his head.

"Just tell us his initial, then," several insisted.

"All right, I'll satisfy you in that," he replied. "He has the same initial as the name of Mary."

The disclosure spread like wildfire, but a guess was still difficult. More than thirty boys had surnames beginning with "M."
There were some skeptics too because a boy named Louis Marchisio was seriously ill and there were grave fears for his life. In fact, the following day, April 18, he was taken home. These skeptics, guessing that Don Bosco had been alluding to him, remarked, "Well, we too can predict that someone whose name begins with 'M' is going to die!"

... Bonnetti goes on to record:

A month had gone by since the prediction, and the healthy apprehension it had generated was now waning. Yet many kept wondering, "Who will die and when? *Pasqua* [Easter]—the first 'P'—is gone!"

Quite unexpectedly, on April 25, Victor Maestro of Viora (Mondovi), thirteen, died of a stroke. He was a very fine lad who went to Communion several times a week. To the very day of Don Bosco's prediction he was well, but two weeks before his death his eyes began bothering him and his vision dimmed in the evening. Two or three days before the stroke, he complained of slight chest pains, for which the doctor prescribed longer sleep.

One morning Don Bosco met him on the stairs. "Would you like to go to heaven?" he asked.

"Of course," Maestro answered.

"Then get ready!" The boy was startled for a moment, but then, thinking that Don Bosco had spoken in jest, he regained his composure. However, Don Bosco, keeping close to him for the next few days, prepared him properly and induced him to make a general, most consoling confession.

On April 24, a boy noticed Maestro sitting on the infirmary balcony. Impulsively he approached Don Bosco. "Is it true that Maestro is the boy who wants to die?" he asked.

"How would I know!" Don Bosco replied. "Ask him!"

The lad went up to the balcony and did just that. Maestro broke into a laugh and, going downstairs, asked Don Bosco to let him go home for a few days. "Surely," Don Bosco agreed, "but before you go, have the doctor give you a written report on your illness." The boy felt relieved. He had said to himself, *Someone is to die at the Oratory. If I go home, it can't be me. I'll have a longer [Easter] holiday and come back in perfect shape.*

The next day, Friday, April 25, Maestro got up with the others and heard Mass; then, feeling quite tired, he returned to bed, after telling his schoolmates how glad he was that he could go home.

When the bell rang for classes at nine, his friends wished him a happy vacation and a safe return, said good-bye, and went to school. Maestro was left alone in the dormitory. Toward ten, the infirmarian looked in to tell him that the doctor was expected soon, and that he should get up and report to the infirmary.

The doctor arrived shortly. A boy in the adjoining dormitory, who also had to see the doctor, went to Maestro's dormitory and called him loudly from the doorway. Hearing no answer, he called again. There was still no reply. Thinking that Maestro was sound asleep, he went to his bedside and shook him, calling his name. Maestro was motionless. Frightened beyond words, the lad screamed, "Maestro is dead," and dashed out to call someone. The first one he met was Father Rua who ran to Maestro's bedside in time to give him absolution as he died. Father Alasonatti, the prefect, was informed immediately, and I (Bonetti) went to call Don Bosco.

The news spread like lightning through classrooms and workshops. Boys came running and knelt down in prayer. Others, hoping that Maestro might still be alive, brought bedwarmers and cordials to revive him, but it was all useless. On first sight Don Bosco knew the boy was dead. Everybody was heartbroken, particularly because Maestro had died with no friend by him. Knowing the boys' grief, Don Bosco assured them of Maestro's eternal salvation. He had received Communion on Wednesday, and since the feast of All Saints he had especially behaved and was properly prepared for death. A steady flow of clerics and boys paid him their last respects. As they mourned him, they realized that his death had fulfilled Don Bosco's prediction.

That evening Don Bosco's "Good Night" moved all to tears. He called attention to the fact that within the last nine or ten days God had taken two of our companions, and neither had had a chance to receive the Last Sacraments. "How mistaken people are," he exclaimed, "to delay clearing their conscience till the end of their life. Let us thank the Lord for thus calling into eternity two companions who, we are sure, were spiritually ready. How much more would we grieve if others had been taken whose conduct is quite unsatisfactory."

Maestro's death was a blessing of the Lord. On Saturday morning and evening boys in great numbers wanted to make a general confession. With two or three words Don Bosco put their minds at ease. Later he said very plainly, "Maestro was the boy whom I saw receive the note in my dream. What deeply consoles me is that he went to the sacraments that very Friday morning, as several boys have assured me. His death was sudden but not unprovided."

Maestro's body was interred on the morning of Sunday, April 27. A remarkable incident fulfilled the prediction to the last detail. The mysterious stranger of the dream had handed a note to Maestro as he was standing in the portico facing the passageway leading to the orchard. From there he pointed out to the boy the coffin in the passageway only a few feet away.

When the undertaker and his assistants came, they carried the body down the central staircase, along the portico up to that passageway. There they stopped, sent for chairs, and placed the coffin on them as they waited for the priest and students who were to escort the body to the cemetery.

[Thus reads the Bonetti chronicle.]

We must point out too that John Cagliero [then a deacon], passing by, was distressed by this arrangement because, at other funerals, the coffin had customarily been set down at the far end of the portico near the door of the stairs adjoining the church. He was more displeased to learn that the morticians themselves had had the chairs removed from their customary place. He insisted that the coffin be placed at the usual spot, but the men gruffly refused.

Just then Don Bosco came out of church. Looking very sadly upon the coffin, he remarked to [John Baptist] Francesia and others, "What a coincidence! That's the way I saw it in the dream!" (Vol. VII, pp. 76-79, 81-83)

TWO-THIRTY

On Saturday, December 20 [1862], at the "Good Night," Don Bosco said these exact words: "By Christmas one of us will go to heaven." Since no one was sick, each looked rather uneasily after his own affairs. Sunday, December 21, passed uneventfully. No one was in the infirmary, as many of us verified personally. That evening, the play *Cosimus II Visits the Prisons* was presented on the Oratory stage. On December 22, after Christmas novena services, Joseph Blangino, a fine ten-year-old lad from Sant'Albano took sick and went to the infirmary. Within a few hours his condition became critical, and he was given up by the doctor.

What happened next was described in writing by Francis Provera:

The evening of December 23, Blangino received Holy Viaticum. At about ten, Don Bosco was in the infirmary talking with Father Rua about the boy's condition. "If you wish, I'll willingly sit up with him through the night," Father Rua said.

"It won't be necessary," Don Bosco replied. "There will be no danger until two in the morning. Go to bed now, but have someone call you at two. You will be needed then."

In fact, at that hour, Father Rua administered the Anointing of the Sick to the boy. At two-thirty Blangino died. The next morning, Don Bosco revealed that he had dreamed of the dying boy that night:

"I dreamed that Father Alasonatti, my mother (who has been dead these last six years), and I were nursing Blangino. Father Alasonatti was praying on his knees, my mother was smoothing up the bed, and I was sitting nearby. As she got close to the boy, she exclaimed, 'He's dead!'

" 'Is he?'

" 'Yes.'

" 'What time is it?'

" 'Almost three.'

" 'Would that all our boys could die so tranquilly,' Father Alasonatti remarked.

"That's when I awoke. Immediately I heard a very loud

banging on the walk as with a board. 'Blangino is now on his way to eternity,' I cried out. I opened my eyes to see if dawn had arisen but saw nothing. Certain of the youngster's death, I recited the *De Profundis.* The clock struck two-thirty."

(Vol. VII, pp. 204-205)

HE WILL CRY OUT FOR DON BOSCO

Albert C..., a strapping sixteen-year-old student, had taken a turn for the worse through the evil influence of Felix G..., a schoolmate of his native town. As was always the case in such instances, Albert shunned Don Bosco as much as he could. The latter sent for him several times, but Albert always balked. Finally, one November day, as he was rushing down the stairs, he found himself face to face with Don Bosco and blushed red as a beet.

"Albert, why do you keep running away from me?" Don Bosco asked, gripping his hand. "Don Bosco wants to help you. You must make a good confession as soon as possible." The boy pursed his lips. "You refuse?" Don Bosco went on. "The time will come when you'll ask for me and won't find me. Think it over seriously."

At the "Good Night" on Monday, December 1 [1862], Don Bosco urged the boys to make well the Exercise for a Happy Death because one of them would die before he could make another.

"He is right here among you," Don Bosco said, "but I can never get to him because he always steers clear of me. I have tried to speak to him of his soul, but to no avail, and yet one day he will call for me and I will not be around. In his last moments he will cry out for Don Bosco, but Don Bosco will not be found. He will yearn for him but in vain, because Don Bosco will be away, and he will die without ever seeing him again. I would very much like to talk to him, to help him straighten out within the short time left to him, but he keeps dodging me. Still, I'll secretly put a guardian angel at his side to lead him to me. He does not know and does not want to know that he is doomed to die [shortly]. He does not want to die, but it has been irrevocably so decreed. We shall prepare him, we shall remind him. The feasts of the Immaculate Conception and Christmas are propitious occasions. Let's hope that one of them may draw him to a good confession. But let him bear in mind that he will not be here for the next Exercise for a Happy Death."

The next day the whole Oratory was astir with this stunning prediction. Meanwhile Don Bosco told Francis Cuffia, the infirmarian—a student himself—to look after him prudently and try to persuade him to receive the sacraments, especially to go to confession as soon as possible since time was running out. Cuffia understood and strove to be a guardian angel, but his efforts failed.

Notwithstanding Don Bosco's frightening prediction, Albert was not troubled. His thinking went somewhat like this: *Don Bosco has the reputation of being a prophet. He said that someone would lead the doomed boy to him and that he would warn him. But I won't let myself be caught. Since he won't be able to warn me, I can't be the one he is talking about.*

His unfortunate ruse succeeded all too well. Through that entire month not once could Don Bosco even get a glimpse of him. The feasts of the Immaculate Conception and Christmas came and went, and Albert never even thought of mending his ways or going to confession.

According to the Oratory's time-honored custom, the Exercise for a Happy Death was scheduled for New Year's Day. Don Bosco was on the alert for a chance to be with Albert at least in his last moments. Unfortunately, at this very time Duchess [Laval] Montmorency invited him on behalf of the pastor of Borgo Cornalese, her property and residence, to preach the Forty Hours devotion on December 31, 1862, and January 1 and 2, 1863. A distinguished benefactress, she brooked no refusal. Though ostensibly an invitation, this was actually a command.

"I really cannot oblige this time," Don Bosco apologized. "I've something very urgent on hand. Please forgive me. I'll go out of my way to please you next time. . . ."

"Very well," she replied. "When you ask me to help your

197

boys, I too will tell you that I cannot!"

Despite her threat, Don Bosco dared add, "In those very days [of the Forty Hours devotion] the Oratory boys will make their Exercise for a Happy Death and go to Communion. I must hear their confessions. Please understand..."

"Forget it!" the duchess rejoined imperiously.

"In that case, I shall come," Don Bosco resignedly replied.

On Wednesday morning, December 31, Don Bosco sent for Chevalier Oreglia and Father Alasonatti. They knew he had to go to Borgo Cornalese. "I'll be away for three days," he told them. "Is it all right? Is anybody sick?"

"Have no worry. Everything is fine. The infirmary is empty." And so Don Bosco left.

Albert was in excellent health and in high spirits. In the dormitory, he was handed a letter from a certain Moisio, a friend of his who had left the Oratory the year before to enter the diocesan seminary. "Are you alive or dead?" his friend asked. "If you're alive, why don't you write?"

"I'm going to write to him that I'm dead!" Albert remarked after reading the letter to his companions.

So he did to the great amusement of all and mailed the letter. The rest of the day went by uneventfully. Like everybody else, Albert took part in the weekly walk. On their return, he was told to get the bread for the usual afternoon snack. He helped himself generously, eating it with salted fish and drinking plenty of water. Later, he went to supper and then to choir practice. When the bell rang for night prayers, he too went along, but toward the end of prayers he suddenly felt weak and close to fainting. Felix G..., a schoolmate, propped him up and with another boy helped him to the infirmary. No sooner was he in bed than excruciating stomach pains set in, and his throat began to swell. The doctor was sent for and did all that he could, but he soon realized that the case was very serious and that the patient should receive the Last Sacraments without delay. The infirmarian broke the news to Albert. Sensing his critical condition, the poor boy, grieved by his bad conduct, asked to make his confession. "Shall I call Father Alasonatti?" the infirmarian suggested. "No," Albert replied. "I want Don Bosco!" Boys ran all over the house looking for him, while the youngster kept repeating, "I want Don Bosco!

I want Don Bosco!"

He was greatly dismayed when he was told that Don Bosco was out. Uttering a heartrending cry, he broke into a flood of tears. Back into his mind flashed Don Bosco's words a month before. "I'm lost," he cried. "I'll die without ever seeing Don Bosco again! I always kept away from him because I didn't want to talk to him, and now God is punishing me."

He then asked for another priest. Felix G... ran to fetch Father Rua who came at once. Albert made his confession with true sorrow. Father Alasonatti, too, informed of the boy's critical condition, hastened to his bedside.

At peace with God, Albert turned to his two superiors. "Tell Don Bosco I am sorry. Tell him that though I don't deserve his pardon, I hope he will forgive me, just as I hope God has forgiven me. I'm truly sorry. I ask pardon of everybody..." Toward eleven-thirty, he edifyingly received Holy Viaticum, the Anointing of the Sick, and the papal blessing. Meanwhile, Felix G..., who had done his utmost to be helpful, stood in the corridor, looking in once in a while. Albert spotted him.

"Come in, Felix," he called. Felix stepped to the foot of the bed.

"It's your fault if I die without seeing Don Bosco," Albert went on reproachfully, "but I forgive you because I too need God's pardon. You know who is responsible for my becoming bad. But no more of that. You will see my father and mother. Tell them that I repented before dying and that I'll be waiting for them in heaven. But you—it's because of you that Don Bosco is not here now to comfort me!" Deathly pale, Felix could not utter a word.

Albert died around three o'clock on the morning of January 1, 1863. That same day, his friend Moisio, back in Casale, received Albert's letter with the message, "I am dead!"

(Vol. VII, pp. 205-209)

THE EAGLE

On February 1 [at the "Good Night"] Don Bosco had announced: "One of you will die, perhaps even before this month's Exercise for a Happy Death. If he lives long enough to make it, this will be the longest he will live."

The announcement had been prompted by a dream.

One night Don Bosco dreamed that he was walking into the playground with his usual guide during recreation time. Unexpectedly, a majestic, magnificent eagle appeared out of nowhere and began circling over the boys, gradually flying lower and lower. As Don Bosco gazed on in wonder, the guide said, "Do you see that eagle? It is after one of your boys."

"Which one?" Don Bosco asked.

"The one on whose head it will rest. Look!"

Don Bosco's eyes never left the eagle which, after wheeling about a little longer, finally spiraled down and perched on the head of thirteen year-old Anthony Ferraris of Castellazzo Bormida. Don Bosco recognized the boy perfectly and then awoke. To assure himself that he was awake he clapped his hands. Then, mulling over the dream, he silently prayed, "O Lord, if this is really going to happen, when will it be?"

He fell asleep again and once more he dreamed. His mysterious guide reappeared and said, "Ferraris will not live long enough to make the Exercise for a Happy Death more than once." He then vanished.

Ferraris's mother came to visit him. His condition was not then critical. After nursing him for a few days, she took Bisio aside and, believing Don Bosco to be a saint, she asked. "What does Don Bosco say about my son? Will he die?"

"Why do you ask?" Bisio replied.

"To know whether I should remain or return home."

"How do you feel about your son's condition?"

"As a mother I naturally wish him to recover, but I leave it to God to do what is best for him."

"Do you feel resigned to God's will?"

"Whatever God decides, I shall accept."

"And if your son were to die?"

"What can I say?"

At this display of Christian resignation, Bisio hesitated a little and then replied, "You'd better stay. Don Bosco has told me that your son is a good boy and is well prepared."

At these words that good Christian mother silently gave

vent to her grief. "I'll stay," she sobbed.

Bisio had suggested that she remain because, according to Don Bosco's prediction, the next Exercise for a Happy Death was only five or six days away.

Anthony Ferraris died on Thursday morning, March 16 [1865] after receiving the Last Sacraments. As the end came near, Don Bosco was at his bedside, whispering short prayers to him. He then gave the boy final absolution and read the prayers for the dying. The boy's death occurred, as predicted, before the next Exercise for a Happy Death.

John Bisio confirmed the story of his part in this episode by a formal oath, concluding as follows: "Don Bosco told us many other dreams concerning Oratory boys' deaths. We believed them to be true prophecies. We still do, because unfailingly they came true. During the seven years I lived at the Oratory, not a boy died without Don Bosco predicting his death. We were also convinced that whoever died there under his care and assistance surely went to heaven."

(Vol. VIII, pp. 35,39)

REQUIEM AETERNAM

After I told some people that I had had a dream, others kept asking me about it both in person and by mail. Hence, I will tell you about it, but just for the sake of speaking, because dreams come when one is asleep, and we are not to overrate them.

Throughout my illness you were always in my mind. Always, day and night, I talked about you, because my heart was constantly with you. Even when asleep, therefore, I dreamed about you and the Oratory. I paid you several visits, and consequently I can talk about your concerns even more knowingly perhaps than you can yourselves. Of course, I did not come bodily or you would have seen me.

One night, no sooner had I fallen asleep than I immediately found myself in your midst. I came out of our old church [of Saint Francis de Sales] and immediately spotted an individual in the corner of the playground adjacent to the portico leading to the visitors' lounge. This man was holding a writing tablet which listed all your names. He looked at me and immediately jotted something down. Then he moved successively to the corner near the old classrooms and to the bottom of the staircase leading up to my room, and in no time roamed through the whole playground checking things and taking notes.

Curious to know who he was and what he was writing, I tailed him, but he moved so fast I soon had to trot to keep up with him. He also went through the artisans' playground, checking and taking notes with astonishing speed. Anxious to find out what he was writing, I drew closer. Each line bore the name of a boy, beside which he would jot down something. While he gazed off here and there, I quickly flipped some pages and saw that some names had on the opposite page pictures of animals symbolizing the sins of those boys. Opposite one boy's name was the picture of a swine, with the inscription. "Man, for all his splendor, if he have not prudence, resembles the beasts that perish." (Ps 4: 21) Other names were marked on the facing page with a forked tongue and the legend: "... gossips and slanderers ... all who do such things deserve death; yet they not only do them but approve them in others." (Rom 1: 29-32) I saw also pictures of donkey ears, symbolizing evil talk, with the words: "Bad company corrupts good morals." (1 Cor 15: 33) Others had an owl or some other animal beside their names. I turned the pages very quickly and noticed that some names had not been written in ink and so were hardly legible.

At this point I took a close look at that individual and noticed that he had two reddish long ears. His face was as red as fire and his eyes seemed to flash with blood-red fiery sparks. *Now I know who you are*, I said to myself. Then he walked around the playground two or three more times, checking and taking notes. While he was busy with that, the bell rang for church. I headed toward it and immediately he followed me, stationing himself near the door, watching you as you passed through. He too went inside then and stood just in front of the altar rail gate, to keep an eye on you throughout the whole Mass. I didn't want to miss anything and so, noticing that the sanctuary door was slightly ajar, I stood there watching him. Father Cibrario was celebrating Mass. At the Elevation the boys recited the versicle "Blessed and praised every moment be the Most Holy and Divine Sacrament." At that precise moment I heard a resounding roar, as if the church were caving in. Both the stranger and his writing tablet vanished in smoke, leaving but a handful of ashes.

I thanked God for having thus overcome and driven the demon out of His house. I also realized that attending Holy Mass destroys all devilish gains and that the moment of the Elevation is especially terrible for him.

After Mass I walked out, convinced that I had gotten rid of that individual, but, instead, there he was just outside the door, huddled up, leaning with his back against the corner of the church. He wore a tattered red cap through which two long horns protruded from his head. "Ah, you are still here, you hideous beast!" I shouted. My cries startled poor Enria who was standing nearby, half-dozing. At that same moment I awoke.

This is my dream, and even though it was nothing more than a dream, I still learned something which had never before dawned on me. It is this: the devil, not content with keeping a record of the evil he sees being done because the Lord would not believe him on judgment day, uses the very words of Holy Scripture and of God's commandments to condemn [the guilty ones]. Thus he inflicts also the sentence.

Many of you might like to know whether I saw something about you in that tablet and whether your names were clearly legible. I can't talk about that now, but I will tell those who are interested privately.

I saw many other things in this dream. At times that individual hurled angry words at me and at someone who was with me, but since it would take too long, I'll tell you about it a little at a time.

I have many things to tell you about the past and present, but since so many of you keep asking me about that dream, I'll go into some detail, but briefly, lest it take too long.

I was asked whether I saw anything else after the writing tablet turned into ashes. Yes, as soon as it vanished with that ugly rascal, a cloud of sorts arose, and in its midst was a flag or banner bearing the inscription, "Grace Obtained!" I saw other things too which I did not want to tell you, lest you become swell-headed, but since you are all so good and virtuous (don't take me seriously), I'll let you in on the secret. I saw that during my absence you kept yourselves in God's grace. I can assure you that you have obtained many spiritual favors, including my recovery, for which you prayed so much. But this is not all. While I and someone else kept tailing that hideous monster, watching his every move, I was able to see that all your names were written in that tablet. Some pages had only two or three names followed by these dates: 1872, 1873, 1874, 1875, and 1876. Each date was followed by these words: *Requiem aeternam*—"Eternal rest." On another page I again saw those words but no names. I saw only as far as 1876, and counted *Requiem aeternam* twenty-two times, six referring exclusively to 1872.

In trying to understand this, because you know that dreams must be interpreted, I came to the conclusion that by 1876 we shall have to sing *Requiem aeternam* twenty-two times. I was hesitant about this interpretation. All of you being so healthy and strong, it seemed odd that so many should die by that year, and yet I could draw no other conclusion. Let us hope that what follows, i.e., "And let perpetual light shine upon them," may also come true, and that we may be able to say that such light indeed shines before our eyes.

Now I do not wish, nor is it proper, to disclose how many had the *Requiem aeternam* beside their names or who they were. Let us leave this among God's inscrutable secrets. Let us just strive to keep in God's grace so that, when our day comes, we may tranquilly present ourselves to Our Divine Judge.

Life is God's gift. By keeping us alive, He is constantly bestowing a gift on us. On my part, since I regained my health through your prayers—even though I was not too keen about recovering—I shall always strive to spend it in God's service and for your spiritual welfare, so that some day we may all enjoy God, who showers us so lavishly with benefits in this vale of tears.

Patient research into scholastic and administrative records of the Oratory and into the obituary kept by Father Rua revealed that indeed there were twenty-two deaths—six in 1872, seven in 1873, four in 1874, and five in 1875.

(Vol. X, pp. 38-41)

THERE IS NO DEAD BOY HERE

I fell asleep ... and dreamed that I was crossing the playground on my way toward the main entrance. When I got there I met two morticians.

"Whom are you looking for?" I asked in great surprise.

"The dead boy!" they answered.

"What are you talking about? There is no dead boy here. You have come to the wrong place."

"Not at all! Isn't this Don Bosco's Oratory?"

"Yes!"

"Well, we were told that one of your boys is dead and that we are to take his body away."

What's going on? I wondered. *I know nothing about it.* Meanwhile I was looking about for someone to talk to, but the playground was deserted. *Why is no one here?* I asked myself. *Where are all my boys? After all, it is daytime!* Still dumbfounded, I accompanied the two morticians to the portico and there saw a coffin. One side bore the boy's name and the date 1872; on the other were these dreadful words: ". . . this shall lie with him in the dust." (Jb 20: 11)

The morticians wanted to remove the body, but I would not let them. "I will never allow a pupil of mine to be taken from me without talking to him a last time before he goes." So saying, I went all around the coffin trying to pry it open, but I could not do so. I did not give up, however, and stood my ground, arguing with the morticians who were now becoming angry. One of them got so enraged that he dealt the coffin a mighty blow, bashing in its cover. The noise woke me up. Sad and mournful, I remained awake until morning. The first thing I did was to ask whether that lad was already back at the Oratory. Only when I was assured that he was playing with the rest of the boys did my sorrow abate a little.

This hapless pupil, apparently an artisan, was precisely the same youth to whom Father Louis Piscetta—a student at the Oratory in 1872-73—specifically referred during the Informative Process, as follows:

One evening in 1873 Don Bosco spoke to all the students and artisans at the "Good Night" and predicted, in my hearing, that a boy would die and that his death would serve as an example not to be followed. A month later, C...O..., fifteen, died, although at the time of the prediction he seemed perfectly healthy. When he fell ill, several priests approached him and earnestly begged him to set his conscience in order, but he obstinately refused under various pretexts. He lost his hearing and speech, and although he did somewhat regain these faculties shortly before dying, he still would not agree to go to confession and passed away without receiving the Last Sacraments. James Ceva was present at his death, and Charles Fontana and Michael Vigna witnessed his obstinate refusal.

Doubtless, Don Bosco did all he could to prepare the boy for that great step, but unfortunately he had to leave the Oratory for a few days. The hapless lad, who had been quite well, suddenly fell ill. Father Cagliero was notified and very tactfully tried to direct his thoughts to his soul, but the youth, barely fifteen, kept rejecting the urgency, claiming that he did not feel ready and wanted to be left alone. Father Cagliero visited him again and amiably engaged in small talk with him, but when he sought to question the boy about his personal life, the latter, sensing what this would lead to, fell silent after a few answers and turned his back to him. Father Cagliero went around to the other side of the bed, but again the boy turned his back without a word. This happened several times. He died without receiving the sacraments on the same day that Don Bosco was returning to the Oratory. He left a frightful impression on all the pupils which lasted a long time!

(Vol. X, pp. 44-46)

THE BOY WITH BLACK SPOTS

At the "Good Night" on November 11, 1873, Don Bosco narrated a dream he had had on November 8 and 10. We give it in Father Berto's version:

I dreamed that I was visiting the dormitories. You were all sitting up in bed. Suddenly a stranger appeared and, taking the lamp from me, said: "Come and let me show you something!"

I followed him as he went from bed to bed and kept raising the lamp so that I could see each boy's face. I looked carefully and saw each boy's sins written on his forehead. The stranger advised me to take notes, but, thinking I'd remember, I moved along a bit further, ignoring his advice. Soon, though, realizing that I had been overconfident, I retraced my steps and jotted everything in my notebook.

While going down the long aisle, my guide turned to a corner where, to my great joy, we saw a large number of boys whose faces and foreheads were as white and clean as snow. A little further, however, the stranger marked out one boy whose face was marred with black spots; as we went on, I saw many others in the same condition. I noted everything, saying to myself, *This way, I can warn them.* At last, as we reached the end of the dormitory, I heard a loud noise coming from a corner, followed by an awesome singing of the *Miserere.*

"Who died?" I asked my guide.

"The one with the black spots."

"Impossible! Just last night he was alive!"

Taking a calendar, he pointed to December 5, 1873. "This boy shall die before New Year's Day," he said. He then turned his back to me. I turned about too and awoke in bed.

This was just a dream, but similar dreams have already come true on other occasions. Dream or no dream, let us heed Our Lord's warnings to be ever ready.

When he was through speaking, pupils, clerics and priests crowded about him, anxious to know what he had seen on their foreheads. A large number, some of them clerics, did not go to bed until they had talked privately with him. Father Berto made the following entry in his notes:

As I was going with him to his room, he told me that the lamp used during his visit to the dormitories was the one he had in his room. Later, as we were pacing up and down, he added, "How little it takes to shake up the boys. No sermon could do as much. Yes, I must keep telling them these things."

"They will surely do a lot of good," I remarked. "You'll have quite a crowd for confessions tomorrow."

I also heard one boy say, "I don't want to ask him now [what he saw on my forehead] because I wouldn't have the courage to go to confession tomorrow...." The next morning, however, he did go to confession.

Commenting on the boys with spotted faces, he remarked, "One already asked me to tell him [what I saw]. I mentioned two or three things and he stopped me, saying: 'Enough! You know too much!'"

The next morning I saw that he too was going to confession. On December 4 the boy with the spotted face was still playing with his friends, but at five that afternoon he fell sick with the flu and was taken to the infirmary. During the night he made his confession and received the Last Sacraments; by morning the end seemed near. His parents came and took him to Saint John's Hospital, where at 11 that evening, December 5, he passed into eternity. (Vol. X, pp. 59-60)

A SHORT PATH

The following episode is told by Father Berto; we transcribe it from the Informative Process [for Don Bosco's beatification]:

At the "Good Night" on Tuesday, November 17, 1874, Don Bosco told the students that confessions would be heard the next day in preparation for the Exercise for a Happy Death, scheduled for Thursday. As usual, he urged us to make it well, saying: "I neither am nor wish to be a prophet, but I can tell you that one of us who is present will not be here to make it again. But I will not say who it is." As happened on similar occasions, on stepping down from the stand, he was instantly surrounded by the boys who were eager to know if it was their turn to die. His brief words drew a crowd of boys to his confessional both in the morning and on the evening of the following day, as well as on Thursday morning. They told me themselves that they all wanted to make a general confession.

Since I nearly always witnessed such examples of piety, I

can state that such predictions did our boys more good than ten spiritual retreats. And this was the only reason that prompted Don Bosco to foretell events, especially in public. He always urged us to keep these predictions to ourselves and not to write to outsiders about them.

The better to assure myself that his predictions were not just a pious trick on his part for our boys' spiritual benefit, two days later—Thursday evening, November 19, 1874—while speaking familiarly with him in his room, I confidentially asked how he could so boldly predict the death of so many boys at a time when they were healthy and strong. In particular, I singled out his prediction, just two days before, that most certainly one boy would die before the next Exercise for a Happy Death. Rather reluctantly, he answered: "I seemed to see all our boys walking toward a meadow, each on a path marked only for him. Some paths were very long, with signposts indicating the year 1874, 1875 and so on; others were not quite as long, and still others were much shorter. A few paths were very short and ended abruptly, marking the end of the boy's life. There were also extremely short paths that were strewn with snares. I saw one boy standing on the spot where his path ended. The barely legible signpost was inscribed '1875.' This boy will not have a chance for another Exercise for a Happy Death, since he will die in 1874; possibly he may barely see the dawn of 1875, but he cannot make this pious exercise."

As far as I recall—Father Berto continued—the prediction was fulfilled completely. I must add that we were so used to seeing these predictions verified that we would all have been astonished had any of them not come true. It would have been the exception to the rule. (Vol. X, pp. 66-67)

CHAPTER 5

Dreams About Heaven and Hell

The final category of dreams we will consider is of those which revolve around the Last Things: Judgment, Purgatory, Heaven and Hell. These were subjects that were very close to the heart of Don Bosco; he often spoke about them in his talks with the priests and boys of the Oratory. It is to be expected, then, that some of his most powerful dreams and visions concern heaven and hell. The imagery is graphic, the scenes vividly portrayed. We present these dreams for your prayerful reflection.

TO HELL AND BACK!

On Sunday night, May 3 [1868], the feast of Saint Joseph's patronage, Don Bosco resumed the narration of his dreams:

I have another dream to tell you, a sort of aftermath of those I told you last Thursday and Friday which totally exhausted me. Call them dreams or whatever you like. Anyway, as you know, on the night of April 17 a frightful toad seemed bent on devouring me. When it finally vanished, a voice said to me: "Why don't you tell them?" I turned in that direction and saw a distinguished person standing by my bed. Feeling guilty about my silence, I asked: "What should I tell my boys?"

"What you have seen and heard in your last dreams and what you have wanted to know and shall have revealed to you tomorrow night!" He then vanished.

I spent the whole next day worrying about the miserable

night in store for me, and when evening came, loath to go to bed, I sat at my desk browsing through books until midnight. The mere thought of having more nightmares thoroughly scared me. However, with great effort, I finally went to bed.

Lest I should fall asleep immediately and start dreaming, I set my pillow upright against the headboard and practically sat up, but soon in my exhaustion I simply fell asleep. Immediately the same person of the night before appeared at my bedside. (*Don Bosco often called him "the man with the cap."*)

"Get up and follow me!" he said.

"For heaven's sake," I protested, "leave me alone. I am exhausted! I've been tormented by a toothache for several days now and need rest. Besides, nightmares have completely worn me out." I said this because this man's apparition always means trouble, fatigue, and terror for me.

"Get up," he repeated. "You have no time to lose."

I complied and followed him. "Where are you taking me?" I asked.

"Never mind. You'll see." He led me to a vast, boundless plain, veritably a lifeless desert, with not a soul in sight or a tree or brook. Yellowed, dried-up vegetation added to the desolation. I had no idea where I was or what was I to do. For a moment I even lost sight of my guide and feared that I was lost, utterly alone. Father Rua, Father Francesia, and the others were nowhere to be seen. When I finally saw my friend coming toward me, I sighed in relief.

"Where am I?" I asked.

"Come with me and you will find out!"

"All right. I'll go with you."

He led the way and I followed in silence, but after a long, dismal trudge, I began worrying whether I would ever be able to cross that vast expanse, what with my toothache and swollen legs. Suddenly I saw a road ahead. "Where to now?" I asked my guide.

"This way," he replied.

We took the road. It was beautiful, wide, and neatly paved. "The path of sinners is smooth stones that end in the depths of the nether world." (Sir 21: 10) Both sides were lined with magnificent verdant hedges dotted with gorgeous flowers. Roses, especially, peeped everywhere through the leaves. At first glance, the road was level and comfortable, and so I ventured upon it without the least suspicion, but soon I noticed that it insensibly kept sloping downward. Though it did not look steep at all, I found myself moving so swiftly that I felt I was effortlessly gliding through the air. Really, I was gliding and hardly using my feet. Then the thought struck me that the return trip would be very long and ardous.

"How shall we get back to the Oratory?" I asked worriedly.

"Do not worry," he answered. "The Almighty wants you to go. He who leads you on will also know how to lead you back."

The road kept sloping downward. As we were continuing on our way, flanked by banks of roses and other flowers, I became aware that the Oratory boys and very many others whom I did not know were following me. Somehow I found myself in their midst. As I was looking at them, I noticed now one, now another fall to the ground and instantly be dragged by an unseen force toward a frightful drop, distantly visible, which sloped into a furnace. "What makes these boys fall?" I asked my companion. "They have spread cords for a net; by the wayside they have laid snares for me." (Ps 140: 6)

"Take a closer look," he replied.

I did. Traps were everywhere, some close to the ground, others at eye level, but all well concealed. Unaware of their danger, many boys got caught, and they tripped, they would sprawl to the ground, legs in the air. Then, when they managed to get back on their feet, they would run headlong down the road toward the abyss. Some got trapped by the head, others by the neck, hand, arms, legs, or sides, and were pulled down instantly. The ground traps, fine as spiders' webs and hardly visible, seemed very flimsy and harmless; yet, to my surprise, every boy they snared fell to the ground.

Noticing my astonishment, the guide remarked, "Do you know what this is?"

"Just some filmy fiber," I answered.

"A mere nothing," he said, "just plain human respect."

Seeing that many boys were being caught in those traps, I asked, "Why do so many get caught? Who pulls them down?"

"Go nearer and you will see!" he told me.

I followed his advice but saw nothing peculiar.

"Look closer," he insisted.

I picked up one of the traps and tugged. I immediately felt some resistance. I pulled harder, only to feel that, instead of drawing the thread closer, I was being pulled down myself. I did not resist and soon found myself at the mouth of a frightful cave. I halted, unwilling to venture into that deep cavern, and again started pulling the thread toward me. It gave a little, but only through great effort on my part. I kept tugging, and after a long while a huge, hideous monster emerged, clutching a rope to which all those traps were tied together. He was the one who instantly dragged down anyone who got caught in them. *It won't do to match my strength with his,* I said to myself. *I'll certainly lose. I'd better fight him with the Sign of the Cross and with short invocations.*

Then I went back to my guide. "Now you know who he is," he said to me.

"I surely do! It is the devil himself!"

Carefully examining many of the traps, I saw that each bore an inscription: Pride, Disobedience, Envy, Sixth Commandment, Theft, Gluttony, Sloth, Anger and so on. Stepping back a bit to see which ones trapped the greater number of boys, I discovered that the most dangerous were those of impurity, disobedience, and pride. In fact, these three were linked together. Many other traps also did great harm, but not as much as the first two. Still watching, I noticed many boys running faster than others. "Why such haste?" I asked.

"Because they are dragged by the snare of human respect."

Looking even more closely, I spotted knives among the traps. A providential hand had put them there for cutting oneself free. The bigger ones, symbolizing meditation, were for use against the trap of pride; others, not quite as big, symbolized spiritual reading well made. There were also two swords representing devotion to the Blessed Sacrament, especially through frequent Holy Communion, and to the Blessed Virgin. There was also a hammer symbolizing confession, and other knives signifying devotion to Saint Joseph, to Saint Aloysius, and to other saints. By these means quite a few boys were able to free themselves or evade capture.

Indeed I saw some lads walking safely through all those traps, either by good timing before the trap sprung on them or by making it slip off them if they got caught.

When my guide was satisfied that I had observed everything, he made me continue along that rose-hedged road, but the farther we went the scarcer the roses became. Long thorns began to show up, and soon the roses were no more. The hedges became sun-scorched, leafless, and thorn-studded. Withered branches torn from the bushes lay criss-crossed along the roadbed, littering it with thorns and making it impassable. We had come now to a gulch whose steep sides hid what lay beyond. The road, still sloping downward, was becoming ever more horrid, rutted, guttered, and bristling with rocks and boulders. I lost track of all my boys, most of whom had left this treacherous road for other paths.

I kept going, but the farther I advanced, the more arduous and steep became the descent, so that I tumbled and fell several times, lying prostrate until I could catch my breath. Now and then my guide supported me or helped me to rise. At every step my joints seemed to give way, and I thought my shinbones would snap. Panting, I said to my guide, "My good fellow, my legs won't carry me another step. I just can't go any farther."

He did not answer but continued walking. Taking heart, I followed until, seeing me soaked in perspiration and thoroughly exhausted, he led me to a little clearing alongside the road. I sat down, took a deep breath, and felt a little better. From my resting place, the road I had already traveled looked very steep, jagged, and strewn with loose stones, but what lay ahead seemed so much worse that I closed my eyes in horror.

"Let's go back," I pleaded. "If we go any farther, how shall we ever get back to the Oratory? I will never make it up this slope."

"Now that we have come so far, do you want me to leave you here?" my guide sternly asked.

At this threat, I wailed, "How can I survive without your help?"

"Then follow me."

We continued our descent, the road now becoming so frightfully steep that it was almost impossible to stand erect. And then, at the bottom of this precipice, at the entrance of a dark valley, an enormous building loomed into sight, its towering portal, tightly locked, facing our road. When I finally got to the bottom, I became smothered by a suffocating heat, while a greasy, green-tinted smoke lit by flashes of scarlet flames rose from behind those enormous walls which loomed higher than mountains.

"Where are we? What is this?" I asked my guide.

"Read the inscription on that portal and you will know."

I looked up and read these words: "The place of no reprieve." I realized that we were at the gates of hell. The guide led me all around this horrible place. At regular distances, bronze portals like the first overlooked precipitous descents; on each was an inscription, such as: "Out of my sight, you condemned, into that everlasting fire prepared for the devil and his angels." (Mt 25: 41) "Every tree that does not bear good fruit is cut down and thrown into the fire." (Mt 7: 19)

I tried to copy them into my notebook, but my guide restrained me: "There is no need. You have them all in Holy Scripture. You even have some of them inscribed in your porticoes."

At such a sight I wanted to turn back and return to the Oratory. As a matter of fact, I did start back, but my guide ignored my attempt. After trudging through a steep, never-ending ravine, we again came to the foot of the precipice facing the first portal. Suddenly the guide turned to me. Upset and startled, he motioned to me to step aside. "Look!" he said.

I looked up in terror and saw in the distance someone racing down the path at an uncontrollable speed. I kept my eyes on him, trying to identify him, and as he got closer, I recognized him as one of my boys. His disheveled hair was partly standing upright on his head and partly tossed back by the wind. His arms were outstretched as though he were thrashing the water in an attempt to stay afloat. He wanted to stop, but could not. Tripping on the protruding stones, he kept falling even faster. "Let's help him, let's stop him," I shouted, holding out my hands in a vain effort to restrain him.

"Leave him alone," the guide replied.

"Why?"

"Don't you know how terrible God's vengeance is? Do you think you can restrain one who is fleeing from His just wrath?"

Meanwhile the youth had turned his fiery gaze backward in an attempt to see if God's wrath were still pursuing him. The next moment he fell tumbling to the bottom of the ravine and crashed against the bronze portal as though he could find no better refuge in his flight.

"Why was he looking backward in terror?" I asked.

"Because God's wrath will pierce hell's gates to reach and torment him even in the midst of fire!"

As the boy crashed into the portal, it sprang open with a roar, and instantly a thousand inner portals opened with a deafening clamor as if struck by a body that had been propelled by an invisible, most violent, irrestible gale. As these bronze doors—one behind the other, though at a considerable distance from each other—remained momentarily open, I saw far into the distance something like furnace jaws sprouting fiery balls the moment the youth hurtled into it. As swiftly as they had opened, the portals then clanged shut again. For a third time I tried to jot down the name of that unfortunate lad, but the guide again restrained me. "Wait," he ordered. "Watch!"

Three other boys of ours, screaming in terror and with arms outstretched, were rolling down one behind the other like massive rocks. I recognized them as they too crashed against the portal. In that split second, it sprang open and so did the other thousand. The three lads were sucked into that endless corridor amid a long-drawn, fading, infernal echo, and then the portals clanged shut again. At intervals, many other lads came tumbling down after them. I saw one unlucky boy being pushed down the slope by an evil companion. Others fell singly or with others, arm in arm or side by side. Each of them bore the name of his sin on his forehead. I kept calling to them as they hurtled down, but they did not hear me. Again the portals would open thunderously and slam shut with a rumble. Then, dead silence!

"Bad companions, bad books, and bad habits," my guide exclaimed, "are mainly responsible for so many eternally lost."

The traps I had seen earlier were indeed dragging the boys to ruin. Seeing so many going to perdition, I cried out disconsolately, "If so many of our boys end up this way, we are working in vain. How can we prevent such tragedies?"

"This is their present state," my guide replied, "and that is where they would go if they were to die now."

"Then let me jot down their names so that I may warn them and put them back on the path to heaven."

"Do you really believe that some of them would reform if you were to warn them? Then and there your warning might impress them, but soon they will forget it, saying, 'It was just a dream,' and they will do worse than before. Others, realizing they have been unmasked, will receive the sacraments, but this will be neither spontaneous nor meritorious; others will go to confession because of a momentary fear of hell but will still be attached to sin."

"Then is there no way to save these unfortuante lads? Please, tell me what I can do for them."

"They have superiors; let them obey them. They have rules; let them observe them. They have the sacraments; let them receive them."

Just then a new group of boys came hurtling down and the portals momentarily opened. "Let's go in," the guide said to me.

I pulled back in horror. I could not wait to rush back to the Oratory to warn the boys lest others might be lost as well.

"Come," my guide insisted. "You'll learn much. But first tell me: Do you wish to go alone or with me?" He asked this to make me realize that I was not brave enough and therefore needed his friendly assistance.

"Alone inside that horrible place?" I replied. "How will I ever be able to find my way out without your help?" Then a thought came to my mind and aroused my courage. *Before one is condemned to hell,* I said to myself, *he must be judged. And I haven't been judged yet!*

"Let's go," I exclaimed resolutely. We entered that narrow, horrible corridor and whizzed through it with lightning speed. Threatening inscriptions shone eerily over all the inner gateways. The last one opened into a vast, grim courtyard with a large, unbelievably forbidding entrance at the far end. Above it stood this inscription: "Those will go off to eternal punishment." (Mt. 25: 46) The walls all about were similarly inscribed. I asked my guide if I could read them, and he consented. These were the inscriptions:

"He will send fire and worms into their flesh, and they shall burn and suffer forever." (Jdt 16: 17)

"There they will be tortured day and night forever and ever." (Rv 20: 10)

"... and the smoke of their torment shall rise forever and ever." (Rv 14: 11)

"The black, disordered land where darkness is the only light." (Jb 10: 22)

"There is no peace for the wicked." (Is 48: 22)

"Wailing will be heard there, and the grinding of teeth." (Mt 8: 12)

While I moved from one inscription to another, my guide, who had stood in the center of the courtyard, came up to me.

"From here on," he said, "no one may have a helpful companion, a comforting friend, a loving heart, a compassionate glance, or a benevolent word. All this is gone forever. Do you just want to see or would you rather experience these things yourself?"

"I only want to see!" I answered.

"Then come with me," my friend added, and, taking me in tow, he stepped through that gate into a corridor at whose far end stood an observation platform, closed by a huge, single crystal pane reaching from the pavement to the ceiling. As soon as I crossed its threshold, I felt an indescribable terror and dared not take another step. Ahead of me I could see something like an immense cave which gradually disappeared into recesses sunk far into the bowels of the mountains. They were all ablaze, but theirs was not an earthly fire with leaping tongues of flames. The entire cave—walls, ceiling, floor, iron, stones, wood, and coal—everything was a glowing white at temperatures of thousands of degrees. Yet the fire did not incinerate, did not consume. I simply can't find words to describe the cavern's horror.

"Broad and deep it is piled with dry grass and wood in abundance. And the breath of the Lord, like a stream of sulfur, will set it afire." (Is 30: 33)

I was staring in bewilderment about me when a lad dashed out of a gate. Seemingly unaware of anything else, he emitted a most shrilling scream, like one who is about to fall into a cauldron of liquid bronze, and plummeted into the center of the cave. Instantly he too became incandescent and perfectly motionless, while the echo of his dying wail lingered for an instant more.

Terribly frightened, I stared briefly at him for a while. He seemed to be one of my Oratory boys. "Isn't he so and so?" I asked my guide.

"Yes," was the answer.

"Why is he so still, so incandescent?"

"You chose to see," he replied. "Be satisfied with that. Just keep looking. Besides, "Everyone will be salted with fire." (Mk 9: 49)

As I looked again, another boy came hurtling down into the cave at breakneck speed. He too was from the Oratory. As he fell, so he remained. He too emitted one single heart-rending shriek that blended with the last echo of the scream that came from the youth who had preceded him. Other boys kept hurtling in the same way in increasing numbers, all screaming the same way and then all becoming equally motionless and incandescent. I noticed that the first seemed frozen to the spot, one hand and one foot raised into the air; the second boy seemed bent almost double to the floor. Others stood or hung in various other positions, balancing themselves on one foot or hand, sitting or lying on their backs or on their sides, standing or kneeling, hands clutching their hair. Briefly, the scene resembled a large statuary group of youngsters cast into ever more painful postures. Other lads hurtled into that same furnace. Some I knew; others were strangers to me. I then recalled what is written in the Bible to the effect that as one falls into hell, so he shall forever remain. ". . . wherever it falls, there shall it lie." (Eccl 11: 3)

More frightened than ever, I asked my guide, "When these boys come dashing into this cave, don't they know where they are going?"

"They surely do. They have been warned a thousand times, but they still choose to rush into the fire because they do not detest sin and are loath to forsake it. Furthermore, they despise and reject God's incessant, merciful invitations to do penance. Thus provoked, Divine Justice harries them, hounds them, and goads them on so that they cannot halt until they reach this place."

"Oh, how miserable these unfortunate boys must feel in knowing they no longer have any hope," I exclaimed.

"If you really want to know their innermost frenzy and fury, go a little closer," my guide remarked.

I took a few steps forward and saw that many of those

poor wretches were savagely striking at each other like mad dogs. Others were clawing their own faces and hands, tearing their own flesh and spitefully throwing it about. Just then the entire ceiling of the cave became as transparent as crystal and revealed a patch of heaven and their radiant companions safe for all eternity.

The poor wretches, fuming and panting with envy, burned with rage because they had once ridiculed the just. "The wicked man shall see it and be vexed; he shall gnash his teeth and pine away..." (Ps 112: 10)

"Why do I hear no sound?" I asked my guide.

"Go closer!" he advised.

Pressing my ear to the crystal window, I heard screams and sobs, blasphemies and imprecations against the saints. It was a tumult of voices and cries, shrill and confused.

"When they recall the happy lot of their good companions," he replied, "they are obliged to admit: "His life we accounted madness, and his death dishonored. See how he is accounted among the sons of God; and how his lot is with the saints! We, then, have strayed from the way of truth..."
(Wis 5: 4-6)

"We had our fill of the ways of mischief and ruin. We journeyed through impassable deserts, but the way of the Lord we knew not. What did our pride avail us?... All of them passed like a shadow." (Wis 5: 7-9)

"Such are the mournful chants which shall echo here throughout eternity. But their shouts, their efforts and their cries are all in vain... terrors shall fall upon them."
(Jb 20: 25)

"Here time is no more. Here is only eternity."

While I viewed the condition of many of my boys in utter terror, a thought suddenly struck me. "How can these boys be damned?" I asked. "Last night they were still alive at the Oratory!"

"The boys you see here," he answered, "are all dead to God's grace. Were they to die now or persist in their evil ways, they would be damned. But we are wasting time. Let us go on."

He led me away and we went down through a corridor into a lower cavern, at whose entrance I read: "Their worm shall not die, nor their fire be extinguished." (Is 66: 24) "He will send fire and worms into their flesh, and they shall burn and suffer forever." (Jdt 16: 17)

Here one could see how atrocious was the remorse of those who had been pupils in our schools. What a torment was theirs to remember each unforgiven sin and its just punishment, the countless, even extraordinary means they had had to mend their ways, persevere in virtue, and earn paradise, and their lack of response to the many favors promised and bestowed by the Virgin Mary. What a torture to think that they could have been saved so easily, yet now are irredeemably lost, and to remember the many good resolutions made and never kept. Hell is indeed paved with good intentions!

In this lower cavern I again saw those Oratory boys who had fallen into the fiery furnace. Some are listening to me right now; others are former pupils or even strangers to me. I drew closer to them and noticed that they were all covered with worms and vermin which gnawed at their vitals, hearts, eyes, hands, legs, and entire bodies so ferociously as to defy description. Helpless and motionless, they were a prey to every kind of torment. Hoping I might be able to speak with them or to hear something from them, I drew even closer but no one spoke or even looked at me. I then asked my guide why, and he explained that the damned are totally deprived of freedom. Each must fully endure his own punishment, with absolutely no reprieve whatever.

"And now," he added, "you too must enter that cavern."

"Oh, no!" I objected in terror. "Before going to hell, one has to be judged. I have not been judged yet, and so I will not go to hell!"

"Listen," he said, "what would you rather do: visit hell and save your boys, or stay outside and leave them in agony?"

For a moment I was struck speechless. "Of course I love my boys and wish to save them all," I replied, "but isn't there some other way out?"

"Yes, there is a way," he went on, "provided you do all you can."

I breathed more easily and instantly said to myself, *I don't mind slaving if I can rescue these beloved sons of mine from such torments.*

"Come inside then," my friend went on, "and see how our

good, almighty God lovingly provides a thousand means for guiding your boys to penance and saving them from everlasting death."

Taking my hand, he led me into the cave. As I stepped in, I found myself suddenly transported into a magnificent hall whose curtained glass doors concealed more entrances.

Above one of them I read this inscription: *The Sixth Commandment.* Pointing to it, my guide exclaimed, "Transgressions of this commandment caused the eternal ruin of many boys."

"Didn't they go to confession?"

"They did, but they either omitted or insufficiently confessed the sins against the beautiful virtue of purity, saying for instance that they had committed such sins two or three times when it was four or five. Other boys may have fallen into that sin but once in their childhood, and, through shame, never confessed it or did so insufficiently. Others were not truly sorry or sincere in their resolve to avoid it in the future. There were even some who, rather than examine their conscience, spent their time trying to figure out how best to deceive their confessor. Anyone dying in this frame of mind chooses to be among the damned, and so he is doomed for all eternity. Only those who die truly repentant shall be eternally happy. Now do you want to see why our merciful God brought you here?" He lifted the curtain and I saw a group of Oratory boys—all known to me—who were there because of this sin. Among them were some whose conduct seems to be good.

"Now you will surely let me take down their names so that I may warn them individually," I exclaimed.

"It won't be necessary!"

"Then what do you suggest I tell them?"

"Always preach against immodesty. A generic warning will suffice. Bear in mind that even if you did admonish them individually, they would promise, but not always in earnest. For a firm resolution, one needs God's grace which will not be denied to your boys if they pray. God manifests His power especially by being merciful and forgiving. On your part, pray and make sacrifices. As for the boys, let them listen to your admonitions and consult their conscience. It will tell them what to do."

We spent the next half hour discussing the requisites of a good confession. Afterward, my guide several times exclaimed in a loud voice, *"Avertere! Avertere!"*

"What do you mean?" I asked.

"Change life!"

Perplexed, I bowed my head and made as if to withdraw, but he held me back.

"You haven't seen everything yet," he explained.

He turned and lifted another curtain bearing this inscription: "Those who want to be rich are falling into temptation and a trap." (1 Tm. 6: 9)

"This does not apply to my boys," I countered, "because they are as poor as I am. We are not rich and do not want to be. We give it no thought."

As the curtain was lifted, however, I saw a group of boys, all known to me. They were in pain, like those I had seen before. Pointing to them, my guide remarked, "As you see, the inscription does apply to your boys."

"But how?" I asked.

"Well," he said, "some boys are so attached to material possessions that their love of God is lessened. Thus they sin against charity, piety, and meekness. Even the mere desire of riches can corrupt the heart, especially if such a desire leads to injustice. Your boys are poor, but remember that greed and idleness are bad counselors. One of your boys committed substantial thefts in his native town, and though he could make restitution, he gives it not a thought. There are others who try to break into the pantry or the prefect's or economer's office; those who rummage in their companions' trunks for food, money, or possessions; those who steal stationery and books...."

After naming these boys and others as well, he continued, "Some are here for having stolen clothes, linen, blankets, and coats from the Oratory wardrobe in order to send them home to their families; others for willful, serious damage; others, yet, for not having given back what they had borrowed or for having kept sums of money they were supposed to hand over to the superior. Now that you know who these boys are," he concluded, "admonish them. Tell them to curb all vain, harmful desires, to obey God's law and to safeguard their reputation jealously lest greed lead them to greater excesses and plunge them into sorrow, death, and damnation."

I couldn't understand why such dreadful punishments should be meted out for infractions that boys thought so little of, but my guide shook me out of my thoughts by saying: "Recall what you were told when you saw those spoiled grapes on the vine." With these words he lifted another curtain which hid many of our Oratory boys, all of whom I recognized instantly. The inscription on the curtain read: *The root of all evils.*

"Do you know what that means?" he asked me immediately.

"What sin does that refer to?"

"Pride?"

"No!"

"And yet I have always heard that pride is the root of all evil."

"It is, generally speaking, but, specifically, do you know what led Adam and Eve to commit the first sin for which they were driven away from their earthly paradise?"

"Disobedience?"

"Exactly! Disobedience is the root of all evil."

"What shall I tell my boys about it?"

"Listen carefully: the boys you see here are those who prepare such a tragic end for themselves by being disobedient. So-and-so and so-and-so, who you think went to bed, leave the dormitory later in the night to roam about the playground, and, contrary to orders, they stray into dangerous areas and up scaffolds, endangering even their lives. Others go to church, but, ignoring recommendations, they misbehave; instead of praying, they daydream or cause a disturbance. There are also those who make themselves comfortable so as to doze off during church services, and those who only make believe they are going to church. Woe to those who neglect prayer! He who does not pray dooms himself to perdition. Some are here because, instead of singing hymns or saying the Little Office of the Blessed Virgin, they read frivolous or—worse yet—forbidden books." He then went on mentioning other serious breaches of discipline.

When he was done, I was deeply moved.

"May I mention all these things to my boys?" I asked, looking at him straight in the eye.

"Yes, you may tell them whatever you remember."

"What advice shall I give them to safeguard them from such a tragedy?"

"Keep telling them that by obeying God, the Church, their parents, and their superiors, even in little things, they will be saved."

"Anything else?"

"Warn them against idleness. Because of idleness David fell into sin. Tell them to keep busy at all times, because the devil will not then have a chance to tempt them."

I bowed my head and promised. Faint with dismay, I could only mutter, "Thanks for having been so good to me. Now, please lead me out of here."

"All right, then, come with me." Encouragingly he took my hand and held me up because I could hardly stand on my feet. Leaving that hall, in no time at all we retraced our steps through that horrible courtyard and the long corridor. But as soon as we stepped across the last bronze portal, he turned to me and said, "Now that you have seen what others suffer, you too must experience a touch of hell."

"No, no!" I cried in terror.

He insisted, but I kept refusing.

"Do not be afraid," he told me; "just try it. Touch this wall."

I could not muster enough courage and tried to get away, but he held me back. "Try it," he insisted. Gripping my arm firmly, he pulled me to the wall. "Only one touch," he commanded, "so that you may say you have both seen and touched the walls of eternal suffering and that you may understand what the last wall must be like if the first is so unendurable. Look at this wall!"

I did intently. It seemed incredibly thick. "There are a thousand walls between this and the real fire of hell," my guide continued. "A thousand walls encompass it, each a thousand measures thick and equally distant from the next one. Each measure is a thousand miles. This wall therefore is millions and millions of miles from hell's real fire. It is just a remote rim of hell itself."

When he said this, I instinctively pulled back, but he seized my hand, forced it open, and pressed it against the first of the thousand walls. The sensation was so utterly excruciating that I leaped back with a scream and found myself sitting up in bed. My hand was stinging and I kept rubbing it to ease the pain. When I got up this morning I noticed that it was swollen. Having my hand pressed against the wall, though only in a dream, felt so real that, later, the skin of my palm peeled off.

Bear in mind that I have tried not to frighten you very much, and so I have not described these things in all their horror as I saw them and as they impressed me. We know that Our Lord always portrayed hell in symbols because, had He described it as it really is, we would not have understood Him. No mortal can comprehend these things. The Lord knows them and He reveals them to whomever He wills.

The next several nights I could not fall asleep because I was still upset by this frightful dream. What I told you is but a brief summary of very lengthy dreams. Later I shall talk to you about human respect, the Sixth and Seventh Commandments, and pride. I shall do nothing more than explain these dreams, which fully accord with Holy Scripture. In fact, they are but a commentary on the Bible's teachings on these matters. Some nights ago I told you something, but I'll tell you the rest and explain it whenever I have a chance to speak to you.

Don Bosco kept his promise. Later, he narrated this dream in a condensed form to the boys of our schools in Mirabello and Lanzo. In the retelling he introduced variations but made no substantial change. Likewise, when he spoke of it privately to Salesian priests and clerics, with whom he enjoyed greater familiarity, he would add new particulars. Occasionally he omitted details when talking to some people, while revealing them to others. Concerning the devil's traps, while discussing bad habits, he elaborated on the devil's tactics for luring victims to hell. Of many scenes he offered no explanation. For instance, he said nothing about the majestic figures he saw in that magnificent hall, which we are inclined to call "the treasure house of God's mercy for saving boys who would otherwise perish." Were these persons perhaps the principal dispensers of countless graces?

Some variations in his narration stemmed from the multiplicity of simultaneous scenes. As they flashed back into his mind, he would select what he considered most suited to his audience. After all, meditating on the Four Last Things was a habit with him. Such meditation kindled a most lively compassion in his heart for all sinners threatened by such a frightful eternity. This ardent charity helped him overcome any reticence as he prudently but frankly invited even very promiment people to mend their ways. It also made his words so effective as to work many conversions.

We have faithfully recorded what we ourselves heard at length from Don Bosco or what was testified to us orally or in writing by various priests after coordinating it into one single narrative. It was a difficult task because we wished to record most accurately every word, every link between scenes, and the sequence of incidents, warnings, reproaches, and whatever else he said but did not explain and was perhaps misunderstood. Did we achieve our aim? We can assure our readers that we most diligently sought one thing only: to expound as faithfully as possible Don Bosco's long talks. (Vol. IX, pp. 85-100)

THE LAND OF TRIAL

In 1876 Father Joseph Vespignani, who was then new at the Oratory, ventured to ask Don Bosco about his dreams. With the confidence of a son, he inquired what should be made of them. Don Bosco's answer was not specific but satisfactory. He told him that in his circumstances, without money or personnel, it would have been impossible to work for youth if Mary Help of Christians had not come to his assistance with special enlightenment and with abundant help, not only material but also spiritual. Therefore, his dreams are to be interpreted as a special enlightenment and special aids from Our Lady. The influence of Don Bosco's dreams in the life of the Oratory cannot be ignored by the historian. By this time, they were of themselves a domestic institution. The impact and remembrance of earlier dreams were now history, and the expectation of new ones was ever present. News of another dream aroused anticipation among young and old alike: its narration was eagerly listened to: its salutary effects were not long in coming.

In his "Good Night" on April 30, Don Bosco exhorted the boys to make devoutly the May devotions. After urging them, therefore, to greater diligence in the fulfillment of their duties and the choice of some special act of devotion in honor of Mary, he added that he had a dream to tell them, but since it was already late, he would tell it on the following Sunday, May 4.

The boys were beside themselves with impatience. Their curiosity was further aroused by another two days postponement because Don Bosco was too busy. Finally, on the evening of May 4, their curiosity was satisfied. After prayers Don Bosco addressed them as usual from the little pulpit.

Here I am to keep my promise. You know that dreams come during sleep. As the time for the retreat drew near I was wondering how my boys would make it and what I should suggest to make it fruitful. On Sunday night, April 25, the eve of the retreat, I went to bed with this thought in mind. I fell asleep immediately and I seemed to be standing all alone in a very vast valley enclosed on both sides by high hills. At the far end of the valley along one side where the ground rose steeply, there was a pure, bright light; the other side was in semidarkness. As I stood gazing at the plain, Buzzetti and Gastini came up to me and said, "Don Bosco, you will have to mount a horse. Hurry! Hurry!"

"Are you joking?" I said. "You know how long it has been since I last rode a horse." They insisted, but in an attempt to excuse myself I kept repeating, "I don't want to ride a horse; I did it once and fell off."

Gastini and Buzzetti kept pressing me ever more and said, "Get on a horse, and quickly. There's no time to lose."

"But suppose I do mount a horse, where are you taking me?"

"You'll see. Now, hurry and mount!"

"But where's the horse? I don't see any."

"There it is," shouted Gastini, pointing to one side of the valley. I looked and saw a beautiful, spirited steed. It had long, strong legs, a thick mane, and a very glossy coat.

"Well, since you want me to mount it, I will. But woe

to you if I fall. . . ." I said.

"Don't worry," they replied, "We'll be here with you for any emergency."

"And if I break my neck, you'll have to fix it," I told Buzzetti.

Buzzetti broke into a laugh. "This is no time to laugh," Gastini muttered. We walked over to the horse. Even with their help I had great difficulty mounting, but finally I was in the saddle. How tall that horse seemed to be then! It was as if I were perched on top of a high mound from where I could survey the entire valley from end to end.

Then the horse started to move. Strangely, while this was happening I seemed to be in my own room. I asked myself, "Where are we?" Coming toward me I saw priests, clerics, and others; all looked frightened and breathless.

After a long ride the horse stopped. Then I saw all the priests of the Oratory together with many of the clerics approaching. They gathered around the horse. I recognized Father Rua, Father Cagliero, and Father Bologna among them. When they reached me, they stopped and silently stared at my horse. I noticed that all seemed worried. Their disquiet was such as I have never seen before. I beckoned to Father Bologna. "Father Bologna," I said, "you are in charge at the main entrance; can you tell me what happened? Why do you all look so upset?"

"I don't know where I am or what I'm doing," he said. "I'm all confused . . . Some people came in, talked and left . . . There is such a hubbub of people coming and going at the main entrance that I don't know what's going on."

"Is it possible," I wondered, "that something very unusual might happen today?"

Just then someone handed me a trumpet, saying I should hold on to it because I would need it. "Where are we now?" I asked. "Blow the trumpet."

I did and heard these words: *We are in the land of trial.*

Then I saw a multitude of boys—I think over 100 thousand coming down the hills. There was absolute silence. Carrying pitchforks, they were hastening toward the valley. I recognized among them all the Oratory boys, and those of our other schools; but there were many more unknown to me. Just then on one side of the valley the sky darkened, and hordes of animals resembling lions and tigers appeared. These ferocious beasts had big bodies, strong legs, and long necks, but their heads were quite small. They were terrifying. With blood-shot eyes bulging from their sockets, they hurled themselves at the boys who immediately stood ready to defend themselves. As the animals attacked, the boys stood firm and beat them off with their pronged pitchforks, which they lowered or raised as needed.

Unable to overpower them by this first attack, the beasts snapped at the fork prongs only to break their teeth and vanish. Some of the boys, however, had forks with only one prong and these were wounded. Others had pitchforks with broken or worm-eaten handles, and still others threw themselves at the beasts barehanded and fell victims; quite a few of these were killed. Many had pitchforks with two prongs and new handles.

While this was going on, from the very start swarms of serpents slithered about my horse. Kicking and stamping, the horse crushed and drove them off: at the same time it kept growing ever taller and taller.

I asked someone what the two-pronged forks symbolized. I was handed a fork and on the prongs I read these two words: *Confession*, on one; *Communion*, on the other.

"But what do the prongs mean?"

"Blow the trumpet!"

I did and heard these words: *Good confession and good Communion.*

I blew the trumpet again and heard these words: *Broken handle: sacrilegious confessions and Communions. Worm-eaten handle: Faulty confessions.*

Now that the first attack was over, I rode over the battlefield and saw many dead and wounded. I saw that some of the dead had been strangled and their necks were swollen and deformed. The faces of the others were horribly disfigured; still others had starved to death, while enticing food was within their reach. The boys who were strangled are those who unfortunately committed some sins in their early years and never confessed them: those with disfigured faces are gluttons: and the boys who died of hunger, those who go to confession but never follow the advice or admonitions of their confessor.

Next to each boy whose pitchfork had a worm-eaten

handle a word stood out. For some it was Pride; for others, Sloth; for others still, Immodesty, etc. I must also add that in their march the boys had to walk over a bed of roses. They liked it, but after a few steps they would utter a cry and fall to the ground either dead or wounded because of the thorns hidden underneath. Others instead bravely trampled on those roses and encouraging one another marched on to victory.

Then the sky darkened again. Instantly even greater hordes of the same animals or monsters appeared. All this happened in less than three or four seconds. My horse was surrounded. The monsters increased beyond count and I, too, began to be frightened. I could feel them clawing at me! Then someone handed me a pitchfork, and I also began to fight them, and the monsters were forced to retreat. Beaten in their first attack, they all vanished.

Then I blew the trumpet again, and these words echoed through the valley: *Victory! Victory!*

"Victory?!" I wondered, "how is it possible with so many dead and wounded?"

I blew the trumpet once more and we heard the words: *Truce for the vanquished.* The sky brightened and a rainbow became visible. It was so lovely and so colorful that I cannot describe it. It was immense, as though one end rested on top of Superga and its arch stretched and stretched until it reached the top of Moncenisio. I should also add that all the boys who had been victorious wore crowns so brilliant and so bright and varied in color that it was an awe-inspiring sight. Their faces, too, were resplendently handsome. At the far end of the valley, on one side under the center of the rainbow, there was a sort of balcony holding people full of joy and of such varied beauty as to surpass my imagination. A very noble lady royally arrayed came to the railing of this balcony and called out: "Come my children and take shelter under my mantle." As she spoke, an immense mantle spread out and all the boys ran to take cover under it. Some actually flew; these had the word *Innocence* on their foreheads. Others just walked; and some crawled. I also started to run, and in that split second, it couldn't have been more than that, I said to myself, "This had better end or we'll die." I had just said this and was still running when I woke up.

... [Don Bosco] returned to this subject on May 6, the feast of the Ascension. He had the students and the artisans assembled together for night prayers, and then spoke as follows:

The other night I was not able to say everything because we had visitors in our midst. These things must be kept among us, and no one should write to friends or relatives about them. I confide everything in you, even my sins. That valley, that land of trial, is this world. The semi-darkness is the place of perdition; the two hills are the commandments of God and the Church; the serpents are the devils; the monsters, evil temptations; the horse, I think, is the same as the one that struck Heliodorus and represents our trust in God. The boys who walked over the roses and fell dead are those who give in to this world's pleasures that deal death to the soul; those who trampled the roses underfoot are those who spurn worldly pleasures and are therefore victorious. The boys who flew under the mantle are those who have preserved their baptismal innocence.

For the sake of those who might wish to know, little by little I shall tell those concerned the kind of weapon they carried and whether they were victorious or not, dead or wounded. I did not know all the boys, but I recognized those of the Oratory. And if the others were ever to come here I would recognize them immediately the moment I saw them.

Father Berto, his secretary who took down this dream, wrote that he could not remember many things that Don Bosco narrated and explained at length. The next morning, May 7, when he was with Don Bosco, he asked him, "How can you possibly remember all the boys you saw in your dream, and tell each one the state he was in and pinpoint his faults?"

"Oh," Don Bosco answered, "by means of *Otis Botis Pia Tutis.*" This was a meaningless phrase that he often used to evade embarrassing questions. (Vol. XI, pp. 239-243)

A PLACE OF SALVATION

When I went to bed last night I could not fall asleep directly, and so I began thinking about the soul: its nature, mode of existence, structure, activities after its separation from the body, and mobility. I wondered too how we might be able to recognize others after death, since we would all be pure spirits. The more I thought about it, the less I knew.

Finally I fell asleep and dreamed that I was on my way to ... (*and he named the city*). After passing through several unknown towns, I suddenly heard someone calling me. He was standing on the shoulder of the road. "Come with me," he said, "and your wish will be fulfilled." I obeyed. We moved through space as swiftly as thought, never touching the ground until we got to some place totally unknown to me. High above us stood a magnificent palace. I can't really say whether it stood on a mountain or on a cloud, but it certainly was inaccessible. No roads led to it and it was far beyond reach.

"Go up to that palace," my guide said.

"How?" I replied. "I have no wings!"

"Go up!" he repeated imperiously. Seeing that I did not stir, he added, "Do as I do. Lift your arms as high as you can." He showed me how, and at once I felt myself lifted into the air like a thin cloud. In no time we reached the palace gates.

"Who lives here?" I asked.

"Go in and you'll know. At the end of the hall someone will give you information."

He disappeared. Left to myself, I went in, walked along a portico, went up a stairway, and entered a truly regal apartment. I passed through spacious halls, richly decorated rooms, and endless corridors at such unearthly speed that I could not even count them. Each glittered with priceless treasures. But what astonished me most was that, although I was going as swiftly as the wind, I never even moved my feet. I was gliding along over what seemed to be a crystal floor without ever touching it. Finally I came to a door at the end of a corridor that opened into another hall even more magnificent than all the others. At the far end, a bishop sat majestically in an imposing armchair, apparently awaiting somebody. I approached respectfully and was extremely surprised to recognize him as a dear friend of mine—Bishop ... of ... (*Don Bosco mentioned his name*) who died two years ago. He did not seem to be in pain. He looked healthy and friendly and was indescribably handsome.

"Your Excellency!" I exclaimed with great joy. "Is it really you?"

"Can't you see?" the bishop replied.

"But how? Are you still living? I thought you were dead."

"I *am* dead."

"How can it be? You look wonderful! If you are still alive, please say so or we'll have a problem. At [Cuneo] another bishop has already taken your place. How are we going to settle this?"

"Don't worry! I *am* dead."

"That's good! It would hardly do to have two bishops on the same chair."

"I understand. And how about you, Don Bosco? Are you dead or alive?"

"I am alive. Can't you see I am here in body and soul?"

"Bodies aren't allowed here."

"But I *am* here in my body."

"You *think* you are...."

At this point I fired off a lot of questions which went unanswered. "How can it be that I, still living, am here with you who are dead?" I kept asking. Fearing that the bishop might vanish, I begged him, "Please, Your Excellency, do not leave me. There are many things I want to ask you."

"Relax," he said. "I won't run away. What do you want to know?"

"Are you saved?"

"Look at me! See how vigorous, ruddy, and radiant I am." Indeed his whole appearance gave a well-founded hope that he was saved. Nonetheless, I insisted: "Please give me a straight answer. Are you saved or not?"

"Yes, I am in a place of salvation."

"Are you in heaven or in purgatory?"

"I am in a place of salvation, but I have not yet seen God. I still need your prayers."

"How long must you yet stay in purgatory?"

"This will tell you," he said, handing me a paper. I examined it attentively but found nothing on it.

"There is no writing at all on it," I replied.

"Look carefully," he insisted.

"I am looking," I countered, "but I still can't see any writing."

"Look again."

"I only see multicolored floral designs but no writing whatever."

"There are numerals."

"I don't see any!"

The bishop peered at the paper I was holding. "No wonder you don't see any. Turn the paper upside down." I complied and examined the paper even more closely from all angles, but to no avail. The only thing I could make out were floral twists and whorls resembling the figure 2.

"Do you know why you must turn the paper upside down in order to read it? It is because God's judgments are different from the world's. What men hold as wisdom is foolishness in God's sight."

Not daring to press for a clearer explanation, I just said, "Please, Bishop, do not leave me yet. I have more questions."

"Go on. I'm listening."

"Will I be saved?"

"You must hope."

"Please don't keep me in suspense. Tell me straight."

"I don't know."

"At least tell me if I am in the state of grace."

"I don't know."

"Will my boys be saved?"

"I don't know."

"Tell me, please, I beg you."

"You have studied theology and you can answer that question yourself."

"I can't believe it. Here you are in a place of salvation and you don't know these things?"

"It's like this: God reveals these things to whomsoever He wishes. If He wants this knowledge to be imparted to anyone, He gives the necessary command or permission. Otherwise, no one can reveal these things to the living."

Endless questions kept popping up in my mind and I quickly voiced them, fearing that the bishop might disappear.

"Will you now give me a message for my boys?"

"You know as well as I what they must do. The Church, the Gospel, and the rest of the Scriptures are clear enough. Tell your boys to save their souls because that's all that matters. The rest counts for nothing."

"We know we must save our souls. But how shall we go about it? Tell me something special that may remind us of you. I shall repeat it to my boys in your name."

"Tell them to be good and obedient."

"They know that."

"Tell them to be modest and to pray."

"Please be more specific!"

"Tell them to go to confession often and to make worthy Communions."

"Something more specific yet."

"Well, then, tell them this. Tell them that there is fog before their eyes. If they are aware of it, it's a good sign. Let them dispel it."

"What does this fog symbolize?"

"The things of the world which prevent them from seeing the things of heaven as they really are."

"And what must they do to dispel this fog?"

"They must see the world as it really is. '... the whole world is under the evil one.' (1 Jn 5: 19) Only then will they save their souls. They should not let themselves be deceived by appearances. Believing that worldly pleasures, amusements, and friendships will make them happy, the young long for them, while they should rather keep in mind that all is vanity and affliction of spirit. Let them form the habit to judge matters of the world not by their appearances, but as they really are."

"And what mainly causes this fog?"

"Immodesty and impurity, a sin which, like a murky cloud, prevents youngsters from seeing the abyss toward which they are heading. Tell them to guard jealously the virtue of purity. It is the virtue that shines brightest in heaven. 'They will bloom with abundant flowers...' (Is 35: 2)

"How is it to be safeguarded? Tell me and I'll repeat it to my dear boys in your name."

"Four things: flight from worldly things, obedience, avoiding idleness, and prayer."

"What else?"

"Prayer, avoiding idleness, obedience, and flight from worldly things."

"Anything else?"

"Obedience, flight from worldly things, prayer, and avoiding idleness. Insist on these things. They are enough."

I wanted to ask other questions, but I couldn't think of any at the moment. Besides, being in such a hurry to tell you these things, I dashed out and with the speed of wind found myself at the Oratory gate. There I suddenly felt a sense of regret, thinking: *Why did I not stay longer with the bishop? I could have learned many more things. I really blundered in letting such a good chance slip by.* I immediately dashed back with my former speed but with a nagging fear of no longer finding the bishop. Luckily he was still there—but what a change! He was lying in bed, as white as a ghost, with tears welling in his eyes. He was dying. A slight heaving of his chest was the only sign of life.

I stooped over him in utter shock. "Your Excellency, what happened?"

"Leave me alone," he moaned.

"I have many more things to ask you."

"Leave me alone! I am in terrible pain."

"Can I help you?"

"Pray for me and let me go."

"Go where?"

"Where God is leading me."

"But where? Please tell me."

"I am in too much pain! Leave me alone!"

"At least tell me what I can do for you," I repeated.

"Pray!"

"Have you any messages? Anything you want me to tell your successor?"

"Tell him this and this...." However, since the things he told me are not for you, my dear boys, I will leave them out. The bishop then gave me other confidential messages. (*Don Bosco did not reveal them. They seem to have been admonitions or measures to be taken for the good of that diocese.*)

"Anything else?" I asked.

"Tell your boys that they have always been very dear to me. I prayed for them during my life and still do. Let them now pray for me."

"I will surely tell them," I replied, "and we will begin at once to offer suffrages for you. Please remember us as soon as you reach heaven."

The bishop meanwhile seemed to be suffering even more. It was heartrending to see him in such painful agony.

"Leave me," he repeated. "Let me go where God calls me."

"Bishop! Bishop!" I kept repeating, filled with inexpressible pity.

"Let me be, let me be!" He seemed to be breathing his last while an invisible force pulled him out of sight into an inner part of the palace.

Frightened and deeply moved, I turned to get back to the Oratory, but in so doing I bumped my knee into something and woke up in bed.

As you see, my dear boys, this is a dream like many others. What concerns you needs no explanation. It has taught me a lot about the soul and purgatory. Things I had never before been able to grasp became so clear that I shall never forget them.

Perhaps in this two-part dream Don Bosco meant to depict the state of grace of the souls in purgatory and their expiatory sufferings. He did not comment on the state of that good bishop. Some time later, relying on his trust in us, we asked him if he had delivered the bishop's messages. "Yes," he replied. "I did!"

We will further remark that the dream, as recorded above, omits a detail that we remember but perhaps seemed unclear or unimportant at that time. At a certain point in the dream Don Bosco asked how much longer he would live. In reply the bishop handed him a paper full of scribbles and whorls interwoven into the figure *8*, but he offered no explanations. Did these figures point to 1888 [the year of Don Bosco's death]?

(Vol. VIII, pp. 368-373)

HIKING TO HEAVEN

We shall now narrate another inspiring dream of Don Bosco which occurred on the nights of April 3, 4, and 5, 1861. "Its striking details," Father Bonetti remarks, "will aptly convince our readers that this is such a dream as God now and then graciously sends to His faithful servants." We shall report it here as detailed in Bonetti's and Ruffino's chronicles.

"After night prayers on April 7," they wrote, "Don Bosco mounted the little rostrum to give the 'Good Night' and spoke as follows:

I have something very strange to tell you tonight—a dream. It's only a dream, so do not give it more importance than it merits. Let me first tell you, though, that I am quite honest with you, as I would like you to be honest with me. I keep no secrets from you, but what is said within the family should be kept in the family. I don't mean to imply that it would be a sin to tell others, but even so I'd rather you didn't. Talk about it all you want, and laugh and joke to your heart's content among yourselves, or even with those few who may—in your opinion—benefit spiritually from it.

This dream has three parts because it lasted three nights. This evening I'll tell you only the first part, leaving the rest for other nights. Surprisingly, on the second and third night I resumed the dream at the very point I had left off when I awoke.

PART ONE

Since dreams come while sleeping, I too was asleep. A few days ago, having to go out of town, I passed by the green-clad hills of Moncalieri. I was deeply impressed. Possibly this charming scene came back to my mind, stirring a desire to go hiking. As a matter of fact, that's what I decided to do in my dream.

I seemed to be with my boys in a vast plain which stretched out to a massively high hill. As we were all standing there, I suddenly proposed a hike.

"Yes, yes!" they all cheerfully shouted. "Let's go!"

"Where to?" we asked one another undecidedly. While we looked hopefully at each other for suggestions, someone abruptly blurted out, "Let's hike to heaven."

"Yes, yes, to heaven!" the cry arose on all sides.

We started off, and after a while we reached the foot of the hill and began climbing. A magnificent view soon unfolded before our eyes. As far as we could see, the hillside was dotted with trees and saplings of all kinds—some small and tender, others tall and vigorous, none thicker than a man's arm. There were pears, apples, cherries, plums, vines, and other fruit trees. Amazingly, each tree had some flowers just blossoming and others in full bloom, some fruits just forming and others lusciously ripe. In other words, each tree showed the best of each season at one and the same time. The fruit was so plentiful that the branches sagged under its weight. Surprised at this phenomenon, the boys kept asking me for explanations. To satisfy their curiosity somewhat, I remember saying, "Well, it's like this. Heaven is not like our earth with its seasons. Its climate is always the same, embodying the best of every season. It is very mild and suitable for every tree and plant."

We stood entranced by the beauty surrounding us. The gentle breeze, the calm, and the fragrant air about us left no doubt that this climate was ideally suited to all kinds of fruits. Here and there, the boys were plucking apples, pears, cherries, or grapes while slowly climbing. When we finally reached the top of the hill, we thought we were in heaven, but in reality we were quite far from it.

From this vantage point we could see, beyond a vast plain, an extensive pleateau and, in its center, a very lofty mountain soaring straight up to the clouds. Many people were determinedly struggling up its steep sides, while on its summit stood One inviting and encouraging them to go up. We also spotted some persons descending from the top to help those who were too exhausted to continue the steep climb. Those reaching the top were greeted with vibrant cheers and jubiliation. We understood that paradise was at that peak, and so we started downhill toward the plateau and mountain.

After covering a good part of the way—many boys were running far ahead of the crowd—we were in for quite a surprise. Some distance from the foot of the mountain the plateau held a big lake full of blood. Its length would extend from the Oratory to Piazza Castello. Its shore was littered with human limbs, fractured skulls, and remnants of corpses. It was a gruesome sight, a veritable carnage! The boys who had run on ahead stopped in their tracks, terrified. Being far behind and having no inkling of what was ahead, I was surprised to see them stop with horrified looks on their faces.

"What's wrong?" I shouted. "Why don't you keep going?"

"Come and see!" they replied. I hurried over and gazed upon the grim spectacle. As the others came up, they too took in the scene and immediately became silent and dispirited. Standing on the banks of that mysterious lake, I sought a way across, but in vain. Just in front of me, on the opposite bank, I could read a large inscription: *Through blood!*

Puzzled, the boys kept asking one another: "What does all this mean?"

Then I asked someone (who he was I can't remember) for an explanation, and he replied, "This is the blood shed by the very many who have already reached the mountain's summit and are now in heaven. It is the blood of martyrs. Here, also, is the blood of Jesus Christ. In it were bathed the bodies of those who were martyred in testimony of the faith. No one may enter heaven without passing through this blood and being sprinkled by it. It guards the Holy Mountain—the Catholic Church. Whoever attempts to attack her shall drown in it. The torn limbs, mangled bodies, and broken skulls dotting the shore are the gruesome remains of those who chose to fight the Church. All have been crushed to bits; all have perished in this lake."

In the course of his explanation, the mysterious youth named many martyrs, including the papal soldiers who died defending the Pope's temporal power.

Then, pointing eastward to our right, he showed us an immense valley four or five times the size of the lake. "Do you see that valley?" he asked. "Into it shall flow the blood of those who will pass this way to scale this mountain—the blood of the just, of those who will die for the faith in days to come." Seeing that the boys were terrified by all they saw and heard, I tried to encourage them by saying that, if we were to die martyrs, our blood would flow into that valley, but our limbs would not be tossed about like those of the persecutors.

We then hastened to resume our march, skirting the shore of the lake. At our left stood the hill we had come down from; at our right were the lake and mountain. Where the lake ended, we saw a strip of land dotted with oaks, laurels, palms, and other trees. We went through it in search of a trail to the mountain, but only came across another vast lake. Floating in its waters were dismembered human limbs. On the shore stood an inscription: *Through water!*

"What does all this mean?" the boys again asked, mystified.

"This lake," someone replied, "holds the water which flowed from Christ's side. Small in quantity then, it has increased, is still increasing, and will keep increasing in the future. This is the baptismal water which washed and purified those who climbed this mountain. In this same water all who must still climb will have to be baptized and purified. In it must be cleansed all those who want to go to heaven. There is no other way to paradise than through innocence or penance. No one can be saved without being cleansed in this water." Then, pointing to the dismembered limbs, he added, "These are the remains of those who have recently attacked the Church."

Meanwhile, a number of people and some of our own boys, too, were swiftly darting across the lake, skimming over the waters without wetting the soles of their feet. We were astonished at this, but were told, "These are the just. When the souls of the saints are freed from their bodily prison or when their bodies are glorified, they not only can tread lightly and swiftly over water, but they can also fly through the air."

Hearing this, all the boys, eager to cross the lake like the other people, looked at me inquiringly. No one, however, dared attempt it.

"For my part, I don't dare," I replied. "It would be rash to believe ourselves so just as to be able to cross the lake without sinking."

"If *you* don't dare, we dare even less," they all exclaimed.

Continuing on our way, always skirting the mountain, we reached a third lake as large as the first, full of flames and more torn human limbs. On the opposite shore an inscription proclaimed: *Through fire!*

While we were observing that fiery lake, that same mysterious person spoke again and said, "This is the fire of the charity of God and His saints. These are the flames of love and desire through which all must pass if they have not gone through blood and water. This is also the fire with which tyrants tortured and consumed so many martyrs. Many are they who had to go through it before climbing the mountain. But these flames will also serve to reduce their enemies to ashes."

Thus for the third time we were seeing God's enemies crushed and defeated.

Wasting no time, we advanced past the lake and came upon a fourth one, even more frightening, shaped like a huge amphitheater. It was full of dogs, cats, wolves, bears, tigers, lions, panthers, snakes and other fierce monsters eager to pounce upon anyone within their reach. We saw people stepping over the heads of these raging beasts. We also saw boys fearlessly following them and suffering no injury.

I tried to call them back, shouting as loudly as I could: "Stop! Can't you see that those beasts are just waiting to devour you?" It was useless. They didn't hear me and kept treading upon the monsters' heads as if they were on firm, safe ground. My usual guide then said to me: "Those beasts symbolize the devils, the dangers and snares of the world. Those who step over them unharmed are the just, the innocent. Don't you know what Holy Scripture says? 'You shall tread upon the asp and the viper; you shall trample down the lion and the dragon.' (Ps 91: 13) It was of such souls that David spoke. And doesn't the Gospel say: '. . . I have given you power to tread on snakes and scorpions and all the forces of the enemy, and nothing shall ever injure you.' "? (Lk 10: 19)

We still kept asking one another: "How shall we cross over? Do we have to step over these wild beasts too?"

"Yes, let's go!" someone told me.

"I don't dare!" I replied. "It would be rash to believe ourselves so good as to be able to tread safely over these fierce beasts. Do as you wish, but not I."

"Then we won't try it either," the boys concluded.

We left that place and came upon a vast plain crowded with noseless, earless, or headless people. Some, moreover, had no limbs, others had no hands or feet, and still others had no tongue or eyes. The boys were simply struck dumb at such an odd sight. A mysterious person explained: "These are God's friends. To save their souls, they have mortified their senses and performed good works. Many lost parts of their bodies in carrying out harsh penances or in working for God or their fellow men. The headless ones are those who in a special manner consecrated themselves to God."

While we were pondering these things, we could see that many people, having crossed the lake, were now ascending the mountain.

We also saw others, already at the top, helping and encouraging those who were going up, giving them joyous, hearty cheers of welcome as they reached the top. The handclapping and cheering woke me, and I found myself in bed. This ended the first part of the dream.

The following night, April 8, Don Bosco again spoke to the boys, who couldn't wait to hear the continuation of the dream.

... Smiling upon their upturned faces, Don Bosco briefly paused and then went on thus:

PART TWO

You will remember that at the bottom of a deep valley, near the first lake, stood another lake yet to be filled with blood. Well, after seeing all I have already described and going around that plateau, we found a passage taking us into another valley, which in turn opened into a large, wedge-shaped plaza. We entered it. Wide at the entrance, it gradually tapered into a trail at its other end near the mountain. At this point the trail was wedged between two huge boulders so close together that only one person at a time could squeeze through. The plaza was filled with cheerful, happy people, all heading for the narrow mountain trail.

"Could that be the trail to heaven?" we asked one another. As the people reached it and squeezed through single-file, they had to pull their clothes tight, hold their breath, and discard whatever they carried. This sufficed to convince me that surely this was the way to heaven, for I remembered that, to get there, one must not only rid himself of sin, but also give up all worldly ties and desires. "... nothing profane shall enter it ..." says the Apostle John. (Rv 21: 27) We stood briefly watching that scene. Then we did a very foolish thing. Instead of trying to squeeze through the trail, we turned back to see what was happening in the valley past the entrance of the plaza. We had noticed a great crowd of people far off, and we were curious to know what went on there.

We started off on a boundless stretch of land and were faced by the odd sight of people and many of our boys yoked to various kinds of animals. "What can this mean?" I mused. Then it flashed across my mind that the ox is a symbol of laziness, and I understood that those boys were lazy. I clearly recognized them. They were habitually indolent, sluggish in their work. So I said to myself, "It serves you right! Stay where you are! If you don't want to work, that's just where you belong!"

I saw others yoked to donkeys, carrying loads or grazing. These were the stubborn boys who obstinately resist suggestions and orders. Other lads were paired with mules and horses, reminding me of what Holy Scripture says: "Be not senseless like horses or mules . . . " (Ps 32: 9) These were the boys who never give a thought to their souls. Such empty heads!

Still others were feeding with pigs. Like them, they grunted and wallowed in the mire. These were the boys who feed on earthly pleasures by gratifying their lower passions. They are far from their heavenly Father. What a sad spectacle! They reminded me of what the Gospel says about the prodigal son being reduced to that sad state "by dissolute living." (Lk 15: 13)

Finally, I saw a multitude of people—and some of our boys too—cavorting with cats, dogs, cocks, rabbits—animals symbolizing thieves, scandal-givers, braggards, and spineless individuals who don't have the courage to stand up for their religious beliefs. We now realized that this valley represented the world. I took a good look at each of the boys, and then we moved on to another very large area of that boundless plain. The ground sloped so gently that we did not even notice it at first. A little way off there seemed to be a flower garden, and we decided to look at it. We first came across most beautiful red roses. "How gorgeous!" the boys shouted, running to pluck a few. But they were disappointed! Though full-blown and colorful, those roses were rotten inside and gave off an extremely foul stench. Fresh-looking violets were there too, but when we picked a few we saw that they also were blighted and smelly.

We kept going and came to several charming groves of trees

laden with luscious fruit. They were truly enticing orchards. A boy ran up to a tree and plucked a large pear. A more beautiful one would be hard to find. Yet, as soon as he bit into it, he flung it away in disgust. It was stuffed with clay and sand and tasted awful. "How can this be?" we asked.

One of our boys, whose name I well remember, replied, "Is this all the world can give us? It's a worthless sham!"

While we wondered where we were headed for, we became aware that the road was sloping, though ever so slightly. One boy remarked, "We're going downhill. It's no good!"

"Let's take a look, anyway!" I replied.

Meanwhile, a vast multitude of people overtook us and kept going down the road in coaches, on horseback, or on foot. The last-named group kept jumping and running about, singing and dancing or marching along to the beat of drums. The merrymaking was beyond description.

"Lets wait a while and see before going along with them," we decided.

Presently a couple of boys noticed some individuals in the crowd who seemed to be directing various groups. They were handsome, well dressed, and quite gracious in manner, but it was obvious that their hats covered horns. That vast plain, then, symbolized our wicked, corrupt world so well described by the Holy Spirit: "Sometimes a way seems right to a man, but the end of it leads to death." (Prv 16: 25)

Then and there a mysterious person said to us: "See how men almost unknowingly fall into hell." At this I immediately called back the boys who had gone ahead. They ran to me, crying, "We don't want to go down there!" Still shouting, they kept running back to where we had come from, leaving me alone. When I finally caught up with them, I said, "You're right. Let's get out of here, or we too shall fall into hell before we realize it!"

We wanted to return to the plaza from which we had set out and finally get started on the trail to the mountain. Imagine our surprise when, after a long walk, we saw no trace of the valley leading to heaven, but only a meadow. We turned this way and that, but could not find our bearings.

"We have taken the wrong road!" someone cried.

"No, we haven't," replied another.

While the boys were arguing, I woke up. Thus ended the dream on the second night.

Before sending you to bed, though, I must tell you one more thing. I do not want you to give any importance to this dream; just remember that pleasures which lead to perdition are deceitful; they are not pleasures at all! Remember also to be on guard against bad habits which make us so similar to beasts and deserving of being yoked with them. Guard especially against sins that turn us into unclean animals. It is, indeed, most unbecoming for a man to be brought down to the level of beasts, but it is far more unbecoming for a creature made to God's image and likeness, an heir to heaven, to wallow in the mire like swine through those sins which Holy Scripture labels "dissolute living."

I told you only the highlights of my dream—and briefly too—because to narrate it as it was would take too much time. As a matter of fact, last night too I gave you but a hint of what I saw. Tomorrow night I will tell you the rest.

On Saturday night, April 9, Don Bosco continued the narration of his dream:

PART THREE

I would rather not tell you my dreams. In fact, the night before last I had no sooner started my narration than I regretted my promise. I truly wished I had never said a word at all. However, I must confess that if I kept these things to myself I would feel very uneasy. Narrating them, in fact, is a great relief. I will therefore continue with the last part of the dream. Let me first say, though, that the past two nights I had to cut short many things which were better left unsaid, and I left out others which could be seen but not described.

After taking in all the scenes I mentioned, after seeing various places and ways through which one may fall into hell, we were determined to get to heaven at all costs, but try as we might, we always strayed off and came upon new sights. Finally we hit upon the right road and reached the plaza; it was still crowded with people striving to go up the mountain. If you remember, it gradually tapered into a very narrow trail wedged between two lofty boulders. Just beyond them was a rather long, very narrow, railless bridge spanning a frightful gorge. As soon as we saw the trail, we all shouted, "There it is! Let's go." And so we did.

Some boys immediately began running, leaving their companions behind. I wanted them to wait for me, but they had got it into their heads to arrive there first. On reaching the bridge, however, they became frightened and stopped. I tried to urge them to advance bravely, but they refused.

"Go ahead," they replied. "You try it first, Father! The bridge is too narrow. If we miss one step, we're through!" Finally one boy mustered enough courage to attempt the crossing; another followed him and then the rest. Thus we reached the foot of the mountain.

We looked for a trail but found none. We walked around looking for one, but our search was hindered on all sides by boulders, crags, ravines, and briers. The climb looked steep. We knew we were in for a hard time. Nevertheless, we did not lose heart and eagerly began to work our way up. After a short but very exhausting climb with hands and feet, occasionally helping one another, the obstacles began to decrease until we finally found a trail and were able to climb more comfortably.

Eventually we reached a spot on the mountainside where a great many people were suffering such horrible and strange pains that we were filled with compassion and horror. I cannot tell you what I saw because it's too distressing and you could not bear it. I leave this out entirely.

We saw also very many people climbing the mountain on all sides. As they reached the summit they were greeted with loud cheers and applause by those who were already there. We could also hear a truly heavenly music, a most melodious singing, which encouraged us all the more to keep climbing. While we ascended, a thought struck me, and I said to the boys near me, "Isn't this funny? Here we are on our way to heaven, but are we alive or dead? What about the judgment? Or have we already been judged?"

"No," they replied laughingly. "We are still alive."

"Well," I concluded, "alive or dead, let's get to the top and see what's there!" And we quickened our step.

By dint of perseverance we finally got close to the summit.

Those already there were getting ready to greet us, but, as I looked behind to see if the boys were following, I found to my great sorrow that I was almost alone. Only three or four boys had kept up with me.

"Where are the others?" I asked, somewhat upset.

"They stopped here and there," was the answer. "Perhaps they will come up later!"

I looked down and saw them scattered about the mountain trail, hunting for snails, picking scentless wild flowers, plucking wild berries, chasing butterflies and crickets, or just resting on some green patch under a shady tree. I shouted as loud as I could, waved to them, and called them by name, urging them to hurry up and telling them that this was no time to rest. A few heeded me, so that now I had about eight boys around me. All the others turned a deaf ear, busy with silly trifles. I had no intention at all of going to heaven with only a few boys, and therefore I decided to go down and get after those lazy fellows. I told the boys near me to wait and then I started down.

As many boys as I met, I sent up the mountain. I urged, exhorted, reprimanded, even jabbed and shoved, as needed.

"For heaven's sake, go up," I kept saying. "Don't waste time on trifles!"

In the end, after reaching nearly every one of them, I found myself almost at the scarp of the mountain which we had climbed with so much effort. Here I stopped some boys who, exhausted and discouraged, had given up the ascent and were on their way down. As I turned to resume the climb with them, I stumbled against a stone and woke up.

Now that you have heard the whole dream, I ask two things of you. First, don't tell it to outsiders, because they would only make fun of it. I tell you these things just to please you. Talk about this dream among yourselves all you want, but remember that it is only a dream. Secondly, please don't come to ask me if you were there or not, who was or wasn't there, what you were or weren't doing, if you were among the few or the many, where I saw you, or similar questions, because then we would have a repetition of last winter's commotion. For some this could be more harmful than useful, and I don't want to disturb your consciences.

I only tell you that, if this had not been a dream but

reality and we had died then, of the seven or eight hundred boys we have here, very few would have made it to heaven—perhaps only three or four.

Now, lest you get me wrong, let me explain this rash statement. What I mean is that only three or four would make it *straight to heaven* without having to go through purgatory. Some might have to spend only a minute there; others, perhaps a day; still others, several days or weeks; nearly all, at least a short time. Now would you like to know how to avoid that? Strive to gain as many indulgences as you possibly can. If you rightly carry out these practices of piety to which indulgences are attached and gain a plenary indulgence, you will go straight to heaven.

Don Bosco gave no private explanation of this dream to any of the pupils and said very little otherwise on the various meanings of the things he had seen. It would not have been easy. This dream, as we shall show, portrayed a variety of tableaux: the Oratory as it was and as it would be; all the boys who were there now or would come later—each with his moral traits and his future; the Salesian Society—its growth, vicissitudes, and destinies; the Catholic Church—her persecutions and triumphs; and other events of general or particular interest.

With tableaux so bewildering in their vastness and interaction, Don Bosco simply could not thoroughly describe everything he had so vividly seen in his dream. Besides, discretion dictated—and duty required—that some things be kept secret or disclosed only to prudent persons to whom such a revelation might be comforting or serve as a warning.

In narrating to his boys the various dreams of which we shall have occasion to speak in due time, Don Bosco only told them what was best for them, since this was the intent of Him who gave these mysterious revelations. Occasionally, however, because of the deep impression he had received, in an effort to choose his subject matter, Don Bosco hinted vaguely at other incidents, things, or ideas. Occasionally these seemed incoherent and unrelated to his narrative, but strongly suggested that he was holding back much more than he told. Such is the case in his narration of the hike to heaven. We shall attempt to throw some light upon it both by quoting a few words we heard from Don Bosco and also by making a few comments of our own. However, we submit them to the readers' judgment.

1. Seemingly, the hill Don Bosco met at the start of his hike is the Oratory. Its verdure suggests youth. There are no old trees there, large and lofty; rather, youth's blossoms are ever flowering, and flowers and fruit blossom and ripen in every season. Such is the Oratory, or such it should be. Like all of Don Bosco's works it is sustained by charity, which Holy Scripture describes as a garden blessed by God, yielding precious fruits of immortality, similar to Eden's garden, where stood also the tree of life.

2. The mountain climbers are prefigured in the man described in Psalm 84, whose strength comes from the Lord. In this valley of tears he—and many others too—resolved to climb steadily to the summit of the mountain, to the tabernacle of the Most High, that is, to heaven. Our Lord, the lawgiver, will bless them, fill them with His grace, and help them to grow in all virtues until they see God in the heavenly Jerusalem and are eternally happy with Him.

3. The lakes seemingly sum up the history of the Church. The countless severed limbs scattered about the shores are the remnants of persecutors, heretics, schismatics, and rebellious Christians. From certain expressions of Don Bosco in his dream we gather that he saw events both present and future. The chronicle remarks: "Speaking privately to a few about the vast valley near the lake of blood, Don Bosco said, 'That deep valley is to be filled especially with the blood of priests, perhaps very soon.'"

The chronicle continues: "During the last few days Don Bosco paid a visit to Cardinal De Angelis who said to him: 'Tell me something to cheer me up.'"

" 'Very well, I will tell you a dream.'

"Don Bosco then began to narrate his dream, but with more details and remarks. When he came to the lake of blood, the cardinal became serious and sad. Don Bosco cut his account short, saying, 'That will be all for now!'

" 'Go on,' said the cardinal.

" 'Not now,' Don Bosco repeated, and then passed on to

more cheerful topics."

4. The straight, narrow pass between the two boulders, the narrow wooden bridge (Our Lord's Cross), the self assurance of a man of faith that he can cross it, the peril to which a man exposes himself in so doing if he does not have the right intention, the various obstacles before the mountain trail becomes passable—all this, if we are not mistaken, may refer to religious vocations. The people in the plaza may be boys called by God to serve Him in the Salesian Society. In fact, all those waiting to start on the trail to heaven looked happy and content and enjoyed themselves. This would indicate mostly young people. As for the climbers who had stopped in their ascent or were turning back, could this not suggest a cooling in following one's vocation? Don Bosco's own interpretation of this incident could indirectly allude to vocations, but he did not deem it wise to elaborate.

5. On the slope of the mountain, just past the initial obstacles, Don Bosco saw people in pain. Father Bonetti's chronicle offers this explanation: "Several asked him about this privately, and he replied, 'This place symbolized purgatory. If I had to preach on this subject, I'd just describe what I saw. It was simply frightful. There were all kinds of torments. I will only say that I saw people crushed under presses, hands, feet and heads sticking out all around, eyes bursting from their sockets. These people were so badly squashed and crushed that the sight was truly bloodcurdling.'"

We shall conclude with an important observation which can apply to this and other dreams... In these dreams or visions, as they may be called, there nearly always appears a personage who acts as Don Bosco's guide or interpreter. Who can he be? This is the most amazing and consoling part of these dreams, but Don Bosco kept it in his heart.

(Vol. VI, pp. 508-520)

MAMMA MARGARET

Don Bosco's love for his mother did not abate with time. Even in his last days, when he was about to die, he could hardly hold back his tears in reminiscing about her, and at night, in a state of semiconsciousness, he would call her, as those who assisted him have testified. He saw her several times in dreams which remained indelible in his mind and which he at times narrated to us.

In August 1860, for example, he dreamed that he met her near the shrine of Our Lady of Consolation, along the wall surrounding Saint Anne's Monastery at the corner of the road as he was on his way back to the Oratory from the Convitto Ecclesiastico. She looked beautiful. "What? Are you really here?" Don Bosco asked. "Aren't you dead?"

"I died, but I'm alive," Margaret replied.

"And are you happy?"

"Very happy." After several other questions, Don Bosco asked her if she had gone straight to heaven. Margaret answered negatively. He then inquired if several boys—whose names he mentioned—were in heaven, and he received an affirmative reply.

"Now tell me," Don Bosco went on, "what is it that you enjoy in heaven?"

"I cannot explain that to you."

"Give me at least an idea of your happiness; let me see a glimmer of it!"

Mamma Margaret then appeared radiant with majesty and clothed in a magnificent robe. As a large choir stood in the background, she began to sing a song of love to God that was indescribably sweet and went straight to the heart, filling it and carrying it away with love. It sounded as if a thousand voices and a thousand tones—from the deepest bass to the highest soprano—had all been blended together masterfully, delicately, and harmoniously to form one single voice, notwithstanding the variety of tones and the pitch of the voices ranging from loud to the barely perceptible. Don Bosco was so enchanted by this most melodious singing that he thought he was out of his senses, and he was no longer able to tell or ask his mother anything. When Mamma Margaret had finished singing, she turned to him and said: "I'll be waiting for you. The two of us must always be together." After speaking these words, she vanished.

(Vol. V, pp. 375-376)

DOMINIC SAVIO

When I fell asleep the first night I was at Lanzo, I had a dream which is totally different from all the previous ones. I did narrate a dream somewhat like this during the spiritual retreat, but since you were not all present and this is quite different, I have decided to recount it to you. It is quite strange. However, as you know, I bare my very heart to my sons and keep no secrets from them. So give this dream whatever consideration you wish, but because St. Paul says: "Test everything; retain what is good" (1 Thes. 5: 21), if you should happen to find something in this dream that is beneficial to your soul, make good use of it. Those who do not want to believe it don't have to, but let no one ever hold up to ridicule what I am about to say. Furthermore, I ask you not to tell any outsider and not to write home about it. Dreams are to be given the importance they deserve. Those who do not know how close we are to each other might well misjudge the whole thing. They do not realize that you are my children and that I tell you everything I know, and even, sometimes, things I don't know. (*General laughter*) Whatever a father tells his beloved sons for their own good should stay between them and go no further. There is another reason, too. If the dream were to be told to outsiders, more often than not the facts could be twisted or presented out of context. This could be harmful and lead people to regard as worthless what, instead, is important.

As you know, dreams come in one's sleep. So during the night hours of December 6, while I was in my room—whether reading or pacing back and forth or resting in bed, I am not sure—I began dreaming.

It suddenly seemed to me that I was standing on a small mound or hillock, on the rim of a broad plain so far-reaching that the eye could not compass its boundaries lost in vastness. All was blue, blue as the calmest sea, though what I saw was not water. It resembled a highly polished, sparkling sea of glass. Stretching out beneath, behind and on either side of me was an expanse of what looked like a seashore.

Broad, imposing avenues divided the plain into grand gardens of indescribable beauty, each broken up by thickets, lawns, and flower beds of varied shapes and colors. None of the plants we know could ever give you an idea of those flowers, although there was a resemblance of sorts. The very grass, the flowers, the trees, the fruit—all were of singular and magnificent beauty. Leaves were of gold, trunks and boughs were of diamonds, and every tiny detail was in keeping with this wealth. The various kinds of plants were beyond counting. Each species and each single plant sparkled with a brilliance of its own. Scattered throughout those gardens and spread over the entire plain I could see countless buildings whose architecture, magnificence, harmony, grandeur and size were so unique that one could say all the treasures of earth could not suffice to build a single one. *If only my boys had one such house*, I said to myself, *how they would love it, how happy they would be, and how much they would enjoy being there!* Thus ran my thoughts as I gazed upon the exterior of those buildings, but how much greater must their inner splendor have been!

As I stood there basking in the splendor of those gardens, I suddenly heard music most sweet—so delightful and enchanting a melody that I could never adequately describe it. Compared with it, the compositions of Father Cagliero and Brother Dogliani are hardly music at all. A hundred thousand instruments played, each with its own sound, uniquely different from all others, and every possible sound set the air alive with its resonant waves. Blended with them were the songs of choristers.

In those gardens I looked upon a multitude of people enjoying themselves happily, some singing, others playing, but every voice, every note, had the effect of a thousand different instruments playing together. At one and the same time, if you can imagine such a thing, one could hear all the notes of the chromatic scale, from the deepest to the highest, yet all in perfect harmony. Ah yes, we have nothing on earth to compare with that symphony.

One could tell from the expressions of those happy faces that the singers not only took the deepest pleasure in singing, but also received vast joy in listening to the others. The more they sang, the more pressing became their desire to sing. The more they listened, the more vibrant became their yearning to hear more. And this was their song: "Salvation, honor and glory to Almighty God the Father... the Creator who was, who is and who will come to judge the living and the dead forever and ever."

As I listened enthralled to that heavenly choir I saw an endless multitude of boys approaching me. Many I recognized as having been at the Oratory and in our other schools, but by far the majority of them were total strangers to me. Their endless ranks drew closer, headed by Dominic Savio, who was followed immediately by Father Alasonatti, Father Chiala, Father Giulitto and many, many other clerics and priests, each leading a squad of boys.

I kept asking myself: *Am I sleeping or am I awake?* I clapped my hands and felt myself to make sure that I was seeing reality. Once that host of boys got some eight or ten paces from me, they halted. There was a flash of light far brighter than before, the music stopped, and a hushed silence fell over all. A most radiant joy encompassed all those boys and sparkled in their eyes, their countenances aglow with happiness. They looked and smiled at me very pleasantly, as though anxious to speak, but no one said a word.

Dominic Savio stepped forward a pace or two, standing so close to me that, had I stretched out my hand, I would surely have touched him. He too was silent and gazed upon me with a smile. How wonderful he looked! His garments were altogether unique. The snow-white tunic which he wore down to his feet was studded with diamonds, and there were threads of gold running through it. About his waist was fastened a broad red sash, so thickly embroidered with precious gems that they almost overlapped each other, and sewn into such a charming design with such brilliance of colors that, just looking at them, I could feel myself quite lost in admiration. From his neck hung a necklace woven of exotic but not natural flowers whose petals seemed to be clusters of diamonds set into stems of gold. And so it was with everything else. Those flowers flashed with a preternatural sparkle brighter than the very sun, which was then brilliantly burning in all the glory of a spring morning. Their blinding sparkles reflected from Dominic's candid, ruddy countenance in an indescribable manner, so brilliant indeed that their individual species were undetectable. A crown of roses encircled his head. His hair fell down in waves to his shoulders, giving him such a handsome and lovely charm that he seemed... he seemed... an angel!

While enunciating these last few words, Don Bosco seemed to be at a loss for suitable expressions, punctuating them with a gesture which defies description and a tone of voice which moved his listeners. It was as if he had exhausted himself in an effort to find words that would fully convey his idea. He paused momentarily and then went on.

The other persons too were aglow with light, dressed as they all were in different but always glittering garments, some more colorful than others, each garment symbolizing something that exceeded human understanding. However, all wore the same red sash about the waist.

I kept staring and wondering: *What can it all mean? How did I ever manage to get here?* With no idea where I was, beside myself and shaking with awe, I dared not take a step forward. The others all remained silent. At last Dominic Savio spoke. "Why do you stand there silent, as though you were almost devitalized?" he asked. "Aren't you the one who once feared nothing, holding your ground against slander, persecution, hostility, hardships and dangers of all sorts? Where is your courage? Say something!"

I forced myself to reply in a stammer, "I do not know what to say. Are you Dominic Savio?"

"Yes, I am. Don't you know me anymore?"

"How come you are here?" I asked, still bewildered.

Savio spoke affectionately. "I came to talk with you. We spoke together so often on earth! Do you not recall how much you loved me, or how many tokens of friendship you gave me and how kind you were to me? And did I not return the warmth of your love? How much trust I placed in you! So why are you tongue-tied? Why are you shaking? Come, ask me a question or two!"

Summoning my courage, I replied, "I am shaking because I don't know where I am."

"You are in the abode of happiness," Savio answered, "where one experiences every joy, every delight."

"Is this the reward of the just?"

"Not at all! Here we do not enjoy supernatural happiness but only a natural one, though greatly magnified."

"Everything here then is natural?"

"Yes, only enhanced by God's power!"

"Oh," I exclaimed. "I thought this was paradise."

"Oh, no, no!" Savio answered. "No human eye can look upon the beauty of paradise."

"And this music," I asked, "is it the music which you enjoy in heaven?"

"No, no, absolutely not!"

"Are these then natural sounds?"

"Yes, of course, but brought to perfection by God's infinite power."

"And this light which outshines the very sun's brilliance—is it a supernatural light? Is it heavenly light?"

"It is only natural light, fortified and perfected by God's omnipotence."

"Might I be allowed to see a little supernatural light?"

"No one can see it until he has come to see God as He is. The faintest ray of that light would instantly strike one dead, because the human senses are not sturdy enough to endure it."

"Could there possibly be a natural light lovelier than this?"

"Yes, but if you could only see a single ray of natural light increased by just one degree, you would go into an ecstasy."

"Might I not see at least one tiny ray of this brighter light?"

"Yes, of course you may. I'll give you a proof of what I say. Open your eyes."

"They are open," I answered.

"Pay close attention, then, and look out toward the farthest end of that crystal sea."

I looked. Instantly from the remotest heavens a sudden streak of light flashed through space, fine as a thread, but so brilliant, so piercing that my gaze faltered in pain. I shut my eyes and screamed loud enough to wake Father Lemoyne (he is here now) who was sleeping in the next room. In the morning he asked me in fright what had happened to me during the night to have so upset me. That filament of light was a hundred million times brighter than the sun; its brilliance could have lit up our entire universe.

After some moments I opened my eyes again. "What was that?" I asked Dominic. "Was not that a heavenly beam?"

"It was not a supernatural light," Dominic replied, "though ever so much superior in brilliance than the light of the world. It was nothing more than earthly light rendered ever so dazzling by God's power. Even if a vast array of light as strong as the ray you saw at the end of that crystal sea were to cover the whole world, it would still not give you an idea of the splendors of paradise."

"Then what do you enjoy in paradise?"

"Ah, that defies all telling. The happiness of heaven no mortal beings can ever know until they die and are reunited to their Maker. We enjoy God—nothing else!"

By now I had fully recovered from my initial bewilderment and was taken up with admiring Dominic Savio's beauty. "Why are you wearing that white, sparkling robe?" I asked him frankly.

Giving no sign of wanting to respond, Savio remained silent, but the choir, accompanied by all the instruments, sang: "... they have washed their robes and made them white in the blood of the Lamb." (Rv 7: 14)

"And why," I asked as the music ended, "are you wearing that red sash about your waist?"

Again Savio did not reply and motioned that he did not wish to answer.

It was Father Alasonatti who then began to sing by himself: "They are pure and follow the Lamb wherever He goes." (Rv 14: 4)

I then understood that Dominic's blood-red sash was a symbol of the great sacrifices, the strenuous efforts, and the near-martyrdom he had endured to preserve the virtue of purity, and that, to remain chaste in God's eyes, he would have given up his life if the circumstances had warranted it. It was also a symbol of penance which cleanses the soul of guilt. In addition, the shining whiteness of his robe signified the baptismal innocence which he had preserved.

Entranced by the singing and gazing upon those endless ranks of heavenly youths massed behind Dominic Savio, I asked him, "Who are they?" Then, turning, I asked: "Why are all of you so resplendent with light?" Savio continued to remain silent and all his companions broke into song: "They are like God's angels in heaven." I had noticed meanwhile that Savio seemed to enjoy a certain preeminence over that assembly, which kept at a respectful distance some ten paces behind him.

"Tell me, Savio," I said, "you are the youngest of this entire following and of those who have died in our houses. Why then are you at their head as their leader? Why are you their spokesman, while they are silent?"

"I am the oldest of them all."

"Oh, no," I countered. "Many of them are a good deal older than you."

"I am the oldest of the Oratory," Dominic Savio repeated, "because I was the first to leave the world and enter into this life. Besides, I am God's ambassador." This answer made the reason for the apparition clear to me. He was God's envoy.

"Well, then," I said, "let us speak of the things which most concern us at this moment."

"Yes, and be quick. Ask me whatever you wish to know. Hours go by and the time I have been given to speak with you may run out and you might not see me again."

"I am convinced you have something of supreme importance to tell me."

"What could I ever tell you—I, a poor creature?" Savio said with the deepest humility. "From on high I was given the mission to speak with you. That is why I am here."

"Then," I exclaimed, "tell me of the past, of the present, and of the future of our Oratory. Tell me something about my dear sons. Talk to me of my Congregation."

"There are so many things I could tell you about that."

"Reveal to me the things you know. Tell me about the past."

"All the past is your responsibility," Savio replied.

"Have I made any blunders?"

"As to the past," he answered, "I will say that your Congregation has already accomplished a great deal of good. Do you see that countless multitude of boys there?"

"Yes. They are so many," I answered. "How happy they look!"

"Observe," he went on. "Do you see what is written at the gateway of that garden?"

261

"I do. It says 'Salesian Garden.' "

"Well then," Savio went on, "those who are there were all Salesians or Salesian pupils. They were saved by you or your priests and clerics. Or they are those whom you directed on the path of their vocation. Count them if you can! Still, there would be a hundred million times more if you only had greater faith and trust in the Lord."

I sighed in dismay. I had no excuse for his reproach but resolved within my heart: *I shall endeavor to have this faith and trust in the future.*

Then I inquired, "What of the present?"

Savio held out a gorgeous bouquet of roses, violets, sunflowers, gentians, lilies, evergreens, perennials, and sprigs of wheat and he handed it to me. "Look at these flowers," he said.

"I am looking," I replied, "but I don't know what you mean."

"Give this bouquet to your sons so that, when the time comes, they may offer it to the Lord. See to it that everyone has it, that no one is without it and that no one steals it from them. Do this and you can rest assured that they will have enough to make them happy."

"What do these flowers symbolize?"

"Get your theology book," he replied, "and you will know."

"I've studied theology," I objected, "and I still can't fathom any meaning from what you have given me."

"And yet you absolutely should know these things."

"Well then," I pleaded, "ease my anxiety. Tell me what this is all about."

"Do you see these flowers?" Savio obliged. "They symbolize the virtues which most delight the Lord."

"Which are they?"

"The rose is the symbol of charity, the violet of humility, the sunflower of obedience, the gentian of penance and self-denial, and the wheat stalks of frequent Communion. Then, the lily stands for the beautiful virtue of chastity of which it is written: *Erunt sicut angeli Dei in caelo* [They shall be like God's angels in heaven]. Finally, the evergreens and perennials tell you that these virtues must endure forever. They denote perseverance."

"Very well, my dear Savio," I answered. "Now tell me, you who practiced all these virtues in your lifetime, what comforted you the most at the moment of your death?"

"What do you think it was?" Savio prompted.

"Perhaps having preserved the beautiful virtue of purity?"

"Not that alone."

"Having your conscience at peace?"

"That too is a good thing, but it is still not the best."

"Perhaps the hope of paradise?"

"No, not even that."

"Well, was it the treasury of good deeds you had stored up?"

"No, no."

"Well, what was it then?" I pleaded with him, nonplussed at having failed to fathom his thought.

"The one thing that consoled me most at the hour of my death," Savio answered, "was the assistance of the mighty and lovely Mother of the Savior. Tell your sons never to forget to pray to Her as long as they live. But now hurry if you want me to answer more questions."

"What can you tell me about the future?"

"In the coming year of 1877, you will have a painful sorrow to endure. Six and then two more of those dearest to you will be summoned into eternity. But be comforted, for they will be transplanted from this world to the gardens of heaven. They will receive their crown. And do not be worried, for the Lord will be your help and will give you other good sons."

"God's will be done! And what will happen to the Congregation?"

"The Lord is preparing great things for you. In the coming year your Congregation will see a dawn of glory so resplendent that it will light up the four corners of the earth. A great splendor lies in the offing. But see to it that the Lord's chariot is not led by your Salesians off its course, out of its set path. If your priests will guide it in a manner worthy of their lofty calling, the future of your Congregation will be most glorious and will bring salvation to endless multitudes of people. There is but one condition: that your sons be devoted to the Blessed Virgin Mary and that all of them learn to preserve the virtue of chastity which so delights God."

"Now I would like you to tell me about the Church in general," I continued.

"The Church's destiny is in the hands of God, our Maker. I cannot tell you what He has determined in His infinite decrees. To Himself alone He keeps such mysteries, and no heavenly creature can ever share that knowledge."

"What will happen to Pius IX?"

"All I can tell you is that the Church's shepherd will not have much longer to do battle here on earth. Few are the combats he must still win. Soon he will be taken from his see and the Lord will grant him his well-earned reward. The rest you know. The Church will not die. Is there anything else you want to know?"

"What will happen to me?" I asked.

"If you only knew how many tribulations still await you! But hurry now, for the time alotted me to speak to you is drawing to a close."

Impulsively I stretched out my hands to clutch those of that blessed youth, but his hands were no firmer than thin air, and I grasped nothingness.

"How foolish!" Dominic said with a smile. "What are you trying to do?"

"I am afraid to lose you," I exclaimed. "Are you not really here in the flesh?"

"Not in my flesh. One day I will take that up again."

"But what is that I see? You have Dominic Savio's features; you are Dominic Savio."

"Look," he said, "when a soul, separated from the body, is allowed by God to reveal itself to a human, it retains its features just as it had them in the flesh, though considerably enhanced in beauty, until it is reunited to the body on the day of the universal judgment. From then on soul and body will again be together. That is why I seem to have hands, feet and head, but you cannot grasp me because I am a pure spirit. You only recognize me because of the features that I am allowed to retain in order to be seen."

"I understand," I answered. "I have one more question: Are all my boys on the path of salvation? Tell me how to guide them."

"The boys whom Divine Providence has entrusted to your care can be divided into three groups. Take a look at these three sheets of paper." (He held one out to me.)

I looked at the first. It bore one word: *Unscathed*, that is, those whom the devil had not been able to harm, those who had never lost their baptismal innocence. There was a great number of them and I saw them all. Many I personally knew; many others I was seeing for the first time—perhaps boys who will come to the Oratory in future years. They were all moving forward unswervingly along a narrow path, regardless of the arrows and swords and spears that were continually being hurled at them from everywhere. These weapons bristled like hedges on both sides of their path, threatening and harassing but never wounding them.

Savio then handed me a second sheet. It bore the word: *Wounded*, that is, those who had fallen into sin but had risen to their feet again, healed of their wounds after repentance and confession. Their number was considerably greater than the first. They had been wounded on their passage through life by the enemies who lined their way. I scanned the list of their names and saw them all. Many dragged themselves along, bent over and disheartened.

Savio still held a third sheet in his hand, labeled: *"Strayed from the way of truth..."* (Wis 5:6) It bore the names of all those boys who at that moment were in the state of sin. Impatient to know the contents of that list, I put out my hand, but Savio quickly held the note back. "Wait a moment," he said, "and listen. Once you open this note, such a stench will come out that it will overcome us both and make the angels withdraw in disgust and horror. The Holy Spirit himself cannot stand the offensive odor of sin!"

"How can this be," I objected, "since God and his angels are impassible? How can they smell a material stench?"

"They can," he answered. "The purer and holier a creature is, the more it resembles a heavenly spirit, but the filthier and more sinful one is, the further he moves from God and His angels, who in turn withdraw from him, an object of disgust and loathing."

He then gave me the note. "Take it," he said, "and use it for the good of your boys, but don't forget the bouquet of flowers which I have given you. Make sure that everyone has it and does not lose it." Giving me the list, he hastily withdrew and joined his companions. I opened it. I saw no names, but in an instant there flashed before my eyes all the lads therein mentioned, just as real as if they were standing there in front of me. With great grief I saw all of them. Most I knew personally as belonging to this Oratory and to our other schools. I also noticed quite a few who rate as good boys and even some who rank among the very best but are not so at all. Then, as I opened that note, an unbearable stench emanated from it. An atrocious headache immediately seized me, and I felt so sick to my stomach that I thought I would die. The whole sky darkened, the vision vanished, and nothing was left of that wonderful sight. Suddenly a bolt of lightning flashed with a crash of thunder so deafening and frightening that I awoke in a cold sweat.

That stench penetrated the very walls and got into all my clothing, so much so that for days afterward I could still detect its foulness. Even the name of the sinner is truly foul in God's eyes. Even now, no sooner do I recall that stench than I begin to shudder and choke, and my stomach turns over with retching.

There at Lanzo, where I had this dream, I began to call in some boys and soon realized that my dream was no dream but, rather, a very special favor of God that enabled me to know each one's state of soul. Of this, however, I shall say nothing in public. There are also several points which need clearing up, but I will put this off to some other evening. Now, let me just wish you a good night.

Because the dream showed that some Oratory boys who seemed to be among the best were actually morally bad, it gave Don Bosco cause for misgivings that it might be a mere hallucination. That is why [before narrating the dream] he had summoned several boys to his room in order to ascertain its truth. Hence, too, he delayed two weeks before narrating it, and only when he felt quite sure that it had come from above did he speak. As its predictions would be fulfilled, time would corroborate its message.

(Vol. XII, pp. 432-441)

FATHER PROVERA

During the night of January 17, 1883, I dreamed that I left our dining hall with several of our priests. Beside me walked a priest I did not recognize, until I looked at him more closely and saw that it was a former confrere, Father Provera. He was taller than he had been in life, and his face was so youthful-looking and smiling that it seemed to shine.

"Are you really Father Provera?" I asked.

"I certainly am," he replied. And at that moment his face grew brighter and more beautiful, so that it was difficult to look at him.

"If you are Father Provera, then don't go away from me. Stay awhile—I wish to speak to you."

"All right. I'm listening."

"Are you saved?"

"Yes, by the mercy of God."

"What are the joys of the other life?"

"Whatever the heart can desire and the mind imagine; whatever the eye can see and the tongue describe!"

He then made as if to go. I held his hand tightly in mine, but it seemed to have lost its feeling.

"Don't go," I said. "Tell me something that will be useful for me."

"Continue your work; there is much still to be done."

"For how long?"

"Not so long. Anyway, work with all possible energy, as if you will live forever, but always be prepared."

"Anything for our confreres?"

"Insist unceasingly that they be fervent."

"What must we do to obtain this grace?"

"The Master of masters tells us how: take a well-sharpened knife and do what the good vinedresser does—cut off the withered and useless shoots. In this way the vine will become strong and laden with fruit, and, what is more important, it will flourish."

"What shall I tell the confreres?"

"Say to my friends," Father Provera exclaimed, raising his voice a little, "that they must prepare themselves for a great reward, but that God will give it only to those who persevere in the works of God."

"What can you recommend to the boys?"

"They must be hard workers and ever on the watch."

"Anything more?"

"Yes. Watch and work. Work and watch!"

"What must the boys do to secure their eternal salvation?"

"Frequent Holy Communion, the Bread of the strong, and firm resolutions in confession."

"Is there anything they should do more than all else?"

"At that moment, so bright a radiance enclosed my companion that I had to lower my eyes for fear of becoming blind, as when you suddenly look at an electric light—except that it was much more brilliant. His next words were uttered as though they could be set to music:

"Glory to God the Father, to God the Son, to God the Holy Spirit, to God who was and is and shall always be, the judge of the living and the dead."

I wanted to continue the conversation, but he started to sing: "Praise the Lord, all you nations...." His voice was extraordinarily beautiful and solemn. Then, from the porticoes and from the stairs came thousands and thousands of voices joining him in song.

Several times, I tried to open my eyes to see who the people were who were singing, but each time I closed them quickly, for the intensity and the brightness of the light prevented it. At last the "Amen" was sung.

I opened my eyes, but everything was back to normal, and there was no sign of Father Provera. I ran at once to the porticoes to ask the priests and the others if they had seen Father Provera, but they answered "No." They gave the same answer when I asked whether they had heard singing.

I was embarrassed and remarked:

"So I dreamed about Father Provera and about the singing. All right, come along and I shall tell you about it."

I related what I had just seen and heard. Then Fathers Rua, Cagliero and others asked me questions, to which I gave whatever answers seemed appropriate.

I awoke just then, because of a pain in my stomach and a shortness of breath. I heard the quarter of the hour striking, and a little later it was two o'clock in the morning.

(Vol. XVI, pp. 15 ff)

LUIS COLLE

The Colle family played a great part in the work of Don Bosco. Luis, the pride of the family, died on April 3, 1881, and thereafter appeared to Don Bosco many times; some of these appearances are noted here.

The day Luis died, Don Bosco was hearing confessions. He tells us that he saw, in a kind of distraction, Luis Colle enjoying himself in a very beautiful garden with other happy youths. The vision lasted but a moment, but it convinced the saint that the son of his great benefactor was in heaven. So he was able to say in a letter to the Colle family, written on May 4: "I am sure that Luis is eternally saved."

On the morning of the Ascension, May 27, 1881, Don Bosco was saying Mass for the intentions of the Colle family, who were present, when Luis appeared to him at the Consecration. The youth was bathed in light, beautiful of countenance; joy and well-being radiated from him; his clothes were white and rose-colored, and there were gold stripes on his chest.

"Luis, why are you here?"

"There is no need for me to come," he replied. "In my state I can come and go."

"Are you happy?"

"Perfectly."

"Do you need anything?"

"Nothing, except my parents."

Then he disappeared, but he appeared again during the prayers after Mass and again in the sacristy. In this last vision, several Oratory boys who had died appeared with him. The vision gave Don Bosco great comfort.

"Luis," Don Bosco asked, "What shall I tell your parents by way of consolation?"

"Let them live according to their light, and let them make friends with the Blessed."

On June 21 (Don Bosco writes), a little before the Consecration of the Mass, I saw Luis again. His face was radiant, like the bloom of a rose. I asked him if he had anything to tell us.

"Saint Aloysius," he replied simply, "has been a good friend and benefactor to me."

"Is there anything to be done?" I insisted.

He gave the same answer and disappeared.

During the octave of the feast of the Assumption, and again on the 25th of August, I had special prayers offered for Luis. On the 25th, at the Consecration, I was overjoyed to see him appear before me. He was clothed in brilliance; his face was radiant, and he appeared to be perfectly happy. It looked as if he were in a garden, walking with some friends, and all were singing the hymn, "Jesus, Crown of Virgins." They sang with such melodious harmony that I find it difficult to describe. There was a kind of pavillion or tent erected in the garden. When I wanted to approach them to hear the singing better, a very bright flash of light made me close my eyes. On opening them, I found I was at the altar.

One day, while preparing a sermon, Don Bosco felt as if someone was standing near him. He looked to the left, but the presence seemed to pass to the right; he looked to the right, but the presence passed to the left. It all took place in an instant. He demanded to know who was there, and heard the reply:

"You do not know me?"

"Oh, Luis!" exclaimed Don Bosco. "What brings you to San Benigno?"

"It is just as easy for me to be at San Benigno as at my own home, or at Turin, or anywhere else."

"Why don't you let your parents see you? They love you so much."

"Yes, I know they love me, but the permission of God is needed for them to see me. If I spoke to them, my words would not have the same efficacy as when they are relayed through you."

(On July 30, 1882, Don Bosco wrote to the Colles.)

I am happy to tell you that I have seen our dear Luis again. It has made me very happy indeed. I would like to mention several particulars to you.

Once, I saw him playing in a garden with many friends. He was so wonderfully dressed that I cannot find words to describe him.

Another time, I saw him in a garden gathering flowers, which he laid upon a magnificent table in a spacious hall. I asked him:

"What are the flowers for?"

"I have been commissioned," he replied, "to gather flowers and make crowns for my parents, because they have worked so hard for my eternal happiness."

On the feast of St. Joseph's patronage, 1881, the third Sunday after Easter, I was in the sacristy of the chapel near the Church of the Sacred Heart, which was being built in Rome. I saw Luis drawing water from a fountain, so I asked him:

"Why all the water?"

"It is for my parents and for myself."

"So much water?" I asked incredulously.

"Don't you understand? Can't you see that this fountain is the Sacred Heart of Our Lord? No matter how much you draw from it, just as much remains."

"Why are you here?"

"I have come to visit you and to inform you that I am happy."

Don Bosco related these dreams while he was visiting Toulon. He said other things also, but these have not been recorded. He remarked that in the various visions, Luis was dressed differently, and when he asked for an explanation, Luis said that it was simply for the delight of Don Bosco's eyes. The youth's face, however, had the same features as when he was alive, except that his cheeks were of a more healthy hue and he looked happier. His clothes sparkled with gold and with the color of lilies and roses, although to a more perfect degree. His face glowed, until human eyes had to seek shelter from the radiance.

The apparitions that came during Mass lasted a minute, or perhaps a bit more. If they had been any longer, Don Bosco said, he would have swooned, because of the overwhelming contact with the supernatural.

"When I reflect upon these appearances," Don Bosco explained to the mother of Luis Colle, "and study them through and through, I feel that they are not at all tricks of the imagination, but real. All that I see in them is clearly in conformity with the Spirit of God. Undoubtedly, Luis is in heaven. As far as the frequency of these visions, I do not know what God has in mind. I only know that Luis advises me and teaches me things I did not know about Theology and science."

Once Luis gave Don Bosco a rose and remarked:
"Would you like to know the difference between the natural and the supernatural? Examine this rose."

The flower became so brilliant that it seemed like a diamond reflecting the sunlight.

"Now look at this mountain."

The mountain that had been rocky and full of muddy holes just a moment before had now become a thing of beauty, with sparkling mounds of precious stones.

Once, Don Bosco was invited to a dinner in Hyeres. He was in a corridor when he met Luis Colle, who said to him:

"See what an excellent dinner, and such rich foods! Too much money is spent, when there are so many hungry people in the world. You must fight excess in eating and drinking."

Some of the diners addressed Don Bosco, but he seemed to be distracted. They called him: "Don Bosco!" And he became once more aware of his surroundings.

On one occasion, Don Bosco and Luis Colle had the following conversation:

"Are you happy, Luis?"
"Very!"
"Are you dead or alive?"
"My body is dead, but I am alive!"
"Isn't it your body that I see?"
"No."
"Your soul, then?"
"No."
"Your spirit?"
"No."
"Then what am I looking at?"
"Just an apparition."
"How can an apparition speak?"
"Through God's power."
"Where is your soul, then?"
"It stands before God and in Him. Your eyes cannot see it."
"How do you see us?"
"We see all things in God—the past, the present, the future—as though in a mirror."
"What do you do in heaven?"

"I give thanks always to God—to Him who created me; to Him who is master of life and death; to Him who is the beginning and end of all. Thanks! Praises! Alleluia!"

"What shall I tell your parents?"

"That I pray for them continuously, and this is how I thank them. That I am waiting for them in heaven."

"You say that I see only an apparition, a specter, because your soul is standing before God. But how can a specter have the appearance of a living body?"

"Wait awhile and you will have proof."

(The proof came some days later when the deceased pastor of Castelnuovo appeared to Don Bosco one night. The priest seemed to be in the best of health.)

Don Bosco said: "Hello, Father, how are you doing?"

"I am very happy, indeed. Are you walking with me?"

"Do you need anything?"

"In heaven there is all a person can want. Let us walk and talk. Do you recognize me?"

"Undoubtedly!"

"Look at me carefully. Don't you see that I am in the full bloom of youth, and perfectly happy?"

"There is no doubt that you are the former pastor of Castelnuovo."

After a short walk, the specter said:

"Well, have you learned your lesson?"

At that he disappeared.

During Don Bosco's journey to France in 1883, Luis appeared to him many times. On March 4, *Laetare* Sunday, he accompanied Don Bosco by train from Cannes to Toulon and discoursed in Latin on the wonderful works of God. He even turned his attention to the skies and gave him some facts of astronomy that the saint never knew before. He told Don Bosco:

"If you were to go by express from earth to the sun, you would reach it after 350 years! And to cross the sun's face you would need just as long a time. Each nebula out there is 50 million times larger than our sun, and its light needs 10 million years to reach us."

When Luis kept giving him these astronomical figures, Don Bosco cried:

"Enough, Luis, enough! My poor mind cannot keep up with you."

"And yet this is only the beginning of God's greatness."

"How is it that you are here and in heaven too?"

"Faster than light and with the speed of thought, I come here, to my parents' house, and to other places."

Luis appeared to Don Bosco one day at Mass in Hyeres.

"Have you something to tell me, Luis?" the saint asked. Luis showed him a portion of South America where he must send missionaries, and also the beginnings of the river Chubut in the Cordilleras.

"Let me say my Mass now, Luis; otherwise, distractions will annoy me."

"You must see to it," Luis said, "that the boys receive Communion frequently. Admit them early to first Communion; God wants them to feed on the Holy Eucharist."

"They are too young as yet."

"When they are four or five, show them the Host and let them fix their eyes on it while they pray. This will be a communion for them. They must be taught three things: 1) Love for God; 2) Frequency of Communion; 3) Love for the Sacred Heart of Jesus. However, love for the Sacred Heart includes the other two."

In a previous vision, Luis had shown Don Bosco a fountain in the middle of the sea and said:

"Do you see that fountain? The waters of the sea enter it all the time, and yet the sea never decreases. So it is with the graces from the Sacred Heart of Jesus. If you want to receive them, all you have to do is pray."

Don Bosco received another visit from Luis Colle in the Church of Saint Clothilde, where he had gone to say Mass. Many people had crowded into the sacristy to touch the holy priest. Don Bosco could hardly breathe.

"Please leave me," he pleaded in vain. "At least let me say an Our Father."

Then the pastor of the church took him into an adjoining room. As soon as the saint entered, he saw the room bathed in brilliance and Luis Colle slowly pacing up and down.

"Hello, Luis. Why the silent pacing?"

"It is not the time to speak but to pray."

"Say something to me, as you have on other occasions."

"I have something very important to tell you, but now is not the time."

"But you must tell me, because I want to give some comfort to your parents when I see them."

"They will have consolations later. Let them pray and serve God and Mary. I am already preparing their happiness."

"Why pray for you? There is no need, surely. We know you are saved, so why ask your parents to waste time praying for you?"

"Prayer gives God glory."

"Why do you not appear to your parents?"

"That is a secret God has reserved for Himself."

So saying, he disappeared, and Don Bosco realized that the youth had kept his head covered during the entire appearance.

Don Bosco had an important dream at the end of August, 1883. He dreamed that he was among many long-dead friends in a spacious room. A youth radiating a brilliance greater than the sun approached him. It was Luis, although his features suggested a young man in his early teens.

In a flash of light, Luis let the saint see what a glorious heritage was reserved for the Salesians in the Americas, and the sweat and blood that would be required to make those missionary lands fruitful.

Returning one night from Rome—it was in May, 1884— Don Bosco had four hours to wait for his train, so he decided to get some sleep in the waiting room. Luis appeared.

"Is that you, Luis?" asked Don Bosco.

"You haven't forgotten me, have you? Do you remember the journey we made together?"

I certainly do. But how can I carry out all those tasks? I am old, and my health is not too good."

"You are healthy enough, Don Bosco. Tomorrow you must give me your answer."

The following day was the first day of the novena in honor of Mary Help of Christians. Don Bosco felt better than when he was in France, and his health was noticeably improved after that. (Vol. XV, p. 89ff)

SAINTS PETER AND PAUL

On February 13, 1884, Don Bosco had a dream in which he entered a certain house and met Saint Peter and Saint Paul. Each was dressed in a long, flowing tunic that reached below the knees, and on his head was an oriental skullcap. Both smiled at Don Bosco.

He asked them if they had any special communication for him, but they did not answer his question. Instead, they spoke about the Oratory and the boys. Just then a friend of Don Bosco came along.

"Look at these two," Don Bosco said.

"What's this!" the newcomer replied. "Is it really Saint Peter and Saint Paul?"

Don Bosco again posed his question, but the two apostles gently put it aside and spoke of other things.

"What about the *Life of Saint Peter*?" asked the prince of the apostles.

"What about the *Life of Saint Paul*?" asked the apostle to the Gentiles.

"Yes, Yes indeed," answered Don Bosco sheepishly. He had intended to reprint those two booklets, but the idea had slipped his mind.

"If you do not do it quickly, you will not have the time later," observed Saint Paul.

Meanwhile, Saint Peter removed his cap. His head was bald, except for a couple of locks at his temples; yet he looked hale and hearty in spite of his age. He had gone off to the side as if to pray, and Don Bosco was about to follow him when Saint Paul said:

"Let him pray."

Don Bosco said, "I want to see what he is kneeling beside."

Saint Peter was kneeling before an altar that was not really an altar.

"Where are the candles?" Don Bosco asked Saint Paul.

"There is no need for candles," replied the saint, "where the eternal Sun shines."

"Where is the altar?"

"The Victim is not sacrificed; He lives forever."

"So, there is no altar at all!"

"Calvary is the altar for all the world."

Then, in a clear and harmonious voice, Saint Peter prayed:

"Glory to God, Creator and Father, to God the Son, the Redeemer; to God the Holy Spirit, the Sanctifier. To God alone be honor and glory in every age. Praise also to you, O Mary. Heaven and earth proclaim you their queen."

He spoke her name so tenderly that he broke into tears of delight.

Saint Peter returned and Saint Paul took his place. On his knees, he raised his voice and prayed:

"Oh, the depths of divine mysteries! Great God, Your secrets are beyond all mortals. Only in heaven can we grasp the profundity of Your majesty. O God, one and triune, honor be to You, praise and thanksgiving from every part of the universe! Praised and blessed be your name too, O Mary. The blessed sing your praises in heaven and upon earth. You are the help, the consolation and the salvation, queen of all saints. Alleluia. Alleluia."

When Don Bosco narrated the dream later, he remarked:

"The prayers of those two great saints filled me with such emotion that I burst into tears. Then I awoke, but an indescribable joy remained with me." (Vol. XVII, p. 27)

Index

Acts of the Holy Apostle Thomas, xxii-xxiii
Adventure Inward, xl n
Against Celsus, xxiii
Against Heresies, xxiii
Alasonatti, Father Victor. See Personages, in dreams of Don Bosco
Ambrose, Saint, xxvii
Aquinas, Saint Thomas, xxviii
Arphaxad, angel of, 91, 93-95
Athanasius, Saint, xxv
Augustine, Saint, xxvii

Basil the Great, Saint, xxvi
Becchi
  Don Bosco's house in, 23
  Don Bosco's mission begun at, 49
  seen in dream, 68-69
Bible, dreams in, xxi-xxii, xxiv
Blessed Sacrament, devotion to, 108, 203, 214
Blessed Virgin Mary. See also Personages, in dreams of Don Bosco
  devotion to, 16, 18, 51, 106-108, 128-129, 152, 155, 157, 160, 174-180, 214, 225, 229, 263, 275, 277
  hymns to, 12, 127, 152, 176, 178, 180, 225

Cafasso, Father Victor. See Personages, in dreams of Don Bosco
Cagliero, Bishop John. See Personages, in dreams of Don Bosco
Christianity as Psychology, xx
Chrysostom, Saint John, xxvi
Church of Saint Francis de Sales, in dream 201
City of God, The, xxvii

Classification of dreams, xxxii-xxxvi
Clementine Homilies, The, xxiii
Clement of Alexandria, Saint, xxiii
Collected Works of C.G. Jung, xxxix
Colle, Luis. See Personages, in dreams of Don Bosco
Commentary on the Dream of Scipio, xxvii
Conceptual activity during sleep
  alternating with dreams, xv
  description of, xvii-xviii
Confessions, The, xxvii
Conscience, state of, known to Don Bosco, 3-4, 37-38, 129, 135-137, 139-146, 148, 152-155, 159, 169, 182-184, 207-208, 233, 266
Constantine, Emperor, xxv
Cyprian, Saint, xxiv

Daughters of Mary Help of Christians
  advice for, 71-72, 90
  future foretold, 17-18, 71-72, 108-109
Daydream. See Fantasy
Death, predictions of, 49, 121-124, 184-185, 188-189, 195-197, 199-200, 204-209, 264
  Don Bosco's own, 23-24, 41, 48-49, 67, 239, 267, 276
Definition of dreams, xiv
De Magia, xxviii
Devil. See also Personages, in dreams of Don Bosco
  symbols of, 27, 42, 56, 138, 148-152, 173, 214, 244
Dictionary of Symbols, A, xxxix
Dream interpretation, xxxii-xxxiv
  in Christian Church, x, xxi-xxviii
  in modern times, xxix-xxxii

279

Dreams, attitude toward
  Aristotle, xi, xxviii
  at beginning of twentieth century, xviii
  in Bible, ix, 1-2
  in Catholic Church, xxviii
  among Christian clergy, xviii
  in Christian tradition, ix, xiv, xviii, xx
  Cicero, xi
  in Dark and Middle Ages, xxviii
  Dr. Carl G. Jung, xx
  Don Bosco, xvi, xx, xl
  in Eastern Church, xxviii
  in the Enlightenment, xiv, xxix
  among faith healers, xviii-xix
  Jesus of Nazareth, xx
  in major religions, ix, xiii
  in mid-twentieth century theology, xx
  in most cultures, xiii, xvi
  our own, xxxviii-xl
  Plato, xx
  in Protestant Church, xxviii
  among religious groups, xviii
  in the Renaissance, xxviii
  Saint Thomas Aquinas, xxviii
  in scientific community, xiii
  among those who speak in tongues, xviii-xix
  in Western society, xi, xiii, xvi
Dreams: A Way to Listen to God, xxxviii
Dreams, Daydreams and Discovery, xxxv
Dreams, God's Forgotten Language, xl n
Dreams of Don Bosco
  analysis of, xxxvi-xxxviii
  benefits of, 3-4, 190-191, 194, 207-209
  his own view of, 2-3, 37, 53, 152-154
  others' view of, 1-6, 9, 45, 192, 201, 228-229, 239-240
  our response to, xxxvii-xl
Dreams: The Dark Speech of the Spirit, xl n
Dream world. *See* Spiritual world
Edict of Milan, xxx
Exercise for a Happy Death, 196-198, 200, 208-209
Extrasensory dreams, xxxv
  Don Bosco's, xxxvii
Fantasy, relationship to dreams and visions, xvi-xviii
Fascination for dreams, xi-xii
Francis de Sales, Saint. *See* Personages, in dreams of Don Bosco
Freud, Sigmund
  dream symbols in xxxiv
  Interpretation of Dreams, The, vi, xi, xiii, xviii
God and the Unconscious, xix
God, Dreams and Revelation, x
"Good Night," 41, 125, 157, 166, 186, 188, 191, 193-196, 199-200, 206, 208, 229, 240
Gordon, A.J., xxix
Gregory Thaumaturgus, Saint, xxiv
Gregory the Great, Saint
  view of dreams, xxvii
  writings on dreams, xxviii
Hallucinations, distinguished from visions, xvii
Healing and Wholeness, xl n
Heaven, Don Bosco's dreams of, xxxvii, 44-45, 48, 73, 87-92, 139, 161-162, 168, 179, 232, 239-277
Hell, Don Bosco's dreams of, xxxvii-xxxviii, 147, 181, 211-228, 247
Hippolytus, Saint, xxiv
Hymns to God, 47, 63-64, 88-90, 162, 254, 256-257, 268, 270, 277
Hypnagogic, definition of, xv
Hypnopompic, definition of, xv
Informative Process, for beatification of Don Bosco, 184, 205, 208

Interpretation of Dreams, The, xiii, xviii
Irenaeus, Saint, xxiii
Jerome, Saint, xxvii
Joseph, Saint. *See* Personages, in dreams of Don Bosco
Jung, Dr. Carl G.
  attitude toward dreams, xx
  Collected Works of C.G. Jung, xxxix
  collective unconscious in, xiii, xviii
  dream symbols in, xxxiv
  Visions Seminars, The, xxxix
Justin Martyr, Saint, xxiii

Kelsey, Dr. Morton T., books by, x, xx, xxxii, xxxviii, xl n
Kingdom Within, The, xl n
Kleitman, Nathaniel, xiii-xiv, xiv-xv

Les Devins, xxviii
Life of Saint Anthony, xxv

Mamma Margaret. *See* Personages, in dreams of Don Bosco
Martin of Tours, Saint, xxviii
Martyrdom of Polycarp, xxii
Martyrs of Turin. *See* Personages, in dreams of Don Bosco
Mary. *See* Blessed Virgin Mary
Mary Help of Christians
  assistance of, 228
  banner of, 65, 117
  care of, 70
  Church of, 14, 16, 144
  devotion to, 125-129, 183
  inscription, 105
  prayer to, 183, 275
  protects Pope, 115
  statue of, 179
Morals and Dialogues, xxviii
Moretta house, 17

Nazianzen, Saint Gregory, x, xxvi
Newton, John, xxii-xxiii, xxix-xxx
Numinous dreams
  description of, xxxiv

Don Bosco's, xxxvi
Nyssa, Saint Gregory of, xxvi

On the Making of Man, xxvi
On the Soul, xxiv
Oratory
  future foretold, 11-14, 17, 21-22, 29, 68-69
  on spot of martyrdom of Thebian soldiers, 15
  Oratory boys, advice for, 135, 218, 223-226, 236-238, 248, 251, 264-266, 268
Oratory for girls, 69-70
Origen, xxiii
Other Side of Silence, The, xxxii
Otis Botis Pia Tutis, 233
Outsiders, dreams not to be told to, 135, 157, 166, 233, 240, 250, 255

Parapsychological dreams, xxvii
Perpetua, Saint, xxiv
Personages, in dreams of Don Bosco
  Alasonatti, Father Victor, 32, 150, 161, 163, 165, 195, 257, 260
  bishop, 234-239
  Blessed Virgin Mary, 7-8, 10-13, 16-21, 61-64, 130-132, 149-152, 160-166, 180
  brother Joseph, 24, 69, 161, 163, 165
  Cafasso, Father Joseph, 132-135
  Cagliero, Bishop John, 46, 87-91, 129, 140, 144-145, 175, 182, 230, 268
  Colle, Luis, 73-82, 90-93, 148, 269-275
  devil, 42, 138, 164, 201-204, 214, 247
  distinguished person, 211
  Francis de Sales, Saint, 65-68, 148
  guide, 200, 234
  handsome young man, 179
  Jesus, 7-8, 10
  Joseph, Saint, 148

little girls, 69-70
Mamma Margaret, 68-69, 149, 152, 195, 253-254
man of noble bearing, 85
man with the cap, 212-227
martyrs of Turin, 13, 16
mysterious man, 54-60
pastor of Castelnuovo, 273
Peter and Paul, Saints, 276-277
Pius IX, Pope, 121
Provera, Father Francis, 31, 267-268
Rua, Father Michael, 32, 35, 46, 129, 140, 144-145, 230, 268
Savio, Saint Dominic, 148, 181, 255-266
shepherdess, 11-12, 61-64
small boy, 61-62, 64
stranger, 23-34, 43, 52-53, 141, 145-148, 156-158, 167, 184-185, 194, 207
tailor, 9-10
tall old man, 189
a voice, 46
woman gathering chestnuts, 70-72
workingman, 69
young priest, 86-87
Peter and Paul, Saints. *See* Personages, in dreams of Don Bosco
Phenomenon of dreams
frequency, xv
observation, xv
spontaneity, xv, xix
universality, xiii
Physical world, relationship to spiritual world, xvii, xix-xxi, xxix, xxvii, xxxiii-xxxiv, xxxviii
Pinardi house, 185
seen in dream, 16-17, 100, 140, 144
Pius IX, Pope
communication with Don Bosco, 120
death predicted, 121-124, 264
decision to stay in Rome, 119
dream told to, 50
gift for, 103
influence on Don Bosco, 5
medallion in Saint Peter's, 95
ordered Don Bosco to record dreams, x, xxxvi, 5, 9
private audience, 111
in Vatican Council, 114
Prayer
for God's mercy, 168
for one who is to die, 190
gives God glory, 275
in heaven, 272-273, 276-277
importance of, 28, 42, 143, 225, 237-238
relationship to dreams and visions, xx, xxxvi
in time of danger, 176
Precognitive dreams, xii
Don Bosco's, xxxvii
Saint Perpetua's, xxiv
Primary process activity, during sleep, xv
Prophecies of Don Bosco
made, 10-11, 17-18, 38-40, 44, 64-65, 68, 70, 72-73, 78-79, 91, 95, 97-100, 111, 113-116, 119, 121-124, 153-154, 184-186, 188-189, 195-197, 199-200, 204-205, 207, 209
realized, 11, 17-18, 38-40, 44, 64-65, 69, 82-84, 91, 95, 98-100, 118-119, 124, 153, 155, 182, 187-188, 192-196, 199, 201, 204, 206, 208-209
Provera, Father Francis. *See* Personages, in dreams of Don Bosco
Purgatory, 233-239, 251, 253-254
Religious implications of dreams, xiii
Resurrection, xl n
Rua, Father Michael, *See* Personages, in dreams of Don Bosco
Salesian Congregation
advice for, 57-60, 66-67, 86,

90, 93, 267
first mission, 50-52
future foretold, 2, 4-5, 12, 14-15, 20-22, 34-37, 43-46, 50-53, 56-60, 63, 65-68, 72-93, 104, 251, 253, 261-264, 275
official approval, 5
worldwide expansion, 21-22, 49-50
Sanford, John, books by, xxxii, xl n
Savio, Saint Dominic. *See* Personages, in dreams of Don Bosco
Secondary-process mentation, during sleep, xv
Shepherd of Hermas, xxii
Significance of dreams
for Dement, Freud and Jung, xiii
for Don Bosco, 1-6, 17
Sleep and Wakefulness, xiv
Study of dreams
Acts of the Holy Apostle Thomas, xxii
Adventure Inward, xl n
Against Celsus, xxiii
Against Heresies, xxiii
Christianity as Psychology, xx
City of God, The, xxvii
Clementine Homilies, The, xxiii
in clinical psychology, xii
Collected Works of C.G. Jung, xxxix
Commentary on the Dream of Scipio, xxvii
Confessions, The, xxvii
current, xiii
De Magia, xxviii
in depth psychology, xix
Dictionary of Symbols, A, xxxix
Dreams: A Way to Listen to God, xxxviii
Dreams, Daydreams and Discovery, xxxv
Dreams, God's Forgotten Language, xl n
Dreams: The Dark Speech of the Spirit, xl n
in fifth century, xxvi
God and the Unconscious, xix
God, Dreams and Revelation, x
Healing and Wholeness, xl n
Interpretation of Dreams, The, xiii, xviii
Kingdom Within, The, xl n
Les Devins, xxviii
Life of Saint Anthony, xxv
Martyrdom of Polycarp, xxii
in modern society, x-xii
Morals and Dialogues, xxviii
On the Making of Man, xxvi
On the Soul, xxiv
Other Side of Silence, The, xxxii
in psychiatry, xii
in psychology and physiology, x
in the Renaissance, xxviii
Resurrection, xl n
Shepherd of Hermas, xxii
Sleep and Wakefulness, xiv
Testament of Abraham, The, xxiii
Transcend: A Guide to the Spiritual Quest, xl n
Visions Seminars, The, xxxix
Soul, saving one's own, 30, 47, 60, 139, 164, 172-173, 180, 206, 236-237, 244, 268
Souls, saving, 2, 30, 60, 80, 121, 264
Spiritual world
relationship to material world, xvii, xxix, xxi, xxiv, xxvii, xxxiii-xxxiv, xxxviii
revealed in dreams, xxiii-xxiv, xxx, xxxvi
Strenna, 132-136, 148-149, 152
Symbols, in dreams, xxxiv
black-clad cleric, xxxii
death experience, xxxi
father figure, xxx
Indian chief, xxx-xxxi
resurrection experience, xxxi
some useful books, xxxix

283

weed, xxxi
Symbols, in dreams of Don Bosco, xxxvi
- animals, 3, 8, 10-12, 32, 42, 53-56, 81, 126, 148-152, 156-160, 162-163, 172, 177, 181, 230-232, 244, 246
- anvil, 158
- bank of river, 46, 48, 172
- birds, 11-12, 183, 202
- blood, 241-242, 245, 252
- blossoms, 241, 246
- boulders, 249
- buds, 48
- chains, 26
- coach, 53, 58
- cockle, 33
- crown, 232, 257
- crystal, 48
- darkness, 117, 146-147, 229, 233
- diamonds, 48, 162, 256-257
- dirty water, 68
- donkey ears, 202
- eagle, 199-200
- field, 30, 34
- figs, 23-24, 41-42, 52-53, 76
- fire, lake of, 243-244
- fish, 126-127
- flood, 174, 180
- flowers, 31, 43, 126, 252, 255-257, 262, 266, 270-271
- fog, 146-147
- food, 31, 43, 129, 132-134, 137, 175, 180
- forked tongue, 202
- fountain, 274
- fruit, 48, 52-53, 241, 247, 256
- furnace, 177-178, 181
- garden, 20, 61-62, 179, 246, 252, 255-256, 261-262, 269-271
- globe, 166-169
- gold, 3, 48, 134, 162, 256-257, 271
- gorge, 249
- grain, 30, 32-33, 262
- grapes, 24, 33, 41-42, 126, 140, 143-145, 179, 241, 255
- grist mill, 174, 180
- hail, 52-53, 131, 147
- hammer, 158
- handkerchief, 130-132
- harvest, 30, 34
- heads of clay, 133, 135
- hearts of clay, 3
- hearts of gold, 3
- hills, 49, 229, 233, 240, 252, 255
- horns, 27, 56
- horse, 108-110, 229-230, 233, 246
- lanterns, 33
- light, 3, 117, 134, 167, 178, 229, 257, 259-260, 268-269
- lightning, 146-147
- meadows, 178
- mineral spring, 178, 181
- mist, 133, 135
- monsters, 3, 68, 138-139, 156, 159-164, 168-169, 177, 181, 232-233, 244
- moon, 184
- mountain, 248
- mud in mouth, 134
- nails, 58-59, 126, 128
- nuts, 70-72, 126
- orchards, 247
- padlocked lips, 26
- palace, 130
- patches on old cloth, 9-10
- pierced tongues, 25
- pitchforks, 231
- plain, 240, 246, 255
- prairie, 174, 180
- raft, 173-182
- railless bridge, 249, 253
- railway cars, 53-54
- rainbow, 167, 178, 232
- raindrops, 132
- red sash, 257-258, 260
- roses, 18-21, 127, 232, 246, 271-272
- sea, 105-106

sea of glass, 255
seashore, 255
seed, 30
sheaves, 32
shield, 162
ships, 105-106
sickle, 31, 34, 43
silver, 134
smoke, 133, 135
snow, 131-132
sores on head, 25-26
squinting eyes, 25
storm, 131
swamp, 177, 181
tablets, 132-134
thorns, 18-21, 46, 126-127, 215, 232
thunderbolts, 146-147
torrent, 170-173
trees, 178, 256
tree trunk, 174, 181
two columns, 105-108
two pines, 103-104
valley, 46, 48, 229, 233, 246
vine, 137-148, 241
vineyard, 179
wagon, 46-48
water, 271
wide, level road, 46
wide, paved road, 212
wide plank, 174, 181
white robe, 260
wind, 131, 146-147
worms, 71-72, 134, 178
worms in heart, 25-26
Synesius of Cyrene, xxvi

Tertulian, xxiv
Testament of Abraham, The, xxiii
Therese of Lisieux, Saint, xxx
Transcend: A Guide to the Spiritual Quest, xl n

Unconscious
 collective, xiii, xviii
 personal, xxxiv

Value of dreams
 in Bible, xix, xxvi
 in Church history, xix
 for knowledge of future, xxiii, xxv-xxvi, xxxv
 as means of conversion, xxiv-xxv, xxix-xxxii, xxxviii-xxxix
 as means of guidance, xiii, xv, xxiv-xxv, xxvii, xxx, xxxv-xxxvii
 as method of contact with God, x, xiii, xviii, xxiii, xxvi-xxvii
 for receiving instructions from God, xxiv-xxvii, xxxiv-xxxvi, xl n
 for scientific discovery, xxxv
 as source of hope and encouragement, xxiii, xxvii, xxix
 as source of wisdom, xiv-xv, xxiv, xxvi-xxvii, xxx
 for strengthening faith, xiv, xxiii-xxiv
Vices warned against by Don Bosco
 anger, 142, 214
 attachment to possessions, 224
 blasphemy, 142
 capital sins, 56
 disobedience, 127-128, 142, 214, 225
 envy, 142, 214
 gluttony, 60, 66, 142, 164-165, 214
 greed, 81, 224
 grumbling, 60
 human respect, 213
 idleness, 59-60, 66, 142, 164-166, 224, 226
 impurity, 27, 142, 147, 214, 227, 232, 237
 lack of courage, 246
 laziness, 246
 pride, 26, 31, 54-55, 71, 142, 147, 214, 225, 227, 232
 sacrilege, 126, 142
 scandal, 126, 142
 sloth, 166, 214, 232
 stubbornness, 246
 theft, 126, 142, 214, 227

Virtues extolled by Don Bosco
  charity, 34, 40, 110, 127, 224, 262
  chastity, 40, 66, 127, 130-132, 165, 237, 260, 262-265
  faith, 159
  holiness, 84
  humility, 34, 40, 54-56, 86, 127, 165, 170, 262
  innocence, 46, 48-49, 232-233, 260
  knowledge, 31-32
  meekness, 224
  obedience, 55, 66, 127, 143, 237-238, 262
  openness, 60
  penance, 260, 262
  perseverance, 32, 262
  piety, 31-32, 34, 224
  self-denial, 262
  temperance, 57-58, 60, 67, 86, 165-166
  trust, 60
  truthfulness, 60
  zeal, 84
Visions
  relationship to dreams, xv-xviii
  suspicion regarding, xvii
  waking dreams, xvi
Visions of Don Bosco, 111, 113-119, 269-275
Visions Seminars, The, xxxix
Vocations foretold, 29-34, 38-43, 155, 182

White, Victor, xix